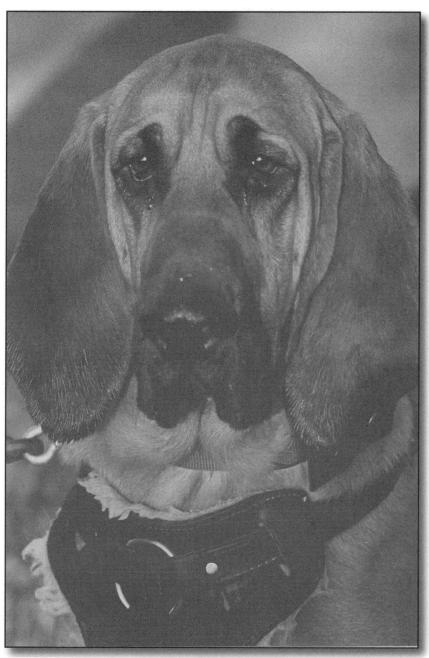

Ronin

RED DOG
RISING

By Jeff Schettler

Alpine Publications
Loveland, Colorado

RED DOG RISING

ISBN 10: 1-57779-104-5
ISBN 13: 978-1-57779-104-1

Cataloging in Publication Data

Schettler, Jeff.
   Red dog rising / Jeff Schettler.
      p. cm.
   ISBN-13: 978-1-57779-104-1 (pbk. : alk. paper)
   ISBN-10: 1-57779-104-5
   1. Police dogs—California. 1. Bloodhound—California.
   3. Police—California. I. Title.
   HV8025.S.28 2009
   363.2'3209794—dc22

2009022727

Names in some cases may have been changed to protect identity.

Cover Design: Kelly Keller, GrafikNature
Cover: Matt Broad with his bloodhound Morgan, and Jim Christman.
Photo by Susan Broad
Editing and Layout: Dianne Nelson, Shadow Canyon Graphics

1 2 3 4 5 6 7 8 9 0
Printed in the United States of America.

Contents

Dedication vii

Foreword by Jamie Hyneman ix

Prologue 1

In the Beginning 4

An Unsolved Mystery 11

The Wandering Samurai 15

Happy Trails 18

Trails and Tribulation 39

Myth Busting 53

The Best Times of My Life 68

The Bank Robbery 83

An Officer Lost 96

A Stolen Car 109

Car Clout 116

A Life Destroyed 121

Manhunt 129

Abandoned Baby Girl 157

Quadruple Homicide 167

Tunnel Vision 178

Colt .45 185

A Hunt for Mushrooms 190

The Last Find 198

The End of an Amazing Career 203

Epilogue 209

Appendix: Trailing Versus Tracking 218

About the Author 241

Dedication

Red Dog Rising *is dedicated to Lisa, Mitsi, Xiana, Christina,
and all of the other 750,000 children reported
missing and exploited every year.*

*"All that is necessary for the triumph of evil
is that good men do nothing."*

Acknowledgments

First and foremost, my sincere appreciation must go to my publisher,
Betty McKinney at Alpine Publications. Betty took a chance on a new
author with little education and less experience in the world of book
writing. I truly hope that *Red Dog Rising* makes you proud, Betty.

I also thank all of the people who worked their tails off on this project:
Dianne Nelson at Shadow Canyon Graphics, who helped with editing
and the overall layout of the book; Tammy Hayes from Alpine, who
constantly fielded my never-ending questions; and Kelly Keller from
GrafikNature for a very cool cover design. I had no idea what a team
project a book could be, and I am grateful for such a wonderful team!

Most important, I want to thank my family for all of their encouragement in this undertaking. My father once told me that our blood is
what binds us; when all else fails, there will always be that.

Jamie from Mythbusters and Kalli, Ronin's "sister."

Foreword

Imet Jeff and Ronin at a point that their time was coming to a close, and Jeff was in the process of handing the torch off to his friend Matt Broad and his dog Morgan. I never had the opportunity to see Ronin in action,

But reading the following story and having worked for a short time with Morgan and Matt, I had no idea at the time what a deep pool I was looking into. I did pick up a clue though: At one point Matt let me have the thirty-foot lead, and I could sense some hesitation in the act that puzzled me. It was just a leash to me, but as you read the following story you will understand that that long line was more like an umbilical thing attaching Jeff and Ronin to each other, and now it was becoming part of Matt and Morgan.

I think the relationship that a man can have with an animal, when it is done right, can be on par with the deepest relationships that people have with each other. It has to do with respect, love, exasperation, affection—all the things that go into great human relationships. Yet at times working with animals can be unique; here is Jeff, a man who grew up on the street in a rough urban setting, he becomes a cop, and is somehow compelled to develop this deep relationship with a dog. The man has issues. How he dealt with them was through Ronin. You can't develop a bond with an animal like this as a casual thing; this requires a level of respect and insight into the creature that one only gets to because he has to for some reason. Both Jeff and Matt wear their hearts on their sleeves when it comes to anything to do with the dogs, and it is not something they came to on a whim.

Great artists are also sometimes compelled in some way. I think they have some bug under their skin that won't leave them alone, and have to get it out. Make no mistake, what Jeff describes in this bond he has with Ronin is an art.

It is a consuming passion, something that Jeff was compelled to do from his youth onward. And it is a joy to read about—in fact, I can't say I have ever read anything like it. The thing that set me off was that while Jeff's recollections read like a page turner of a detective novel, sometimes they just stop. Remember, this is real stuff, and that's how it works. You do your job, things happen, you move on. But then there is that long line and harness hanging on the wall. . . .

— **Jamie Hyneman**

Prologue

I WANT TO TELL YOU A STORY—a story of a time in my life that I'm not sure I'll ever be able to talk about much in the future. For some reason, time is of the essence, and I have a task to complete. I write this now, while I can, as my fingers flow across the keys of my laptop computer. They seem to know the words I want to say before I even think them.

This story, in many ways, is your typical tale of a "boy and his dog." The dog in this story is my retired police K-9, Ronin. Ronin lies beside me as I type, and perhaps, it's his thoughts that guide the tips of my fingers now. Ronin is eleven years old almost to the day on this cold New Years Eve of 2006. His eyes are a little cloudy and his step far from sure, yet Ronin still burns with life as cancer seems to tear and gnaw at his body from the inside. He was not supposed to live past Christmas, yet he is still here with me today. Maybe he is sticking around for a little while just to make sure that I start writing his tale.

Ronin's and my journey began when he was just twelve weeks old, and we lived and worked together for over more than a decade. I spent more time with Ronin than I did with most people, including my family. We worked throughout California and other areas of the United States while we were both young and full of piss and vinegar. Nothing seemed to stop us in those days, and we thrived on the adrenaline rush that was almost a daily occurrence. We were so strong then that it makes it incredibly hard to face what we have become. Ronin and I were manhunters. We were not the first, and we are far from the last. However, we were trained by the best, and Ronin's record was stellar.

Amazingly, both of our careers seemed to end almost simultaneously. Ronin and I worked the streets for the city of Alameda and later, in rural Amador County, California. We rode on patrol together four days a week, ten hours a day, for almost ten years. Our last day working together was after I sustained a career-ending injury on a SWAT test obstacle course in 2004. I was taken to the hospital that day, while a friend and fellow K-9 handler did his best to get into my patrol car and drive it and Ronin home. This was apparently easier said than done. Ronin was a little protective of our car and had no intention of letting anyone inside of it. I was told that my patrol car and Ronin sat in the parking lot for quite some time while everyone debated how best to get them to my house.

At this time, Ronin was getting on in age. Nine for a bloodhound can be considered ancient by working and giant-breed standards. He also had lots of miles on him—kind of like an old car that you absolutely love but it just can't move quite the way it used to. By this time, Ronin had been involved in hundreds of searches, including throughout the state of California and across the country. Ronin had been directly involved in some of the most heinous child abduction cases in California in the 1990s.

The timing was probably good for Ronin, because he was suffering from years of hard miles and strenuous work. Every morning was becoming a little more difficult as he tried to get into the truck for another day on patrol. I didn't want to recognize this and was quite the master of denial in those days. I only wanted to see the spry, young pistol of a puppy with whom I had started working. We humans fear age, declining health, and death—always looking to the future and wondering what is in store for us. Our dogs, on the other hand, seem only to live for the day, not thinking of the future, nor looking back at the past. Perhaps we have something to learn from them.

My story for you now is a chronological history of my time with Ronin, including my tumultuous teenage years that ultimately directed me toward animals, and dogs in particular. I truly hope that it will give you, the reader, a glimpse into our lives. I will do my best to paint this picture as vividly as possible, because Ronin's story should be celebrated. Ronin is a special dog—both hero and companion. There is no hero's funeral in store for him, though. His humble legacy lives in the people he has saved and the criminals he has jailed.

Ronin lies beside me still and, from time to time, picks up his stuffed quail toy and gives it a little squeak. This squeak seems to be a signal for me to get moving because time is short and precious. I know if I cannot do this now, I will never be able to do it in the future. The tears are welling once again as our story begins.

In the Beginning

MY YOUTH AND TIME SPENT MATURING was as much a part of my success and failure as a police dog handler as any training I ever received. My childhood was not exactly normal. My parents split up when I was very young. (Well, maybe that is kind of normal for this era!) I spent a fair amount of time moving to different places, establishing and ending ever-changing friendships, and simply trying to get a sense of who or what my family really was.

I grew up in the 1970s, a time of new music, clothes, and a new society in general. Looking back on it now, I see it for what it truly was. We were shaking off the sheer intensity of my mother's 1960s that culminated in political and social upheaval. People can handle only so much of that type of "heaviness," and I think that everything about my new age was a result of a desperate need to move on.

As a teenager growing up during this time, I experienced everything the 1970s had to offer and more. I moved out on my own when I was about fourteen years old and really never went home again. I grew up on the streets of Berkeley and Oakland, California, loving it and hating it all at the same time. My friends and fellow street urchins became my family. With all the friendships during those years, I learned that they were not always what true friendship was supposed to be. Drugs, partying, and being wild were the names of the game where I lived.

I moved more as teenager than I did at any other time of my life. I moved so often because I either wore out my welcome or I ran out of money; it seemed to be equal on both ends. At first, I stayed with friends but later had to make it on my own. Things started out okay at first but quickly went from bad to worse. I rented rooms in sleazy hotels on Telegraph Avenue in Berkeley, and when my weekly money ran out, I was quickly evicted.

Before I continue here, I think I have to qualify things a little. Many might believe that I had it really rough and that life really wasn't all that fair. Well, it may not have been very fair, but I don't believe that it is for most folks. We all go through trials in our lives based on many of the decisions we make along the way. This just happened to be my trial, and much of it was because of my own decision making. I do not and will not blame my family.

During this entire time, I maintained one sense of order in my life—my employment as a busboy at Kip's Restaurant on Durant Avenue in Berkeley. The owner of the burger and pizza joint was a jewel of a man named Joe. Joe was never exactly a father figure, but he was an anchor who kept me from drifting off into a sea of complete lawlessness. Joe made sure that I always had all the work I wanted and a place to crash if I needed it. I spent many nights sleeping on a pool table at the back of the restaurant. I was not exactly a special child for Joe; it was simply a matter of the goodness in one man's soul. He had performed similar acts of random kindness to many people I knew along this portion of my life's journey.

Kip's was an iconic restaurant, favored among the college crowd from the nearby University of California at Berkeley campus. There was a burger joint serving handmade charbroiled burgers and steaks downstairs, topped off by a pizzeria and beer bar on the upper floor. I bussed tables and washed dishes for three or so years for Joe, and he paid me well for my time along with giving me tons of sage advice. Everyone loved Joe, including all of the students. His place was a legend going back to the radical 1960s—a time that Joe would reminisce about fondly. I remember him telling me how Kip's was the only storefront to survive the many antiwar riots that raged up and down Telegraph Avenue. Joe took me to the attic above the pool hall one day and showed me stacks of bricks backed up against the ceiling of the attic. I asked him what they meant, and he replied, "Those bricks, or what's left of 'em, are what saved each and every one of my windows during the riots." Joe then laughed and said that he used to pile the bricks at the front of the store for all of the students to throw, and they left his business alone because of his generosity.

Most of my time was spent downstairs bussing the tables of the burger part of the joint. "Downstairs" was my place primarily because beer and wine were served upstairs and I was just a kid. I had to make sure that all of the tables were cleared quickly and that the dishes were always clean and stacked. Customers began filtering into Kip's by 11 A.M.-ish and lined up at the grill near the front window.

I also spent a lot of time hanging around and working for specialty pet stores. I was really into tropical fish and exotic birds. Animals in general were my thing, and I found it far easier to deal with them than with people. My self-esteem was always questionable, at best, and working with animals was the one thing I could do really well. A couple of years earlier I had met a kid just about my age who lived under circumstances that were similar to mine. Danny and I became friends the instant we met and stayed close for years to come. I first met Danny when he came into a pet store where I was working. He had an easy manner about him and connected well with the large hook-billed parrots in the shop. He handled each and every one of them, tame or not, with absolutely no fear. This was no easy feat, as a large Amazon double yellow head or macaw could easily break or remove a finger with its incredibly powerful beak. Danny and I went on to become "bird tamers" for an exotic parrot importer in Berkeley not too much later.

I was supposed to be attending high school, but Berkeley High School was really not an option for me even if I *wanted* to attend class. It was a rough place with many street-savvy kids, and I was far from the roughest of the bunch. I had my job, but I was only making minimum wage, and I had no idea how to budget what little I made. It wasn't long before my paychecks were spent. For many of my friends, slinging a little dope was fast money, promising coffee in the morning and a slice of pizza for dinner every night. The problem was that I was a white boy, none too large at that, in a primarily black neighborhood. Most of my friends were black and so, too, were just about all of my enemies who hated me because of my lack of a tan. I ran a gauntlet of robbers every time I tried to make it to school. They were on and off campus, and making it through all of them was incredibly dangerous. If I was with my crew, I was fairly safe; if I was alone, I was prey—most of time, that is.

My living arrangements changed quite a bit during this time, as did many friends with whom I shacked up. We lived a pretty lawless life with little to no parental or adult involvement. Brushes with trouble were so numerous that I lost count, and the allure of the street was a constant siren's song. I wore out my welcome with almost everyone, and I was beginning to live a street person's life in all its glory.

Enter Belit. Belit was a little Chesapeake Bay retriever puppy hauled along by a homeless guy on Telegraph Avenue with a little kite string. She was a beautiful little girl, and I loved her even though she wasn't mine. I tagged along with the guy who had her for a while until he got sick of dealing with puppy issues; then I took her.

Belit was my constant companion. I named her after the girlfriend of a fantasy, sword-wielding barbarian featured in graphic novels of the time. Belit is pronounced "bay-lee." The basic rule of thumb was that if Belit didn't go, neither did I. Belit went to parties, to every friend's house in town, and even to work. Joe was remarkably tolerant of my new acquisition and allowed her to stay in the pool room when I worked in the restaurant. I look back on it now, and I think that he somehow knew that Belit was just about the only real companion or family I had at the time. My first K-9 training began with Belit when I was just about seventeen years old. I noticed that she absolutely loved to chase squirrels on the Berkeley college campus. She used to speed up to the squirrel at Mach one, and as the little rodent scampered up the large oak trees, Belit would run up the tree a few steps, turn around, and jump off! It reminded me of skateboarders in empty swimming pools or ramps.

We started to work on her tree-climbing prowess every day for hours. Belit never grew tired of running, and I was soon the talk of the campus. People would gather all around to watch the amazing tree-climbing dog. It got to the point that she could run ten to fifteen feet up the vertical face of a large tree, and if a branch was close by, she would grasp it with her forelegs or teeth, then haul herself up.

Belit soon graduated to climbing anything vertical. One of her favorite games was to run along the length of a wall, leap sideways, and run perpendicular to the ground for about ten feet. Speed and momentum were the keys to her success. The amazing thing is how she learned this particular trick. Belit learned through observation. The modern era of skateboarding was just beginning during my teenage years. Large, ten-inch-wide boards were replacing the skinny things the beatniks used to ride. And with the advent of the urethane wheel, it was now safe to ride most streets without too many road rashes in the process. It was the urethane wheel that modernized roller skates as well. Some of the best street skaters around wore ski boot–type affairs with super-wide trucks and fat urethane wheels.

Belit used to run alongside me while I was on my Dogtown twelve-inch board, often amongst a large group of other skateboarders and roller skaters. We made quite an impressive posse of youth speeding down the avenues of downtown Berkeley. Some of our favorite haunts were the angled walls in front of the museum on University Avenue just east of Telegraph and any empty backyard swimming pool we might find. The roller skaters soon started up a trick that we skateboarders couldn't quite duplicate. As they sped along the sidewalk next to the walls of local shops and buildings, they would leap sideways onto the wall and skate that way for several feet before dropping off onto the sidewalk again. The first time Belit saw this, she didn't even hesitate. She simply duplicated the maneuver with much more finesse and greater length of the run.

Belit was absolutely amazing. I never had any idea how intelligent a dog could be until I met her. She was responsible for shaping my earliest K-9 training philosophies. I learned through observation. I honestly believe that it's my greatest strength. Perhaps this is one reason why I did so poorly in school, where theories were played out in books and by the spoken or written word. I seemed to learn best simply by watching others doing their thing.

Belit was responsible for my first training rule: that all dogs should be trained in accordance with their capabilities. In other words, train them to do what they like to do the best or already do naturally. Just as humans excel at specific jobs, so, too, do dogs.

Belit became my family and I talked to her constantly. She shared my every misery and often helped me to stay warm at night. My first rule about Belit going everywhere with me ensured that I never really had a home in which to live. I did rent a series of hotel rooms but would be promptly kicked out when the hotel manager caught me sneaking Belit into my room. We soon wore out our welcome with all of our friends, and every hotel in town knew who we were. I had simply run out of options.

This is when I began to camp out in true homeless fashion on the UC Berkeley campus. My campground was in a secluded wood next to a small seasonal creek on the north campus. It was also the area where Belit liked to chase squirrels, so it served a dual purpose. It was not very comfortable and far from clean, but it was all I had. I did my absolute best to get as clean as possible before work every day and to pretend as if my life was as normal as the next guy, but it was tough.

After several months of camping, I decided that I had had enough and needed to make a positive change in my life. The problem, though, was that I didn't know what a positive life might be all about. I was getting close to eighteen years of age now, and I was anxious to do something with my life. The old ways were bound to get me killed or thrown into jail, so I was rather desperate. The problem was that there really wasn't much available to a high school dropout who hadn't even made it past tenth grade. I had hair almost to the middle of my back and a razor's-edge attitude. I saw an advertisement on TV for the army and I thought, why the hell not?

One thing led to another, and I met with a local army recruiter who lined up an entire battery of tests to determine what I would be best at in my new military career. Lo and behold, they determined that law enforcement was my path to enlightenment. My recruiter said to me that I was meant to be a military policeman (MP). What an irony! After everything I had done and been through, the last thing I ever thought I might be was a cop.

I talked to my recruiter in depth about my interest in handling military K-9s and, of course, he massaged my ego in this regard. He stopped short of promising me a position as a handler but did lead me to believe that it was in the cards. To make a long story short, I had a pretty great, albeit short, career in the army as an MP and I thoroughly enjoyed it. I never did get a chance to work a military K-9, but it was still a dream. I matured in the army. I really didn't have much of a choice. It was the army's way or the highway. I chose the army, and I'm glad for it.

Yes, you are probably wondering what became of Belit when I became a soldier. She went with me, of course. Remember? If my dog didn't go, neither did I. Belit accompanied me to Fort Polk, Louisiana, and to Baumholder, Germany. She became quite the world traveler.

My background as an MP and the solid foundation provided to me by the military gave me the incentive to really change my life for the better. I knew that, after everything was said and done, the best career for me was as a cop. My street experience, coupled with what I learned as an MP, gave me an angle on this business that most of my peers didn't have. I had street smarts above and beyond my years, and now I had an education and experience to go with it.

An Unsolved Mystery

FAST FORWARD TO 1994 and things had changed immensely. I had just graduated from the police academy in Pittsburgh, California, and was starting a new police career with the city of Alameda. I was married and I had an eleven-year-old son whom I doted on constantly. We lived in our first home that we actually owned, and it was new, too. We were living the American dream and I couldn't be happier. I had not been on the job for much more than a year when I made my first move to become a real K-9 handler.

I remember the first time that I ever considered getting a bloodhound. My wife, Judy, and I were sitting on the couch in our living room watching one of the murder mystery shows on TV. This particular case was about the Allie Berrelez abduction in Aurora, Colorado. A bloodhound named Yogi had taken the scent of the missing girl and followed it for more than fourteen miles through city streets, crowded business districts, and ultimately up and onto the freeway. Yogi trailed to the point of exhaustion, and his handler, Jerry Nichols, was forced to stop and give Yogi a break. In the interim, ground searchers started up where Yogi had left off. In relatively short order, they discovered Allie in a wooded canyon. Unfortunately, she was not alive. However, the simple fact that she was found at all was amazing. I found it fantastic that a dog would have the ability to take a specific scent of just one person and follow it for miles. This was able to bring some semblance of closure to the Berrelez family and gave the police a few clues to help track down the suspect. In the not-too-distant future, I would meet Yogi and the Berrelez family. Little did I know at the time, but I was headed down a pretty wild career path.

Yogi, owned and handled by Jerry Nichols, takes the scent for a trail in Rocky Mountain National Park. Yogi followed the scent of Alie Berrelez along city streets and busy Interstate 70. Yogi got close to Alie's body but did not find it; he was forced to stop due to exhaustion. The ground pounders picked up where Yogi left off and found her a short distance away. Yogi had trailed more than fourteen miles. As a result, Yogi gained national recognition.
Photo by Kent and Donna Dannen.

I guess my eyes really lit up or something visible must have had happened, because Judy turned to me and simply said "No!" in no uncertain terms. I knew that tone of voice all too well, and it normally means I'm not going to win. Judy went on to tell me that she had had experiences with bloodhounds in the past and that they stank and slobbered horribly. She said she did not want them in our house—not now, not ever, not even as a guest.

We talked and we argued and then we talked some more—for about a week. Judy probably thought that I'd eventually come around to her way of thinking and allowed me the ability to at least do some research. The

Internet was just becoming popular and we were online. Many of the current search engines were not quite as savvy as they are now, but I was still able to negotiate myself through some useful information on bloodhounds. One of the first people whom I talked to was Larry Harris in Southern California. Larry was a longtime bloodhound advocate and had connections to many of the top bloodhound handlers in the country at the time. His closest friend was a famous handler by the name of Bill Tolhurst. Many people credit Bill with being the father of the modern bloodhound as a tool. Bill was working on scent evidence and had even written two books on the subject.

Larry encouraged me to get copies of the books and to get into the business if at all possible. In those days, there were very few bloodhound handlers in California, and those who were available were almost always volunteers. I ran into very few California law-enforcement agencies that had ever heard of deploying bloodhounds, let alone having one in the agency. I took Larry's advice and bought the books he had told me about. I read them several times, but there was still nothing physical to go with the theory that I was reading.

Larry pointed me in the right direction again and recommended that I do two things. First, he suggested that I talk to a handler by the name of Kat Albrecht, who worked her bloodhounds AJ and Chase on a volunteer basis in Santa Cruz. Second, he recommended that I go see a new litter of pups that just happened to be available in Susanville, California. Larry said something to the effect that the Susanville dogs came out of one of the better bloodhound lines called "Rimbey." Not knowing anything about hounds, I assumed that Rimbey was a type of bloodhound and went on my merry way. This was going to become a major name in my phonebook one day.

Judy rolled her eyes when I mentioned going to see the bloodhound puppies; however, she did one amazing thing. She agreed to go along with me. To this day, I'm not sure if she agreed to the trip just to support me or if she had an interest. Judy would never admit that I had a good idea even after the fact. Any concession would be tantamount to an admission that I might actually have a great idea. Don't get me wrong.

I loved my wife dearly and we were the best of friends, but she really liked to have the last word.

I also called Kat Albrecht and spoke to her about what she did. She was most kind and seemed to be excited about my interest. She readily answered my every question and invited me to visit her and her hounds. We had to see the puppies first, though. At this point, unbeknownst to Judy, I was already committed to getting a bloodhound. Judy is well aware of my ways now; however, back then, she was still learning how I operated. Judy and I took the long drive to Susanville and were just in time to see a couple of the last puppies available.

There was one little male dog that seemed a little shy at first but eventually made his way over to check me out. I had the smell of our other dog, Tse-ka, all over me, and the little puppy seemed to be intrigued by the odor. It might have been a little different than that of other dogs he might have smelled, because Tse-ka was a wolf hybrid—part wolf, part dog.

This little bloodhound puppy had his nose plastered to my leg and was making noises similar to those of a clogged vacuum cleaner. I thought that he was adorable and fell in love with him immediately. This little red pup with long ears and a far-too-wrinkled face was incredible. He had a light in his eyes that I remember to this day, and it said that he was something special. Judy seemed to feel the same way. I was truly amazed, because I honestly thought that I was going to have a fight on my hands if I even broached the subject of buying the bloodhound puppy. Believe it or not, Judy even offered to get the checkbook from the car.

We had not performed any "puppy testing" and really had no idea what to look for in a potential working bloodhound. We were going simply on intuition that this was the right thing to do. Everything seemed to be clicking into place with this deal—not necessarily buying a dog, but everything that led up to the acquisition. Everyone has times in their lives when the planets seem to align just so and everything you dream about seems to fit into place seamlessly. This was one of those times. This puppy was supposed to be part of our family, and more importantly, he was to fulfill a crucial role in assisting mankind.

The Wandering Samurai

IT WASN'T LONG BEFORE WE HAD THE LITTLE BOY HOME and immediately set about discovering a name for him. Names are incredibly important and empowering. Careful thought went into the selection of a name for our new bloodhound. From the beginning, I had determined we were going to be a crime-fighting team. I knew almost instinctively that great things were in store for us. I am convinced that fate was responsible for Judy and me, and this bloodhound puppy was another precious moment not to be squandered.

My current standing at the police department was also part of my thought process in determining a name for my dog. I had already decided that we would be a team in Alameda. Although I had made the decision in my mind, I knew that it wouldn't be easy. I had an uphill battle with little chance at success, yet I prepared for this battle as if I had already won it. I honestly believed that I was unstoppable. I was prepared to do whatever I had to do to make this bloodhound a police dog.

My plan was to have a police bloodhound partner, but my police department had absolutely no idea what I was up to. I can say with a great deal of certainty that a bloodhound was not on their agenda for a new project. I was still a rookie police officer with no credibility. Alameda Police Department is an "old school" agency with roots that run very deep. There is a tremendous amount of well-deserved pride that came along with employment at this department. Many officers had preceded me who had exemplified themselves in ways I could not imagine. I was one of the new kids on the block, and any respect or special attention I might hope for had to be earned many times over before it would ever be given.

15

The trouble with my plan was that it had no precedent. Through all of my research, I had never found a single officer who had put together a full-time police bloodhound program in the state of California. I had no model for success, and the burden was entirely on me. This was a little strange, because I had always viewed California as the model for everything modern in law enforcement. It seemed that California law enforcement viewed the bloodhound as an antiquated tool from a bygone era. German Shepherds and Belgian Malinois were part of this new age, but there seemed to be little room for a droopy-eared, slobbering hound dog.

My plan for this puppy was for him to become a four-footed resource to find suspects or victims of crime and mischance when all other methods of detection had failed. My imagination was greater than the reality, but I was a very idealistic police officer. I viewed my position as that of a knight of old, more so than just a method to make money. I felt that being a police officer meant that I was to protect those who could not protect themselves. I had been exposed to a lot of what mankind could do by this short time in my career, but many of the true horrors were yet to manifest themselves.

The Allie Berrelez case, coupled with my new endeavor, made me take a closer look at many of the child abductions that we had in our own state. If my dog could truly have an impact on just one such case, I would be satisfied. Child crime was a pet peeve of mine. To hurt a child for self-gratification was the ultimate evil in my book. Perhaps this was due to all that I had been exposed to while growing up. I don't really know what fueled this fire, but I had an incredible desire to deal some semblance of justice to the monsters preying on our children. Little did I know at the time what this new partnership would carry with it. I didn't realize—not yet—what an awesome burden and gift I had just been given. I would learn in the years to come that, although our work was good, it could also be deeply painful. I did not realize the extent of the commitment that our work would entail. But, I am getting ahead of myself.

I needed a name for this puppy that embodied everything that he would eventually become, coupled with the obstacles we would both have to overcome while trying to get there. The name had to be strong and generate a feeling of righteous purpose.

There is an ancient story from Japan that is viewed by many as the embodiment or soul of the Japanese spirit. It is the true story of the forty-seven Ronin warriors who were left leaderless when their master was forced to commit suicide for assaulting a court official who had wronged him. The warriors avenged their master by killing the court official after years of patient waiting. These warriors knew that, in attacking this man, they would themselves be killed or forced to commit suicide, yet they remained true to their course. The story of the forty-seven Ronin warriors is indicative of the loyalty, persistence, and honor that were meant to be the backbone of the samurai spirit, or *bushido*.

Thus Ronin was named. I knew immediately that this was the name for this puppy. I could feel his spirit whenever I played with him. He was on this earth for a reason, and I knew it. Ronin showed a desire for training that bordered on fanatical. He loved to look for people and would literally stop at nothing to find what he was looking for once he had started.

Happy Trails

WE REALLY HAD NO TEXTBOOK OR TRAINING MANUAL to learn how to train Ronin. We had read two books on the subject and had found various training outlines on the Internet. There was only one national organization for police bloodhounds at the time, and it predominantly catered to handlers on the East Coast. We had learned of a few local handlers, but only one seemed to be fairly active.

Kat Albrecht was a police officer for the University of Santa Cruz Police Department. She had been handling working dogs, especially bloodhounds, for a few years already and had some good work already under her belt. Kat routinely trained other K-9 handlers in my new field of work—trailing. So far, I had only talked to Kat on the phone, but she seemed anxious to work with me. Kat immediately started to steer me in the right direction for training material and set up a date when we could join her for training. I was chomping at the bit. We had already started basic runaway training with Ronin but really had no role model. I desperately wanted to watch someone else do this with a seasoned dog.

Lack of other handlers was my biggest obstacle to overcome. I had nobody else other than Kat to talk to, and I had no idea what I was doing. With standard police K-9s there are numerous schools, trainers, other handlers, manuals, national conferences, and organizations to draw on for expertise. None of this applied to bloodhound work. Throughout history, dating back to our nation's beginnings, there had been bloodhound handlers. However, they were few and far between. Many of the famous handlers also seemed to have a halo of almost supernatural ability that went along with their accomplishments. I was desperate to tap into this resource.

I was to learn that bloodhound handlers, at least the very good ones, underwent what I can only describe as an informal, yet strict, apprenticeship program. New handlers had to prove themselves to the veteran handlers and gain acceptance. This is what I had to do with Kat. From the very first time I met her, I made absolutely sure to be prompt and always true to my word. I latched on to her every sentence and treated her not only as my instructor but also as my mentor.

Kat is an honorable woman and an excellent handler. I was very lucky, or fate was in my corner again when I met her. Our relationship was incredibly close, and in the early years, I spoke to her almost every day on the phone. Frankly, I am surprised that she never got sick of me. Kat was the foundation for everything that we would become. She stuck with me through every phase of my early training all the way up to my first case. She also was with me on the day we made our first find of a missing person.

I will always remember my first training day with Kat. Judy, Ronin, and I drove down to the University of Santa Cruz brimming with anticipation. Kat had planned a training day for us that included puppy trails for Ronin and some advanced work that she was doing with her hounds, AJ and Chase. AJ was Kat's veteran dog, and Chase was a young adult female bloodhound just starting to work her own cases. Judy and I drove onto the campus and met Kat near some dormitories. We were in our brand-new Dodge Ram pickup truck and hadn't even stopped the motor yet when we were greeted by Chase jumping onto the passenger side. The sound the big dog's claws made as they scraped down the side of my beautifully painted, fire-truck-red door panel was horrifying!

Kat had not even met me and she was mortified. She apologized profusely many times over, and I had to continuously assure her that there was no problem. This was going to be just the first of many nasty scratches to this truck over the next few years. I really had no other choice but to get used to it. Bloodhounds are large—plain and simple. They slobber and have little physical grace, and your possessions are ultimately shared with them—vehicles especially.

Most of our first day of training involved discussing how our dogs worked and helping Judy and me to grasp basic scent-discrimination applications. Our dogs were being trained to do something that they already did quite well. We were just teaching them to do it in a specific way so that we could read their responses. We were also teaching them to stick to one human's particular scent so that they could follow it to the source. The two words—scent discrimination—were going to become the most important ones of my vocabulary.

Learning how to work a trailing bloodhound involves understanding the terminology as well as the methods. It is a difficult task, because you are placing your thought processes in a completely new realm. Scent is the dog's world. Yes, they do have good eyesight, and many breeds have phenomenal hearing, but scent is really what makes everything work for them. Think about your own dogs, past or present. Did you ever find it interesting that they could determine who was behind a closed door long before you did? The dog readily reacts to noise on the walkway outside or to the sound of knocks at the door, but what makes him calm around some noises and more alert around others? It is scent. The dog smells the source of the disturbance and immediately catalogs it as friend, foe, or an unknown.

I had to get out of the human paradigm of an audio and visual world and enter a realm about which I had little knowledge—and in which I had absolutely no ability. I learned that dogs can determine age, sex, and infirmity of other animals through scent alone and that this ability also applied to human detection. Every living creature produces scent of one sort or another. Every creature's scent is similar to a blueprint of its general makeup. The dog can determine an amazing number of things about an animal or a human by scent alone. Kat helped me to understand this and apply it to the working bloodhound.

Working with a scent dog opened my mind to this new world. I began to look at scent as not only a tool, but also as an essential element to natural life. I have always been an outdoorsman, hunter, and fisherman, and I knew how prey animals reacted to my own odor when they encountered it. I always did my best to use the wind in my favor when stalking game. However, I never really knew the details of how they utilized the scent that ruled their entire world. I began to observe animals in the wild closer than I ever had before. I could sit for hours and watch a single coyote as it hunted a pasture or field. As a matter of fact, it was a coyote that gave me my first lesson on scent discrimination in the wild.

I had been scouting deer and wild boar on a mountainside in Northern California near the town of Willits when I had this first wild encounter. I watched a small herd of Columbian blacktail deer as they worked their way across a draw below my perch. They were taking their time but were obviously moving with a purpose and direction in mind. It was early morning, and they were coming up out of some alfalfa fields below the dark timber on the mountain for their daytime slumber. The herd was made up of several does and a couple of fawns. They did not always travel in a straight line but more in the way natural land features presented themselves or where certain edible plants were located. The fawns were playing the entire time—running alongside their mothers then dashing a short distance away. There was a certain hierarchy to the troop's movement, with a lead doe paving the way forward and a trailing doe that seemed to be watching the back trail. There were a couple of younger does in the middle who often took up flanking positions, especially when they paused to browse. It reminded me of a small squad of soldiers maneuvering in the field. It was not long before they made it to another ridge top and out of my view.

I decided to stay on the mountaintop and watch the sun come up completely. It was a beautiful picture, with the sun rising in the east above golden mountains edged with pine trees while the inky fog bank rolled back toward the sea to the west. I loved this moment and thanked God for every morning that I was blessed to see. Just as I thought about moving, I detected a flash of movement about 1,000 yards below me from an area whence the deer had come. I glassed the area with my binoculars and noticed two coyotes running in my general direction. They appeared to be following the same general path that the deer had taken, and I noticed that their noses were on the ground as they ran.

As the coyotes closed the gap between us, I quickly realized that they were on the exact trail that the deer had been traveling. They seemed to be re-creating the trail that the fawns had taken as they had dashed away from the herd from time to time. The pair completely ignored the older does' trail and seemed to be strictly concentrating on the fawns. I was amazed, because I had no idea that animals could isolate one particular scent among many and follow it with any degree of proficiency. The coyotes were also hunting these fawns by scent at an almost breakneck speed. Their noses were plastered to the grass as they ran up the mountainside. They were making really good time on the deer herd and it wasn't long before I lost them, too, on the same ridgeline where the deer had disappeared from sight. It was an equally beautiful scene that left me laughing in childlike wonder.

This lesson was probably one of Mother Nature's first of many scent classes for me. I believe that nature played a part in my training, just as much as any person did. I was an apt pupil and took every lesson to heart.

As mentioned, most of my early training and experience revolved around scent discrimination and how it applied to police work as evidence. This is tough conceptually, because so few people actual practiced the art of "trailing"—the art to which I was subscribing. There is court-accepted precedence in the field, and there had been many successful handlers before me, but so little was to be learned about all of those accomplishments. It was like reinventing the wheel for each and every new handler, I was soon to discover.

The other problem was that even though we were such a small group of people, there was no tribal cohesiveness. We were separated by everything from dog type to scent theory, and very few subgroups of man-hunters ever really got along. I found the entire affair factional and divisive.

We did have one thing in common—it seemed that most people had similar roots or foundations in their training. Obviously, something had worked very well for someone else in the past, and it had been handed down to new generations. However, very few people would ever admit where they learned what they now do. My opinion on the subject has always been plain and transparent: Honor and harness our history in order to shape the future.

We all worked our dogs in a similar fashion, which meant that we all had a similar theory on scent; however, few would deign to admit it. I learned that every human produces scent particles that are specific to that one human—perhaps similar to DNA. These scent particles are actually dead and dying microscopic skin cells or rafts, which slough off the body. The rapidity of the loss of skin cells is dependent upon exertion, mental state, age, and physical condition. (Mind you, this definition did not come to me easily, and in no way could have I recited it then as I do now. My thoughts here are based on many years and miles of experience with Ronin. However, for the sake of understanding, I believe it is important to lay the scent foundation as I eventually knew it to this very day, in the early part of this book.)

Certain people simply smell more or, perhaps better, to dogs. They just seem to produce more scent. This can occur due to major physical exertion, such as running from the police after a suspect has dumped a car, to the adrenalin-producing fear exuded by a victim of violent crime. On the other hand, and completely to the opposite extreme, I found that mentally incapacitated people—in particular, Alzheimer's patients—seemed to produce far less or far less acceptable scent to the dog. Dogs just had a heck of a time finding these people, far more so than, let's say, a criminal.

This leads me to the best type of scent: fear scent. The fear dripping off of a fleeing felon is sweet, indeed, to the nose of a trailing dog. There is something primordial about fear scent and the canine, probably harkening to a time when large canids hunted humans as a food source. Fear has led to more successful finds for Ronin and me than all other types of scent combined.

Scent is biological in nature and is therefore subject to the same laws of biodegradation as any other living matter. It is affected by extremes of heat, cold, and chemical contamination. Other odors can mask and confuse a certain scent, and time is the killer of it all. Water in limited quantities seems to accentuate scent, and some of the best hunts occur when people think that they can cover their trail by running through creeks and streams. Nobody knows for sure how long a human scent trail can last. The trail's life span is completely dependent upon all of the aforementioned factors, and then some. It is safe to say that it can last for several days to varying degrees. Conditions have to be optimum, though. The best conditions for human scent longevity are cool, dark, and moist conditions with little contamination or cross traffic. Regardless, handlers can have all of the best conditions in the world, so they assume, yet still the dog may not always pick up the trail. There is an X-factor involved with working scent dogs that often defies human reasoning.

There are moments in a handler's career when everything is just right and the dog simply loses the scent, and there are others that are all wrong, yet the dog performs in stellar fashion. Reasoning tells us that if we could do what our dogs do so well, we would simply harness ourselves and leave them home. Dogs have abilities with scent identification, discrimination, and trailing that defy all human definition.

The key to every trail is a good scent article or start point with the victim's scent. The article can be anything the victim has worn, handled, or touched. It should be as free from other human or contaminating scents as possible. The scent article is given to the dog at the beginning of the trail in order to help him detect the scent trail that the subject left behind.

Trailing is often confused with tracking, and the two titles are often used interchangeably. I feel that tracking is really not the proper word. Tracking is based on the human visual perception of an event through tracks or visible spoor. I believe that the word is used mistakenly to describe our human interpretation of events of which only the dog can know. K-9 tracking is also a method that most often involves having the dog follow a specific set of footprints without deviation. Often, the dog's nose is forced to the ground with a lead running under his leg to the neck. When the handler exerts tension, the lead pulls the dog's head downward. This is done, presumably, to keep the nose of the dog in the scent zone of the footprint. My argument has always been, how do you know that there is scent left in the print?

Officer Brian Kiel and K-9 DaSilva practicing scent presentation.

Ground disturbance in and of itself can help a dog "track," and this may be where the tracking concept came from. If a patch of earth is moved, disturbed, or flipped over, its smell changes. Humans can often detect this scent change, and it is easy to test for; simply smell a patch of undisturbed grass, step on it, then smell it again. Dogs can smell this change even better, and ground disturbance is a real assistant to the dog. However, this change of odor is probably limited in its life span and not that important to a dog that is working off of an individual human odor.

Trailing, on the other hand, is the K-9 art of following a particular scent—i.e., scent discrimination—from the beginning of a person's path to the end. The terrain can vary from pavement and dirt to grass and creek beds. Picture a man holding a smoke bomb and simply standing in one spot. You can easily imagine how the smoke will pool and eddy about the man's feet or spread out with the prevailing wind. Now picture the man walking from one point in an open field to another as the smoke trail follows behind him. The scent may move to the left or right and be constrained by rocks, grass, leaves, trees, and buildings. Sometimes the smoke stays low to the ground, and other times it drifts just above it. How the smoke moves, pools, or collects is dependent upon environmental conditions. It is safe to surmise that the smoke will rarely follow or collect in the exact footsteps of the man on a constant basis.

I believe that scent moves in a fashion that is similar to the visual interpretation I made before. In light of this interpretation, I've concluded that a dog that follows a particular human's scent will follow that scent wherever it might lie, whether or not it is in the actual footsteps. The scent may, in many cases, be extremely far away from the actual path of the human. A good example might be on a paved road in the middle of a city. If a man walks down the center of a paved street with cars, people, wind, etc., the scent he leaves behind will have tremendous difficulty sticking to the pavement beneath his actual footsteps. The scent may collect in small cracks but will primarily be blown to the sides of the street and collect in gutters, against the sides of buildings, etc.

Trailing is simply training a dog to follow a particular human's scent pattern wherever it might lie, rather than following a specific set of tracks.

The dog is allowed to use all of his senses to locate his quarry, and, when scenting, he may find the scent on the ground or in the air. If, for example, the dog is following a trail of scent on a path along which the person was known to have walked, and suddenly the dog detects the same odor on the wind coming from a direction where the suspect currently is located, the dog is allowed to follow the air scent and deviate from the footpath, even if the person did not walk in this new direction.

In my opinion, trailing epitomizes the dog's natural instincts to scent patterns and replicates or approximates what a wild canid such as a coyote or a wolf might do when following prey based on scent. The human addition to the equation is ensuring that the trailing dog stays on one particular scent for as long as it might last.

Trailing is a natural activity for dogs. They all do it whether they are domestic or wild. The difference is that wild canids trail for sustenance hunting, while their domestic cousins trail from basic genetic programming without a real need for food. However, food is a primary motivating factor when you are training a trailing dog. It is my belief that, if a domestic dog is encouraged to trail for work, then the use of food as a motivator will assist as a trigger to stimulate natural responses to the requested behavior. In other words, if food is the reason why dogs are programmed to trail, then it stands to reason that it might be important to use a tool to motivate them.

Some dogs do not require food to learn to do their job, as they are high-prey-drive animals to begin with. The simple act of trailing is exciting and a game that they love. Sometimes, only praise is necessary to reinforce the trailing training. Other dogs appear to enjoy a continuation of the game at the end of a trail by chasing a ball or other toy that you throw for them. The bottom line is that positive reinforcement is the key to a successful trailing dog training regimen.

I use food as a motivator for the most part. I've given the nickname of "Scooby snacks" to the treats that my dogs especially like. I give my dog several Scooby snacks at the successful end to a mission. If he finds what he looking for, he gets the reward. If he fails, he will try harder next time.

Some recommend placing food in the steps of the trail layer. I do not like this method, because it relies on the belief that scent is in the track, when I know for a fact that it is not always there. Furthermore, I believe that placing food in a track encourages the dog to only look for food. Anything along a city street might do.

To properly train a trailing dog, you must have a basic understanding of scent, but you also need a continuous list of new volunteers and work environments. A trailing dog used for police work or for search and rescue will be forced to follow any number of people, often in extreme locations. A downtown city street can be considered extreme when the dog is used to training only on a grassy field.

New handlers can quickly wear out the welcome of friends, family, and neighbors alike when those folks begin to learn that they are nothing more than dog fodder at the end of ever increasingly long trails. As the dog matures, the age and length of the training trails increase significantly, and once-good friends can quickly become just associates when they are forced to sit in a freezing rainstorm for hours while a trailing dog in training tries to find them. Family members will also find many excuses not to participate in your training once the novelty and family spirit wear off.

During my time as a handler, it often got to the point that I had to rely on new handlers who were just getting into the business to be my "victims," as we commonly referred to them, or go to the extreme of paying the neighborhood kids. This can be tough on the budget when a new handler is training five days a week. And, in the beginning stages, training can truly take this much time.

Consequently, the next thing a new handler requires is a strong constitution and a commitment to the long road. A long road it really might be, especially when there is nobody backing your play from the agency for which you work. At this stage in the game, I was looked upon as slightly touched in the head. I lived and breathed trailing and did something with it on a daily basis. I also wore out many a co-worker's ear, as well as their patience. Nobody in Alameda really knew what I was doing, and my fellow K-9 handlers already on the street practiced the footstep-to-footstep method that I spoke of earlier. Everything I was doing was strangely foreign. The beginning trails on which I started Ronin were referred to as "puppy trails" or "fire trails." Where Ronin was concerned, fire trails was a better term, because he literally caught on fire and was unmanageable when we ran them. Fire trails are used in the beginning of training and later as a motivator for complex problem solving in the dog.

A fire trail starts when the trail layer, referred to hereafter as the "victim," takes a scent article that is impregnated with the victim's scent (normally a large piece of clothing), waves it in front of the dog, drops it, then runs a short distance away. The dog watches the article fall to the ground in front of him, but he cannot smell it yet because it is just out of reach. The dog's attention is now split between two objects of desire—the "toy" on the ground and the person who just ran away. The handler sweeps his hand toward the article and allows the dog a little slack in his long lead. As the dog's nose touches the article, or the nose is just slightly above it, the handler gives the command to trail. This command can be anything, but it should be used only once upon the initial scenting of the dog.

Once the dog takes the scent, the handler allows the dog to run forward toward the victim, letting the long lead out before him. These first puppy trails are often sight oriented only when it comes to following the victim. The dog does smell the article, which equates to the victim at the end of the trail. This reinforces the fact that the scent on the article and on the victim himself match. The purpose of the fire trail is to establish the scent article with the dog and encourage the hunt.

Fire trails are high-drive affairs. Puppies and adult dogs alike don't like it when they are restrained and someone is running from them. The adrenalin increases, as does the desire to catch the victim. Everything is a fun game when establishing this prey drive. You want the puppy to thoroughly enjoy himself and want to do it more often. I believe that it is always best to stop the training when the pup is at the peak of his game. When the last trail run was good, and just before the puppy gets tired, you should call it quits for the day. If the timing is correct, the puppy only wants to play more and is doubly enthused the next time the training equipment comes out. I call this keeping the edge. It keeps the pup at the top of his game and always wanting more. The ultimate challenge is to maintain the edge to adulthood, when there comes a time that the dog has a burning desire to search—a desire that rivals all other instincts. It happens, and when it does, the dog is unstoppable.

I've spoken of commitment, drive, equipment, and learning how to do this new job, but I haven't spoken of the relationship. And it is this relationship that was the catalyst for everything I have written so far and for all of our success to follow. Perhaps I should have broached this subject in the beginning, but, as with all things, I believe I had to work up to it. To speak of it too early was simply too painful, and words wouldn't come to my lips let alone to the tips of my fingers.

This relationship is so incredibly rare and special that it is hard for me to describe. Many of my peers will understand immediately, but to the uninitiated, it can be difficult to fathom. After all, it is only a dog, and yes, we love our animals dearly, but they are not people. We take them into our families and often speak of them as our children, but their passing rarely can eclipse the loss of your own kin—your own blood. The two were never equal—or so I believed.

It's unusual to think of a dog as kin—to be related to each other by more than just circumstance. Not blood, of course, but connected nonetheless by the path that fate or God has placed before us. I did not consciously think of this bond until after months or perhaps years of working with Ronin, and I'm not really sure exactly when it became apparent. I just recall a time when things suddenly became in sync. Everything clicked, and I "knew" him. I could feel what he would do before he would do it. And I'm absolutely convinced that he could read me equally as well. There was very little verbal communication; everything was conveyed through and along the length of the long lead.

My long lead was a thirty-foot length of three-eighths-inch rolled bull hide that was once used for the belts on industrial sewing machines. It was incredibly strong and resilient, ultimately outlasting both Ronin and

Placerville Police Department's Hank at the end of a long lead.

me. My long lead was our umbilical cord, and it connected us in ways I could not imagine until today. Everything was fed up and down the length of that lead to the point that I could read my Ronin in complete darkness only by the feel and tension. I knew when he was close to his target by feel alone, even in the stygian darkness of an underground creek tunnel beneath the cruel city streets of downtown Oakland, California. By this time, I had learned that illuminating yourself while hunting an armed criminal during the hours of darkness could draw bullets. I relied, then, on Ronin. His keen sense of smell became my eyes. But I have moved too far ahead.

When I realized this bond with Ronin, I was immediately struck by a loathing fear of losing it. I had never encountered anything remotely like it, and the thought of it breaking sent chills up and down my spine. It was a visceral, physical response to loss that bordered on physical sickness. I could not begin to analyze this concept, let alone dwell on the feeling for any length of time. How anything like Ronin could be taken away from me, I couldn't begin to understand. This was really a strange feeling for me, because I had learned as a teenager that sometimes my own personal pain was the only feeling I had in life. It was far easier to accept loss, because it was simply accepted as normal. But no—this was new and I had trouble with it. In retrospect, I realize that it was also a growth pattern as an adult that should have simply occurred when I was a child.

It was ultimately the relationship that I shared with Ronin that made possible all of his many amazing feats.

All training must have progression and growth. To do less is stifling and self-destructive. The puppy trails needed to progress from the point of the puppy's visual attempt to find the victim to the point when the puppy could do it by scent alone. This step is neither quick nor easy. It is accomplished with simple baby steps. The transition is done slowly over short distances and on soft surfaces, such as damp grass.

Shortly after the puppy can consistently smell the scent article and run and jump on the victim a few yards away, you should increase the distance by several more yards. Do this until the puppy loses the victim simply due to distance. By now, the pup should be using his nose to acquire the trail of the victim at least part of the time. The next step is to assign a gradual left or right turn to the trail and then lengthen the turn in intervals. The first turn for the puppy is really confusing, because he is running fast and invariably runs right past the turn. You should know the precise spot where the turn began by sighting a marker left by the victim. As the puppy passes the marker, you need to exert pressure on the lead by simply slowing down, then stopping. The pup normally recognizes that the victim isn't there, and he will start to cast about, attempting

Jeff and Ronin on an early training session when Ronin was about one year old.

to acquire the victim by sight, sound, and scent. There should be sufficient scent left by the victim's passing so that, when the puppy begins to quarter into the turn (because the handler is motionless), he detects the odor and begins again in the direction of the turn. At times, I found it necessary for the victim to drag a well-worn jacket or shirt along the trail turn to reinforce the odor and increase the amount of ground disturbance for the puppy.

The next step is to add more turns and distance. Once the puppy can run a trail that is 75 to 100 yards, it is time to move past the fire trail stage. The puppy should understand that the scent article has the scent of the target and be able to match it to the scent on the trail. I like to start aging the trails to about five to fifteen minutes at this point. I have the victim lay the trail out of the sight of the puppy and start using the scent article alone. I also use this time to transition to holding the article for the puppy rather than having him take it from the ground. I do this because the article will not always be large, with an abundance of odor, and often the ground will have more scent than a scent article you might hold in your hands.

As the puppy progresses, so, too, should the difficulty of the trail. Every time the puppy encounters a problem that is a little too difficult, it's important to take one step back and do something that the puppy knows well. Do this over and over again if necessary. Just remember that it's crucial not to move on until your dog understands the new problem completely.

Once my dog can run trails one-half mile or more with several turns on a soft surface, it is time to start changing things up. By now, the young dog is used to finding his victim standing or sitting all alone somewhere in a park or field. How does the dog respond to another person near the victim or walking across his trail? The natural instinct for exuberant puppies seems to be to jump on the first thing that moves on two legs, regardless of scent. The problem I faced was that it was counterproductive to throw a new person on the trail whom I knew the puppy was going to misidentify, because then I'd have to correct the dog. He had no chance to make a "right" decision.

I found that the best way to handle this situation is to use those baby steps I've talked about. I place a human distraction near the puppy's trail so that the puppy will see or smell the person without physically contacting him. He has a chance to identify two odors—the one on the trail and the one coming from this new person. Often, a new dog makes the right decision and the distraction is ignored. If the pup pays a little too much attention to the distraction, I give the command to "get to work" or "leave it," signaling the puppy that he has made a wrong choice and encouraging him to get back on the trail.

Once the puppy can consistently run past a motionless human distraction near the trail, I slowly move the distraction in closer with each progressive trail. By now, it is a "no brainer" for the puppy, and he will often just walk around the distraction even when it is standing right on the trail—which is our ultimate goal.

The next step is a little more difficult. As soon as the puppy encounters the human distraction, the distraction turns and walks in the opposite direction. Up until this time, the puppy has been dealing with non-moving human distractions; now one is moving. An instinctual response can be to chase the moving distraction. If this occurs, I simply remind the dog to get to work and keep him on the trail. We continue this step until the puppy is running it flawlessly.

Next is a running distraction, followed by a noise-making distraction, and then animals of various sorts on the trail. I repeat the same procedure for each consecutive step in training. If I have a problem, I simply step back a little, remembering that baby steps and repetition are the keys to success.

It has been important over the years for me to change every facet of training imaginable. I had to take into consideration everything that Ronin and I had been up against to date and imagine those things that we might encounter. Training was one thing, but real-life scenarios were my greatest teacher. I learned that I had to re-create in training situations what my dog and I had encountered on real cases. What would my dog do if he encountered a dead body? What happens if we get shot at? How does my dog react to a busy metropolitan city? Every new scenario often requires the baby-step approach. Other scenarios are a breeze; it simply depended upon the given situation.

One of the hardest situations to overcome was urban work. The city streets, with all of the traffic, people, garbage, and just "stuff" in general, are really hard on the dog. Imagine all of the distracting and contaminating odors. Sometimes, I could have all of the best conditions in the world for a trail and, simply due to the urban condition, the dog's job was impossible.

One of the most important roles that I had to teach Ronin was an identification move. In other words, he had to perform some act that I could articulate, and which said that the person he found was the one for whom we were looking. The normal response for puppies when they find their victims is to jump all over them. This can become a little hard on the victim when a bloodhound gets older and weighs in at about 100 pounds. People have a tendency not to like to be bowled over by large, slobbering hound dogs. I had to teach Ronin something a little more civil.

Thankfully, Kat helped me here, too. She had come up with an ID that she called the "California push." Kat put the California designator on it because all of her peers on the East Coast simply let their hounds jump up, and when her fellow handlers saw what she was doing, they said it must be a California thing. What Kat's dog did when he found the right person was to sit nicely and simply put a paw on the victim. Thus, the California push was born. Of course, I copied it, and that was what Ronin did from then on.

The training for this particular ID was pretty easy. Every time Ronin wanted to eat his dinner, he had to sit and paw me before he got the bowl. I had to sit him down a couple of times and put his paw on my leg just to show him what I was after, but it wasn't long until he pawed without thought. We simply moved this training to the ID of the victim at the end of the trail. Ronin would not get his Scooby snack reward until he sat and pawed. Since Ronin was a chow hound, I think we had to practice this twice.

My training was really varied at this point. Judy and I were working Ronin about five days a week, with an hour or two allotted for each session. We were also traveling weekly to meet and train with Kat from Livermore to Santa Cruz. This was about 100 miles round-trip. We knew by now that varied training scenarios, conditions, and environments were the key to our success, so there were times we would joyfully await the heaviest rainstorm of the season so that we could run the dog in it. Most of our neighbors thought we were crazy.

My son, Shayne, was probably one of the most important assistants I had in those days. When all of my neighbors and friends hid from me, Shayne was always there to lay a trail. He enlisted the aid of school friends from elementary school all the way to his high school years. Never once did he argue, and he always had a smile on his face. I think I have the best son in the world. Shayne had to really put up with a lot. This was not just *my* sacrifice of time but my family's as well. I was not getting paid or compensated in any way for this work, and I still had my regular police job to contend with. I was also the physical fitness coach for Shayne's youth football league. I look back on it now and often wonder how we ever did it.

Our entire vacations during those early years revolved around dog training. I received a certain amount of vacation days for every year of

Jeff and Ronin with Glenn Rimbey boarding a helicopter for training in Santa Fe, New Mexico.

police work in Alameda. I also accrued quite a bit of what is called comp time—overtime hours that collect over time—and I could either cash them in or use the time for days off in the future. I used all of my comp time and my vacation days on training.

Judy and I were now gallivanting around the country attending bloodhound seminars from New Mexico, Texas, and Kansas, to Wyoming, Colorado, and, of course, back in California. We seemed to have a school to attend two to three times every year. I put more than 30,000 miles on my Dodge in the first year alone. I was absolutely crazy!

But, it all paid off in the long run. I honestly believe it was my bottomless pit of passion for training Ronin, and the fact that he was simply a great dog, that carried us into the future.

Trails and Tribulation

I WAS SOON TO FIND OUT HOW MUCH MORE OF A COMMITMENT I would have
to make when we became an operational team. I was chomping at
the bit to work real cases, but I had no idea what I was asking for.
Ronin wasn't even ten months old yet, and I honestly believed that he
was God's gift to the bloodhound community. I didn't believe that there
was anything we could not do. Yes, I was incredibly arrogant and over-
bearing, but I couldn't help myself. I knew so deep in my soul that I had
a mission with this dog that nothing would stop us. The problem with
this situation was that Ronin was still a novice dog, and I couldn't even
begin to consider myself more than, perhaps, a rookie. However, I believe that there is a certain power in just being headstrong. I look back
on it now and see that, if I did not have conviction, there were simply
some hurdles that I never would have crossed—in particular, the issue
of the inordinate amount of time I was spending on Ronin's training. It
was commitment and faith that pulled us through every setback and
naysayer that Ronin and I ever encountered.

One of the first hurdles I had to cross was Ronin's puberty, which is
the only thing I can call it. He was ten months old and just kicking ass
on every trail he ran. Kat was really getting excited about our prospects,
and people in my department were even starting to come on board.
Then the hormones struck with a mighty vengeance that could have top-
pled buildings. Ronin went from a focused manhunting machine to a
critter hound overnight—or so it seemed. He wouldn't even sniff the
scent article I presented to him because the bush with another dog's pee
on it smelled oh so much better.

If I was lucky enough to get Ronin to start to run a trail when he was this age, I was equally lucky if he didn't stop to pee on a tree within the first five feet. This went on and on and on and on. He peed so much that he could have filled a five-gallon bucket. I didn't know how a dog could have so much pee in him. I was simply flabbergasted! Oh! And God forbid that a bitch in heat was anywhere within 100 miles. If there was even the prospect of that happening, we were going nowhere. What a mess we were. I was so upset but could do absolutely nothing about the situation . . . or so I thought.

Thankfully, I had a wife in the veterinary business. Judy had recently taken a job as a veterinarian technician after about twenty years in the pet retail industry. She knew the dilemma I faced and had just the cure. She said it very well when she told me that where there are no hormones, there is no distraction. Of course, it had to be a woman who thought of this theory. Judy told me that if we neutered Ronin all would be well within a few weeks. In hindsight, I'm glad my parents didn't consider this for me when I was a kid!

The decision was made, and the day came when Ronin underwent a minor, albeit radical, medical procedure. When he returned home, Ronin was minus a couple of parts, but seemed none the worse for wear. Within a very few days, he was up and running minor trails and doing very well again. As time went on, his distraction level returned to a normal low, and I could trust him again. His energy level was a little low at first, but that was due to the surgery. I didn't expect anything less. Ronin was working his trails smoothly, and the bushes in the surrounding area were staying somewhat dry.

It was around this age, that Kat and I began to make some serious inroads with certain search-and-rescue venues. Kat had a number of contacts and was well respected in the field. When I say "Kat and I," I really should be saying Kat. Kat had the connections and arranged the meetings, and I came along for the ride. I had input on everything we were doing, but she was the expert and I deferred to her judgment. We made an arrangement with a couple of local police departments and a search and rescue (SAR) group to assist them with missing person cases in Santa Clara County. They had been using dog teams for a number of years, but bloodhounds were still a little new. This was a dream come true for me, because I had not even had the opportunity to work my first case yet. Here I was running with Kat, and we just seemed to land a pretty big job. How little did I know about how big this venture was going to be. The general plan was that, when there was a significant missing-person case in the area, either Kat or I would be called to respond. The only drawback was that any response was on our own time, on a strictly volunteer basis, and without the blessings of our respective departments. This was only a drawback in the sense that our time would be limited due to our workloads. We were both more than willing to volunteer our time for what we considered to be the worthiest of all causes—we just needed the time!

I don't believe that we had even finished shaking hands with the representatives of the Santa Clara County Search and Rescue Group when the first call outs came in. We were in an interesting situation in that regard as well. Kat and I were rogue handlers in a way. It was common for volunteers involved in the SAR trade to be associated with a particular search and rescue group and to be certified in a wide variety of activities. It was just this certification about which Kat and I had reservations. SAR groups have to work diligently to ensure that their members are, at minimum, sane and able to do the job asked of them. They also have to make darned sure that their people can work a wide variety of SAR call outs. Consequently, considerable training and tests are required.

Kat and I, on the other hand, were already certified peace officers, with much of the training already under our belts, and we were only interested in one mission—to work our bloodhounds. At the time, there were absolutely no bloodhound programs in existence in the area other than ours. I guess that we could certify ourselves, but what would be the point? There were other dog certification programs for these SAR groups, but we did not feel that they really had our methods and goals in mind.

We bypassed this process primarily because we were peace officers working for other police agencies. This streamlined our deployment and smoothed any ruffled feathers we may have encountered on the civilian side of the situation.

Our first deployments involved mostly missing children and Alzheimer's patients. Both of these cases are tough no matter how you slice it. Add a search dog team into the equation and it gets tougher, mainly for the search dog team. I didn't realize it when I first got into this process that we would end up being the last people called in for the majority of our searches. Even though search dogs are featured on TV regularly and the various agencies for which we worked knew of our services, it seemed like we were always the last to be invited to the party. There are probably two reasons for this. First, the dog is just often over-looked. It is human nature to think in terms that we can understand, and that primarily has to do with in how we visually identify and interpret things. Dogs use scent to follow and locate prey or people, and scent is just too foreign of a concept for most people who would normally never think twice about it. Many of the concepts of which I have already written, coupled with many of those on which I haven't even touched, make it difficult for any search manager who is not knowledgeable about search dogs to make a decision to call for them. Similarly, if you have no knowledge of the dogs or how they work, it is very difficult to prepare a scene for a search dog's arrival.

The second reason, in my opinion, is sheer stubbornness. Many agencies loathe the thought of calling for mutual aid in their own back-yard. They may have the misconception that assets from other agencies constitute a threat to their order of business or that they simply can do things better. The solution to the problem, as I see it, is simple. When there is a missing child or endangered person, no stone is left unturned. You have to do whatever it takes to find that person. There is often very little time to find missing children or endangered persons before some-thing dreadful happens to them. It takes skilled search managers with ex-perience to form a search plan in an expedited fashion. There is no time to lose or waste. It is the responsibility of every law-enforcement agency to have a plan in place to deal with these circumstances and to have trained managers already designated to manage the operation. Knowledgeable search managers know when and when not to call in the dogs. They understand the variety of search dogs available, be they expert in trailing, air scent, cadaver, or avalanche. All trained search dogs are not created equal. There is a significant difference in skills and training. A good search manager knows immediately what assets he has at his disposal and how to deploy them.

In the case of a missing person at risk, a trailing dog should be one of the first assets on the scene. Everything else can evolve as time and resources dictate, but the trailing dog needs to be there first. I've already written about many of the problems for which a trailing dog needs to be trained; however, the one factor that can never be completely accounted for is time. Time is the killer of scent, plain and simple. It is impossible for a handler, or anyone else for that matter, to say how viable a trail is based on the age. It is always safest to assume that the fresher the trail, the easier it will be for the dog to follow it.

The other issue, besides age of the trail, is contamination. The more people at the scene looking around, the more confusing it is for the dog to unravel the scent picture. Remember the smoke bomb scenario I described with the trail layer walking down a path with a certain colored smoke bomb? Think of that same scenario and thirty more people, all with their own color of smoke on the same trail. Add that to urban conditions with the thousands of other people who came and went before, during, and after the missing person traveled there, and you can see the scent dilemma a dog can face. Why add to the problem?

In the case of a trailing dog, the handler needs to acquire a good scent article that has not been contaminated by other people. The scent article is crucial for the dog to find the correct scent of the person on the trail. If a tremendous amount of investigation has occurred prior to the arrival of the dog handler, there is a good chance that quality available scent material may have already been contaminated. The last thing a handler wants to do is follow the trail of the wrong person. It is embarrassing and takes time away from the real investigation.

I had just this scenario play out on one evening in Alameda in the case of a car thief who had fled the stolen car when he was stopped by a patrol. I was one of the last people on the scene with Ronin, but thankfully, most of my fellow officers were cognizant of saving scent material. The officer who stopped the suspect gave me a breakdown on who may have touched what items in the car. I thought that I had accounted for all of the officers when I collected my article.

It can be hard to locate items in stolen cars, believe it or not. The car actually belongs to someone else, and that person's scent permeates the car. The suspect may have been in contact with the car for only a short time, and his scent signature may not be as strong as that of the owner. Therefore, I try to obtain scent from something that has been in direct contact with the suspect's skin, such as the steering wheel, a tool used to punch the ignition, clothing he left behind, etc. In this case, I discovered some papers on the floorboard that appeared to identify the suspect. This person happened to be a regular customer of ours and was relatively well known anyway. Technically, even if Ronin couldn't find the guy, his paperwork would identify him later. We weren't spinning our wheels, as it would be nice to catch him that evening with a dog, but it wasn't all-consuming either.

Probably because of this lazy attitude of mine, this became an embarrassing trail rather quickly. I simply grabbed the papers on the floorboard, not inquiring as to whom might have already handled them, and started Ronin next to the car door. I wanted to get this case over quickly, because I was backed up on reports and needed to go home at a reasonable hour. Ronin picked up the trail quite easily and with good speed. He was trotting at a good pace with his nose plastered to pavement, alternating back and forth to patches of grass or vegetation.

Ronin quickly established a pattern, which should have been my first clue that there was also a problem. Patterns on a trail down a city street on which a fleeing felon is running really don't happen—at least in

Alameda. These knuckleheads typically find the best backyard where they can hop over a fence, and then they continue to hop subsequent fences until they are gone. Looking back on it now, I can easily see what the mistake was, but back then, I was just following my dog—deaf, dumb, and blind as a bat.

The pattern Ronin was running went a little like this: He started by the car, which was in a residential section of downtown Alameda. Houses are butted up right next to each other for the length of every block. In front of each house is a little patch of lawn, and in front of that is the sidewalk, which runs the length of the street. Ronin trotted down the sidewalk to the walkway or grass lawn of every house without fail and checked the front door. He would then turn around, go back the way he came, and continue down the sidewalk. Every now and then he would cut diagonally across a patch of lawn, but for the most part, he trotted in and out of each walkway from the sidewalk to each and every front door on that block. Not exactly something a criminal would do. However, as I said before, I was oblivious.

This pattern lasted for about a block and a half when Ronin started to pull and strain at the lead with a sense of urgency. He was whining a bit and his head was up. This was a sure sign that we were close to what he was looking for. Stupid me—I still hadn't connected the dots on this caper and I, too, began to get excited. I called in on the radio and let my brother officers know that we might be close to the suspect while simultaneously asking for backup and giving my exact location. Of course, this created a flurry of police activity punctuated by squealing tires and the occasional "whoop, whoop" of someone cycling their siren to move traffic. All the noise was converging on me, and that was a good thing, because it meant that the cavalry was coming.

The cavalry is a nice thing for a bloodhound handler; especially for this bloodhound handler, because Ronin did not bite. I had been in many a fight in his presence in the past, and the only thing he did was sound off with "whooo, hooo" repeatedly while wagging his tail. (I call this Ronin's seal pup impersonation.) Even when things started to go badly, he was still just the happy-go-lucky Ronin. Everyone was his friend, including the guy who was trying to kick my ass. On many of these little foot chases of fleeing felons, there was always the possibility of a fight. These men just didn't seem to want to go to jail all the time. Ronin was useless in a fight, because he would simply sit there and howl, expecting me to throw a cookie his way while I was blocking punches. We actually began to have patrol dogs run behind Ronin for just these situations; I always had a backup officer in tow, too.

Well, here we were, getting close to the front porch of a house where I expected to find the suspect, and the cavalry was surrounding me on all sides. As we lit up the porch with a plethora of handheld flashlights, who walked off the porch? Just another brother in blue! He looked up at all of the commotion while jotting something in his notebook and exclaimed that he was wondering what the heck was happening with all the radio traffic and noise. Ronin ran up to the officer, sat down, and tagged him in good identifying fashion and looked at me for a cookie. I asked the officer if he had been in the stolen car, and he replied that of course he had and wondered if I had taken a look at the suspect's papers that he had used to identify the suspect in the first place. He said that once he discovered the information, he decided to conduct a neighborhood check with all of the residents on the block to see if they had heard or noticed anything suspicious in their yards that evening. I gave Ronin his cookie while the suspect was probably already at home watching us on the 11:00 news.

My only excuse is that there was no instructional manual for what I was doing. Yes, by now I had run into other people doing the same thing, and I had done a lot of training, but there was really no police academy for bloodhound handling. I may not have been a pioneer, but there certainly wasn't anything I could use as an officer-safety guideline. We had to make it up as we went along our merry way. I made a lot of mistakes and I learned from them, rarely making the same one twice.

That last story was a perfect example of why it was important for a handler to use a good, uncontaminated scent article. If he didn't, he could end up finding something unexpected.

The last thing I needed to have was a good location where the person for whom we were looking was known to have been. You might think that this was relatively easy, but I am here to tell you that even when things appear plain on the outside, they can be complicated on the inside.

Take, for example, a case fast-forwarded to, again, in the future. Ronin and I were working in Alameda on a Friday night some summer a few years ago. The night was a little balmy, and things had been a little slow so far, and I was getting a little bored. Just as I was thinking how bored I really was, I received a call to respond to the home of a victim who had reported a 261 PC—a rape.

All sexual crime cases have to be treated with the utmost care and sensitivity. It is easy to destroy evidence and even easier to bruise the already traumatized psyche of the victim. A lot of specialized training goes into preparing for these investigations, but that still doesn't really quite help an officer on the first few cases with which he or she might have to deal. By this time, I had worked quite a few sex cases and knew what procedure to follow. I called for my supervisor, a civilian counselor just for these circumstances, and a female officer to help me with questioning if necessary.

I had everything lined up for my interview with the victim and her family when I arrived at her house within a few minutes of the call out. Ronin waited in the car as usual, and I wasn't prepared to use him at this point anyway. I didn't know what kind of case I had. I was met at the door by the victim, who did not look disheveled at all. For that matter, she appeared to be pretty happy and healthy. She seemed completely normal, did not seem withdrawn in any way, and was even smiling from time to time. A rape victim's look can be deceiving, though. No two victims are ever the same, and it can be hard for a victim to get a handle on what is going on inside her own head. Patience, care, and complete understanding are mandatory.

The story came quite easily for the teenage girl, and she had little trouble in relaying what had happened to her that night. She told me that she had been walking to her boyfriend's house several blocks away on the west end of town when she noticed a dark-colored, late-model sedan rolling up behind her. She watched the right, rear passenger throw out gang signs to her as the driver drove past her very slowly up the street and around the corner. She advised me that her boyfriend belonged to a rival gang of the men in the car and that they were obviously targeting her because of the boyfriend. She said that suddenly, the men in the car jumped out and ran up to her, pinning her up against a wooden fence on a residential sidewalk. She told me that the guy who threw the gang signs ripped off her pants, threw her to the ground, and raped her right there on the pavement. She said that she screamed for help, but nobody responded or even looked out their window to see the commotion. As suddenly as the men appeared, they ran back to their car and sped away.

I immediately called for an ambulance to respond, evaluate the victim, and take her to the hospital for an exam. I conferred with my supervisor and asked for my female partner to finish with the interview while I responded to the scene. We have only a short time in which to gather evidence in situations that occur in public places before that evidence is ruined.

The girl was apparently still wearing the pants from the time of the crime, and I had my partner obtain them as evidence. I placed them in a bag and brought them with me. My plan was to use Ronin at the scene to see if I could get a trail to the location to where the men had run or to where the car had been parked. A couple of other officers responded as well to help collect more evidence and conduct a neighborhood check for witnesses.

I went to the area of the fence that the victim had told me about and started Ronin on the pants. He smelled the scent article, took a couple of steps, stopped, and just started to whine. This is an indication that he does not have a trail from the article. I moved him around to a couple of other places on the sidewalk, thinking that I may not have had the correct location. There were several more starts and no luck. Ronin was going nowhere fast. This was really strange, because, at minimum, he should have followed the victim's trail to her family's apartment. But he had no scent trail at all. This was really strange. Normally, with crimes of a terrifying nature, there is plenty of scent for Ronin to pick up. He had nothing here—not even the victim's scent.

Shortly after I tried to work Ronin, one of my fellow beat officers reported that he talked to the neighbors who lived behind the wooden fence. They had been watching television in their family room directly behind the wooden fence, and their windows were open. They heard nothing.

The facts in this case were not adding up at all. The girl's attitude was nonchalant, there was no evidence at the scene or scent trail from anyone, and none of the neighbors heard or saw anything. I recommended to my supervisor that we take another crack at interviewing the victim. This would not be easy, however. The victim had her counselor present, and she was being prepared for an exam. All of the wheels were turning for a proper rape investigation. We had to let them play out.

In the end, it was discovered that the girl had fabricated the story to get the attention of her boyfriend, whom she felt was cheating on her. This was a lesson in many senses of the word, but it was also directly relative to working my dog. If the person for whom you are looking was not in the area where you start your dog, you will not have a trail. My luck was that Ronin was able to tell me this through body language.

To recap, what is needed for a good trail that may or may not be successful are the following:

- A timely call out within a couple of hours of the missing person's disappearance.
- Little to no contamination of the area and the scent article.
- A location where the person was known to have been.
- Lots of luck.

Even when the situation seems perfect, a handler cannot always be sure that the dog will have a good scent trail. Many times, the trail simply peters out for a myriad of reasons. The bottom line is that we cannot detect what the dogs smell, nor can we measure the scent for our own benefit or satisfaction. We have to be able to read our dogs' behavioral patterns and interpret them.

Consider what might happen when everything is all messed up and nothing is in the handler's favor. Technically, the handler should think about packing up and going home. However, if the case is of a missing person at risk or a very serious crime, the handler might have to suck it up and give it the old Boy Scout try. If everything fails, however, and there is just nothing to be found, it is OK to say that you gave it your best shot but the dog couldn't find anything. A veteran handler learns this sometimes years after he or she starts working a dog. I always have encouraged new handlers to accept the fact early to save heartache and frustration later. The simple truth of a trailing dog's career in an urban environment is that there will be more failures than finds. If a new handler expects fame and fortune out of this job, then he or she is in for a major disappointment.

I am guilty of producing a behavior in my dog during my early years that I see duplicated quite often even amongst senior handlers. I was guilty of making my dog run what I call "ghost trails." I define a ghost trail as an imaginary trail; no particular scent is being followed and the dog is simply running to please his handler. Remember when I wrote about the lead being an umbilical cord connecting the dog and handler and of a relationship that is incredibly close? Well, this same relationship can cause a good dog to run bad trails. All working dogs desperately want to please their handlers, and they pick up on little cues and human signals exhibited through our own body language that indicate, to them, a course of action. Sometimes it can be as little as a slight change in tone of voice that will trigger a response from the dog.

I remember the time well when this began for me. Ronin was working well and we already had made a few good finds, and I was anxious to work more complicated cases. I volunteered for anything that I could—good, bad, or just stupid. I'd try to work Ronin on cases that he had absolutely no business working, because nothing was there for him to work with in the first place. When he could not find a trail, Ronin would immediately key in on my disappointment. My feelings were worn on my long lead, and he felt everything that I did. I could tell this by his demeanor when we failed. Yet, I would encourage him and cajole him into trying to work just a little more, even when I knew it was pointless. I did this out of my own vanity and self-absorbed pride, and my dog suffered for it. Ronin quickly learned that I was pleased if he seemed to be working. He started to mimic his own working behavior as if he was on a real trail. There were telltale signals that this was exactly what he was doing, but I was oblivious at first because I so desperately wanted him to run the trail.

I remember the first time Ronin ran a ghost trail as if it were yesterday. We were working a robbery case on a beachfront road in Alameda during a late afternoon shift. The suspects had physically assaulted the victim and taken some money (probably drugs as well), then fled on foot to a waiting car. I knew that there was little in the way of a viable trail, but I decided to try it anyway. And, in a way, this was a victimless crime. The "victim" was nothing more than an upset drug dealer who wanted to use the police for his own tool of revenge. As I knew would happen, Ronin picked up a short trail to where the car had been parked, and then it promptly petered out. At this time, I was under the mistaken belief that bloodhounds could routinely follow car trails. In other words, the scent of the person would escape as the car went down the highway. Many other bloodhound handlers supported this theory heavily and preached just as strongly. Being relatively new to the job, I believed it, too.

I pushed Ronin even when I knew that the trail was going sour. He was showing me all of the telltale signs of a bad trail, such as whining, looking around, and simply stopping. I continued to push and prod even when I saw that it was confusing him. I was so stuck in the paradigm that my dog should do this type of trail that I was oblivious to everything he was telling me. Something clicked in Ronin, and I'm not sure if it was plain exasperation with me and he wanted me to shut up, or if he just wanted to make me happy. I like to think that it was the former, but knowing dogs as I know them now, he wanted to please me. His world was making me happy. Nothing is more selfless; nothing human, that is.

Jeff and Ronin working a crime scene at an unknown location.

Ronin dropped his nose slightly and pulled into his harness and just started to run down the sidewalk. He did not look left. He did not look right. He did not change his speed or effort. He simply trotted down the way. Still in a state of self-absorption, I was happy that he was going. The problem is, we went nowhere and wasted a lot of time doing it.

It did not take me long to figure out what was going on. It took far longer to correct it. Ronin now thought that if he just ran, I was happy. He continued this behavior for weeks, and it took countless training sessions to curb him of a problem that I had created. This is the sorry truth of the matter. Ronin was a wonderful dog and worked exceptionally well. I was really lucky to have him as my first working dog, because he carried me through each and every mistake I made in training and through real-life cases—and he still wanted to run with me. I know I could never ask for a better coworker, and I wonder if there is friend who would ever do as much as Ronin did for me.

Myth Busting

I'M GOING TO TELL YOU THE TRUTH ABOUT POLICE BLOODHOUNDS. I won't pull any punches, and what I write about here is based upon my own training and experience. I came to know this breed quite intimately, probably better than anything I have ever known, because I lived and breathed bloodhounds and trailing for more than a decade of my life. As with everything I do passionately, I became obsessive. I read, I wrote, I worked, and I spoke about bloodhounds only for much of my police career. I really didn't care about anything else, and everyone knew it. I hung out with police officers and K-9 handlers, and all of my vacation or off-duty time was spent training bloodhounds or going to bloodhound seminars. I had such a one-track mind that I was very difficult to be around—unless, of course, you wanted to hear about bloodhounds.

I do not believe there is another breed of dog that is more surrounded by myth than the bloodhound. Perhaps this is because the breed is so ancient. However, I also think that the reason is because bloodhounds were the original purebred dog specifically bred to find people, criminals, or missing persons by scent. The breed was recognized as far back as the Dark Ages as being a phenomenal scent hound. The bloodhound was given carte blanche in seventeenth-century England to pursue its quarry through any land holding, property, or home. It had a "King's warrant" for lack of better words.

During the birth of our own country, the bloodhound was a necessary tool used to hunt marauding bands of Indians who attacked early American settlements on the East Coast. I remember reading a very old advertisement or want ad from an eighteenth-century America village requesting the aid and importation of bloodhounds from the English homeland just for this purpose.

It is said that bloodhounds were used to pursue runaway slaves up to the end of our American Civil War. How much of this is true will never really be known, as there is so little in the way of historical references or documentation to support the claim. I am sure that bloodhounds were used for this purpose, but to what extent, I remain skeptical. The breed was not common in olden times, and purebred bloodhounds commanded a heavy price. The name "bloodhound" is from the term "pure of blood." Furthermore, what is written of these runaway slave dogs often refers to mixed-breed curs that were bred not only for their ability to follow human scent but also for their sheer ferocity. For the most part, bloodhounds do not make ferocious dogs, and the breed has never been known for this trait.

Still, movies new and old often portray the bloodhound in whatever theatrical light best suits the film. Rarely is any effort made to accurately show the bloodhound for what the breed truly is. Some films, such as *Cool Hand Luke*, produce their own set of myths that actually help a bloodhound handler. There have been many convicts who, after seeing the tricks played on the bloodhound on film, attempted to duplicate them for their own escape or evasion purposes. I absolutely loved it when a criminal decided to use a stream or creek to mask his scent. Ronin worked better around water than anywhere else.

Then there are stories such as *Uncle Tom's Cabin* that evoke a fear of the breed that transcends the ages and polarizes races. I encountered the race-card hurdle during my efforts to establish Ronin as a police dog. Some members of the community looked at the bloodhound as the epitome of slavery and racial discrimination. Thankfully, these people were relatively few, but they did make their voice heard.

The bloodhound is actually the quintessential American police dog. This might be hard to believe for many who recognize the German shepherd as the poster dog in police circles. However, long before the German shepherd ever hit American shores, the bloodhound was being used by law enforcement for one purpose only—to find people. Moderniza-tion and new law-enforcement practices changed the situation dramati-cally in the twentieth century. The bloodhound, although still present, slipped almost into obscurity. The droopy-eyed, long-eared, slobbering, goofy bloodhound moved aside for the sleek and intimidating German shepherd, along with a few other breeds. This has remained so to the present. For the most part, the majority of police departments or sheriffs' offices know little about the capability of the bloodhound. Fewer still have access to a hound or have one on their staff.

Over the last twenty years or so, the bloodhound has made a come-back—not a strong one, but a recovery nonetheless. I attribute this to dog handlers simply branching out and reevaluating old ideas. I also believe that the media had something to do with it. No longer do we get our news from the local village crier—we get it from a global, mass-market-ing television screen that tells us everything we need to know about the world from Moscow to San Francisco. A horrendous crime that occurs in the backwoods of a small town in Florida is flashed across TV screens long before the police reports are even written.

Throughout the ages, there have always been relatively few dedicated bloodhound handlers who used their dogs for their own communities. Some of these new, modern pioneers were directly responsible for solv-ing some of the most heinous crimes in our history. Names such as Bill Tolhurst, Jerry Yelk, Glenn Rimbey, Larry Harris, Jerry Nichols, John Luten-berg, John Salem, and Doug Lowry immediately come to mind. I was for-tunate to train with and learn from all of them. Their exploits were commemorated by their local news agencies and communities but were also broadcast nationwide. These exploits are what have gained the ad-miration and interest of so many new bloodhound recruits—me included.

Little of the way in which bloodhounds are worked has changed over the generations. We still need the hound, the harness, the long lead, and the scent article. What has changed is the environment. Soggy bay-ous have given way to paved suburban neighborhoods, and small vil-lages in pristine, forested mountains have evolved into monstrous urban jungles filled with pollution and every noxious odor imaginable. Yet, the bloodhound remains relatively unchanged—a large breed with a sensitive nose, stubborn beyond thinking, but generally loving and loyal. The environment has not changed the bloodhound, but it has affected the way the bloodhound works.

Any canid excels in a natural environment, one filled with nature rather than man-made objects and materials. Massive concentrations of humanity do affect the way in which a bloodhound works, and it is confusing. Bloodhounds can be trained to work in city environments, but it is never easy regardless of what anyone might profess. The bloodhound, as with all trailing dogs, works far better in a rural environment. If a handler plans on working in an urban area, it is absolutely crucial to train the dog in the environment in which it will work—slowly and with baby steps. Even then, the success of an urban dog will normally not equal that of a rural dog.

There are many urban myths surrounding the bloodhound, primarily because of media hype and blind devotees who believe that the bloodhound is unsurpassable in all venues. The myths simply help to promote the bloodhound mystique.

Some myths have a basis in truth, however. Car trails come immediately to mind. A car trail is a situation where a person leaves the scene in a vehicle of some sort, and his or her scent is blown through the vents or windows on the car back to the street. This appears plausible on the surface, considering how sensitive a dog's nose is, but it is incredibly difficult for a dog to do in real situations. I was taught that car trails were a normal course of business for a bloodhound handler, and we practiced them in seminars and on our own. Practice and training are one thing, but real life is something altogether different. During training, handlers can make their dogs do anything they want and discover as many ways to rationalize whatever behavior the dogs exhibit. I know this because I did it. It took real-life cases and crimes to prove to me that what we trained for and how we actually worked were two separate conditions. Thankfully, I recognized the futility of some of my early training methods and mended my ways. I believe that this came about due to my experiences as a soldier and a police officer. In order to survive, training had to be realistic.

Once Ronin and I began to work real cases in the urban jungles of the Bay Area, I quickly learned that most criminal trails eventually became car trails, and that the majority simply ended nowhere in particular. Sure, Ronin seemed to follow the trail for a short distance after the car drove off, but the trails invariably ended after a few hundred yards. Out of the hundreds of real-life trails that ended with a car, only one might have been successful. This was the case not only for my dog, but for every dog I saw work across the country. I concluded that car trails might be possible from time to time, but the success rate was so low that it was irresponsible for me to say that we could do them. It was far more ethical to ignore the topic and simply say that we'd do our best.

The car trails case that I mentioned above might have been successful. I know this because someone shot at us very close to where the suspect was finally caught—several miles from the crime scene. This story is difficult for me to tell, because it is about the death of a brother officer, and it was the sheer madness of this crime that initiated our call out.

A police officer was shot and killed by a gang member from the overpass on a freeway in Oakland, California. The suspect fled in a vehicle but left behind a piece of evidence that was later used to convict him. It was a 7.62 x 39 mm empty bullet casing found on the sidewalk of the overpass. This bullet is commonly used by various Eastern Block countries, pre– and post–Cold War. The most common rifles that use this bullet are the SKS and the AK-47.

I received the call out while I was on patrol in Alameda on a midnight shift. I was called into the office and told that an officer had been shot in Oakland and that Ronin's services were required. Upon arrival, I was met by several Oakland Police Department officers and detectives at the scene. They told me they had called for us because they had heard that bloodhounds could follow the scent of a suspect who had fled in a car. I didn't want to argue with them, because I could see that they'd attempt anything necessary to find the suspect. When a fellow officer is killed, no stone is left unturned. I would try to help them in any way I could.

Thankfully, we arrived at the location very quickly, long before the crime scene was processed. I was allowed access to the overpass first, which was important if we were to get any decent scent material. Unfortunately, the only scent article I had was the spent cartridge case left on the sidewalk after it had been ejected by the semi-automatic weapon. The casing had been recovered as per my directions and placed in a bag with a sterile gauze pad. I allowed the two some time to commingle, then extracted the pad and placed it in a heavy-duty Zip-Lock bag.

A spent shell casing is one of the most extreme forms of scent articles that there is. It is a small piece of brass that has been cycled through a weapon and exposed to extreme heat and pressure. Couple these problems with the fact that the shooter probably had very little contact with the cartridge except when he loaded it, and you have a recipe for no trail. As a matter of fact, that was how most of those types of incidents resulted for us in real life. Training was easy, because we controlled many of the variables. In real cases, you just didn't know what had happened to the scent article before you got it.

And I had no idea what had happened to this shell casing before we got there. It may have been stepped on by a pedestrian, or it may have been there for some time before the shooting. It was really a crap shoot, and I didn't know what to expect. I was anxious, though, because of the nature of the crime and the fact that all eyes were on us. Talk about a load of pressure. It was enormous, and I could feel my bulletproof vest soaking up the sweat. There was nothing to go on at this point other than the fact that an officer had been killed. I didn't know the man, and neither did the majority of us at the scene, but he was still a brother and deserved whatever we could do.

I had impressed upon the scene commander the absolute need for lack of human traffic. The location was in downtown Oakland, which was already contaminated, and a lot of officers and crime scene technicians would make it even worse. I had my doubts about this trail, but couldn't talk about my feelings. As far as everyone was concerned, we were going to find the trail, and they gave me every accommodation I asked for.

I started Ronin in the area where the shooter should have been using the pad that I had extracted from the shell casing bag. In theory, I should have some scent on the pad to identify the shooter and the trail. I scented Ronin on the pad and gave him the command to search—"Skit it!" I'm not sure to this day why things started off so well in this case, but I could tell by Ronin's demeanor long before he took scent that he was going to do something good. He had an aura about him that was so confident that everyone around us seemed to visibly relax as he trotted up to our starting point. His confidence buoyed mine, when it actually was supposed to be the other way around.

Ronin took the scent and was onto a trail before I could finish the command to search. In some ways, I think he may have known who we were looking for before we started. Perhaps the overwhelming emotional state that the suspect must have been in permeated the area with fear scent. I'm not really sure what happened, but we took off like the space shuttle. We headed west down High Street at a good clip, with a full contingent of tactical officers pulling up the rear.

Most of the guys behind me were from my own department and were good friends. I knew I could count on them if the shit hit the fan. I had a vague, uneasy feeling about this trail. Aside from the pressure of the sheer madness of the crime, something else was bothering me there. Ronin was moving far too well and seemed to have relatively few problems, if any. It was dark on this trail, even though the streets were lit by streetlights. Perhaps the darkness was also due to the general feeling of anger, fear, and hate that accompanied this trail. I know that we all felt something because of the way we looked at each other. Maybe it was for comfort or simple camaraderie, but deep down inside, I knew it was because of the brotherhood that bound us in moments such as these, and nothing could get in our way.

Ronin must have felt something from all of us. I know that he was tuned into my own tension and sense of commitment, and his every movement was indicative of this. Ronin was an extension of me but was also connected to the men who followed me. We were a team—or perhaps a pack—in his mind. Each of us had a purpose and role to play on this dark night when even the streetlights could not pierce the blackness. None of this really mattered to him, because we were on the hunt and only the prey was in mind. The officer who had been killed this night would be avenged. We all knew this, and Ronin was leading the way.

We headed north along a side street to the main highway and trotted with determination. There was no rest or pause. We just ran, silent and with single-minded purpose. Ronin did not stop to pee on bushes or check out the most recent dog spoor in the neighborhood; he just ran with his nose hovering a foot or so off of the ground. Occasionally, I heard a feint snuffling from him as he attempted to gain more scent, but the trail was eerily quiet. The rest of the noises were nothing more than the slap of booted feet following behind, punctuated by a muffled cough from time to time. It was as if the sound of human voices would break the spell or rhythm that we seemed to be under.

Up until this point on our path, we had been ruled by stealth and quiet. We practiced noise and light discipline as best as possible, because we had no intention of giving ourselves away. Our advantage was Ronin's nose, speed, and relative quiet should we come upon the creature that had committed this crime. However, once Ronin ran into a neighborhood park, our speed slowed to a walk and Ronin began casting about. I could not see him well; he was nothing more than a dim shape or shadow, for there was nothing left of the streetlights that were now behind us. Still, I could feel his intention as his head cast from left to right. Something was here—maybe not very close—but it was something nonetheless.

The team spread out a little as everyone tried to get an idea of where we were and what, if anything, we might encounter. I had not said a word to our small squad, but they seemed to instinctively know that something was amiss, and the inky blackness only accentuated the feeling. Suddenly, Ronin pulled hard into the harness as if he had made a conscious decision about where it was we needed to go. Because it was so dark, I had no sense other than being attuned to Ronin. My steps over barriers or debris were made by almost a type of braille. I could feel Ronin move left and right, and increase or decrease speed, but I could also feel what he ran over through the length of the long lead. My steps were co-ordinated with this feeling through the line. It was almost like a telegraph wire signaling to us back and forth. The only obstructions that the lead did not account for were the limbs and brush that Ronin went under and did not detect himself. Those normally hit me right in the face.

The darkness became too much for one member of the team. I don't know to this day who it was, and I do not hold him accountable in any way. I really don't blame anyone for using a flashlight here. The park through which we were traipsing was a hornet's nest of crime and "crack" cocaine dealing. Just because it was night didn't mean that the "kids" had all gone home. For this park was not a park for children at all. This had ended many years earlier when the neighborhood had changed hands to the thugs who ruled it now. Police presence was nothing more than an annoyance for most people here, and a lone officer should never feel safe. We were not in our element, and we all knew it.

I was in some kind of zone, running behind Ronin that night. I didn't hear much of anything, and I was only seeing what I could of my dog. It was almost a form of tunnel vision. This tunnel vision is exactly why a bloodhound handler should always run a case with a cover man. The cover man is a team member whose sole focus is to be the eyes and the ears of the handler. It was my cover man who may have saved my life that night. I say "may," because to this day, I have no memory of what happened. I was literally deaf, dumb, and blind to the moment. What I do remember is being yanked savagely backward and told to take cover behind a boulder. I hadn't even noticed the flashlight being extinguished. I remember feeling my cover man's breath on my ear as he hissed that we were being shot at and seeing the shadowy form of his hand pointing in front of us. I saw it then—the hot flash of a muzzle blast pointed in our direction. I could not really say how far it was—maybe thirty or forty yards. Darkness confuses your vision, and depth and distance can be deceiving. I saw a couple of shots but had no memory of how many had come before.

I reeled Ronin in almost as fast as I fell down behind the boulder. I could tell that he didn't like it, because he was howling in frustration and leaping at the end of the lead. I tried to hush him, but he would have nothing to do with it. He, too, now heard the shots, and he wanted at them. I had no way to determine if the shooter here was the same as the shooter at the bridge, because gunfire was definitely not uncommon in this park. It could be anyone shooting at us. However, we had to assume that it was the same person and take the appropriate action to protect ourselves. We were armed with pistols and a couple of Remington 870 shotguns with low-recoil 00 buckshot. An SKS or AK had us outgunned, plain and simple, and it would be suicide to move forward. We could only take cover and call for the cavalry. Hell, we couldn't even shoot back for fear of hitting the homes behind the suspect.

It took a little while to get the backup we needed to extract ourselves because of the massive police presence at the crime scene. I think that, once we were out of the area of the crime scene, we were no longer the focus of attention. Consequently, we hid behind boulders and trees for a long time before we were rescued. By the time everything was said and done, I was unable to start Ronin again on any meaningful search. Much of the focus of the investigation now switched to the area of the park, and we went back to Alameda to finish our shift. Finishing my shift was pretty anticlimactic. Adrenalin was still pumping and my hands were visibly shaking—not from fear, but from all of the energy and then the sudden letdown of the evening. I had a hard time concentrating on anything.

It was not until my next shift on the following evening that I received the news. The sergeant of the special squad who ran our tactical team told me that a suspect had been arrested. He was beside himself with the news and hurriedly told me the story. Apparently, after our little one-sided firefight and extraction, the detectives on this case went to work with vigor. They located and arrested the suspect in a home right around the corner from the park where we had been pinned down.

I don't know to this day if the man who was shooting at us was the same person who shot the officer from the overpass that night. I do know that it was determined that our shooter was probably using a handgun. I don't believe that any casings were found; therefore, the gun was probably a pistol. The general consensus was that our shooter was probably a passenger or accomplice of the suspect who was trying to keep us off of the trail. Frankly, I don't give a rat's ass as long as the murderer is behind bars—and that he remains there to this day.

That particular case was a bad one of many soon to come. It seemed like every time Ronin caught a suspect or his trail led to an arrest, we got ten more call outs. Each call out seemed to be a case more heinous than the prior one. I didn't know it at the time, but the evilness of it all was affecting me—making me a little more callous and cynical about everything and everybody around me, including my own family. There is only so long that you can stare into the eyes of the beast. I just didn't know it at the time.

The car trail that we had just run was also disturbing to me, because it was around this time that I had stopped believing they were possible. Of course, I would attempt them if the need was there, but I had no faith in them. I had worked at least 100 trails that ended up in cars, and they all just petered out—all but this one. How was I to deal with this anomaly? It took some time to fully think this out, and now—a decade later—I have trouble explaining it. I've come to the conclusion that this trail was one of those X factor trails that simply defies explanation. I have to take it for face value and move on. I still do not subscribe to car trails as a viable method to catch suspects or obtain evidence, because I know in my heart that they don't work most of the time. However, they are possible, be it through sheer determination or divine intervention. I will never know.

Over the years I've watched several interviews on various news channels featuring the comments of other bloodhound handlers. For the most part, most seem to represent themselves and our work honorably and honestly. I am proud to hear of their exploits. However, there are

High Sierra SWAT Challenge participants; Ronin is in the foreground.

times when I have seen the occasional handler make statements that I believe are less than honest and ultimately a detriment to our efforts. Probably the most glaringly overstatement I ever heard was when a nameless handler told a reporter on a national cable news channel that his bloodhound could reliably work six-month-old trails. This is not the first time that something along these lines has been said, and it irks me to this day.

The simple fact of the matter is that scent degrades with age and circumstance. Everything environmental and manmade has an affect on scent. Because of my job as a K-9 handler, I documented in writing everything I did—from the time and date to the weather conditions. I discovered that the best time to run a bloodhound on a trail was a case that was one to six hours old. If I had a good scent article and a location to start where the subject was known to have been, we could run success-ful trails more than 57 percent of the time. By successful, I mean a trail that ended with a subject in hand, physical evidence, or witness-corrob-orated statements. Fifty-seven percent is a pretty good number consid-ering all of the factors that go into trailing work.

Trails that were more than six hours old degenerated quickly, de-creasing the success rate exponentially. There seemed to be little rhyme or reason to the quality of the trail at this point. Our averages dropped off to the low thirtieth percentile. Once our trails aged more than twelve to twenty-four hours, our success rate dropped off to the teens and worse. If more than twenty-four hours passed, I could count the quan-tity of walk-up finds of people on one hand. In an urban environment, there are far too many variables involved with aged trails to ever be able to accurately predict how a dog will work. I do not count training trails when I'm working with these averages. Training trails are not an accu-rate representation of what trails a dog can successfully complete. Train-ing, although it is designed to replicate real-life scenarios, never quite accomplishes the task and is never subject to the same set of intangibles or variables.

Does scent last longer than twenty-four hours? I'm sure it does, but the degree to which it is available to the dog is subject to debate. Because we cannot accurately detect or measure it, we are limited to the behav-ioral changes we read in the dog, which tells us whether he has a scent trail or not. It is easy to simply run behind a dog and say that he is work-ing. Anyone can do this. However, to prove that the dog has found the trail and can reliably get from the beginning to the end is another mat-ter. A handler can easily rationalize everything his or her dog does and dress it up to match just about any scenario that has played out, but ul-timately, the proof is in the pudding. Did the dog find the prey or some-thing connected to it other than conjecture? These are the hard questions that handlers must ask themselves.

I took meticulous notes during my tenure as a bloodhound handler. I also worked behind some of the best handlers and dogs across the country at the time I was running hounds. Based on this experience, I've concluded that scent is such a fickle phenomenon, there is absolutely no way to gauge how long it really lasts. An honest handler can only determine age by what his or her dog is doing, and that is subject to debate if the handler cannot read his or her own dog.

Search dogs can switch to a trail of an animal or another person more quickly than the handler can blink. If the handler cannot tell the difference between the trail of the original person and the trail of, let's say, a deer that just ran across the path, how can that handler honestly say that he or she knows if the dog is on the correct trail? I am not leveling this charge at any handlers in particular but rather make this statement from my own personal experience. There was a time when I made these mistakes and had no idea I was making them. One human's trail was exactly the same as another. When I learned to read my dog properly, I began to understand the nature of scent and the time frames during which it might stay viable.

My experience and training, but most important, my need to be honest with myself, changed my way of thinking. I made a lot of mistakes as a handler—made numerous claims, and I believed that everything my dog did was correct. The harsh slap in the face by reality is what changed my course. I was faced with overwhelming facts about how my dog performed, and if I did not accept them and change my tune, I was bound for trouble. Ronin and I were working a job that required honesty and integrity. If we didn't have that, everything for which we worked so hard would be ruined. More important, if I lived a lie about the abilities of my dog, our ultimate success rate would be reduced. I also began to see that the less actual success we had, the more room there was for rationalization. I could make up any scenario to fit what my dog did. The hard part was saying that we had nothing at all to begin with.

Imagine the position in which you, as a dog handler, can find yourself. You have a case of a missing child with little to no evidence; investigators and parents alike are looking for and grasping at every bit of hope that comes their way. Along comes a canine handler with a bloodhound rumored to find people after all else has failed. Television and the movies helped to spawn that myth, as did a few bloodhound handlers themselves. All eyes are upon you, and you are offered every tool or asset available for your mission. Imagine the pressure of being in that position. It is easy to feel that you must perform, because that is what is expected of you. The hard part—the honest part—is to be strong enough to say that sometimes you cannot find what you are looking for. You will do your best, but things don't always work out. What else can mortals do but their best? It is perfectly fine to fail.

One of my early police mentors was famous for stories that related to the job of a police officer. He used to tell me that it would be great to be rated as a police officer in a fashion similar to that of a baseball player. If a baseball player had a batting average of .500, he was considered a phenomenal hitter worthy of every imaginable accolade and pay scale. On the other hand, a police officer was expected to be correct 100 percent of the time, be happy with a marginal wage, and live with considerably more pressure and scrutiny. It was exactly this situation that made it so hard not to pull a magical rabbit out of my top hat every time Ronin and I worked a difficult case. I learned to say that we would simply do the best we could. And, to say that we would do our best, but may not find what it was we were asked to find.

Thankfully, I learned my lessons early in my canine career. Yes, I made mistakes, but I learned from them and became a better handler in the process. I learned that the biggest myth that handlers can encounter is the myth they, themselves, created.

The Best Times of My Life

I STARTED RONIN ON REAL CASES EARLIER THAN WHAT I WOULD CONSIDER BEST. I look back on it now (hindsight is always 20/20), and I see that I thought that we were far better than we really were. However, this is the consequence of an extremely competitive nature. I had very few supporters, no compensation for my time, and a burning desire to succeed at what it was I had started. I also had a very good dog that I was dying to show off. We just weren't ready, though. Knowing all that I know now, and thinking about all of the training that I make my own students endure, Ronin and I would have been far better off waiting for another six months or so. I also took on every case that came my way, no matter how impossible or ridiculous it might have been. Regardless, the situation eventually began to turn for the better.

Our best find was our first find. I think it is that way for every trailing dog handler. The first find is always the best, because it is a moment in time when everything for which you have worked so incredibly hard finally pays off. It is an overwhelming sense of pride and accomplishment that you will never lose. Ronin's and my first find was by far not the most spectacular case, but it will always be fresh in my mind as if we had just run the trail this very day. Writing about it now makes me feel a little younger and stronger, too. I can almost sense the heat of that day and taste the dust from every footstep we took in that farmer's field. May 25, 1997, will be a timeless moment for me.

I received the call out for a missing-person case on a summer afternoon while living in Livermore, California. Ronin and I had been training for over a year, and I was pretty proud of him. The only problem we had was due to hormonal changes that I fixed by neutering him. Ronin had been out of commission for just more than two weeks due to the surgery when we were asked to work this case. His stitches had just been removed and he really had not worked anything too strenuous up to this point. I was a little concerned about his health, even though Judy assured me that he'd be fine. She just said to keep him at a little slower pace and out of the water.

The call out was for a missing thirty-year-old female who had disappeared under suspicious circumstances. The woman's car had been found in a farmer's field in Gilroy, California, on May 22, 1997. The farmer had reported the car to the sheriff's department on May 25. Ronin and I arrived around 5 P.M. that day. Homicide and robbery detectives had been called to the scene, and that was the FBI clue to me that this case may have gone sideways. Detectives are not normally called to the scene of simple missing-person cases, especially in the very early stages.

Thankfully, this was one of the few cases where everything seemed to be prepared just for a trailing bloodhound. The scene was relatively uncontaminated. The weather was a little warm but still good, and the detectives had preserved the scene for my arrival. I was one of the first people on the scene and had carte blanche with the vehicle. Nobody had mucked with it, and everything had been left relatively untouched. The woman's car was parked in a plowed farmer's field just off of the highway in Gilroy. There was a canal with slow-moving water flowing in a northwesterly direction to a containment pond just a few yards from the parked car. The canal was lined with cattails, and they were thick. I noticed several sets of footprints in the dirt around the car, and it was difficult to determine exactly how many people had been around it. The car itself was wide open. It was a newer model, compact, Japanese car, and both of the front doors were open.

When I looked at the interior of the vehicle, I knew immediately why the detectives had been called. The car appeared to have been ransacked. Clothing was strewn all around the back and front seats, and the keys were still in the ignition. To make matters worse, there was a bloodied feminine napkin on floorboards of the driver's side. My initial thought was that this was a kidnap and rape case and that we had a body in the pond.

Because there was the potential for a major felony and a person's life may have been taken or seriously at risk, I had to be very careful with everything that I did. I took one path into the driver's side door of the car and one path out. I had to quickly determine the best scent article available for the missing woman and get out of the car so that it could be processed by crime scene technicians, popularly referred to as CSI guys. I had a lot of choices for a good scent article, but it was possible that most of it had been touched by an assailant if one was involved. The clothing would easily have the scent of another person on it, as would most of the interior of the car, especially if the woman had been kidnapped and transported in her own car. I decided that the best article to use would be the feminine napkin, because even if it had been handled by another person, the woman's scent should be very strong. I collected that napkin with a pair of hemostats and placed it in a freezer-type Zip-Lock bag.

I got Ronin out of my truck and let him canvass the area on his own for a little while. Many people now refer to this as a "scent inventory," and perhaps that is a good name. I really liked the time, because it allowed Ronin enough time to urinate as much as he could before we started to run. I brought him to the area of the parked car and harnessed him up. The harness is always the signal that we are going to work. I then snapped in his long lead to the big D-ring on the top of his harness and gave it a little tug. The tug was the signal that things were about to get hot. I remember always feeling the tension building in Ronin whenever he felt that tug. It seemed that a little electricity would course through his muscles and ignite in his eyes. His desire to trail was palpable.

The next step was presenting the scent article to Ronin. This was always the most crucial step in our little preparation to dance. The scent article is the most important part of the package, and if Ronin could not get a good scent off of it, then there would be no trail. When opening the bag, I used to always make it a little game for him. I wanted him to be excited about smelling something in the bag, and it had to be a surprise. The last thing I wanted to happen was for Ronin to somehow get a whiff of the article before I presented it to him. For some reason, this anticipation really helped to fire Ronin up for the trail. I started by straddling Ronin with a leg over each shoulder, almost like riding a horse. Hell, he was big enough at this point to be considered a horse. The long lead attached to his harness D-ring was stretched short and taunt over his right shoulder and was held down by my right boot. The pressure of my knees on his flanks, coupled with the lead being held down by my foot, kept him locked into place. This was not easy, because, depending on the trail, he was a ball of canine energy just waiting to explode. Thankfully, I have always been fairly strong and could manage Ronin to a certain extent. By now, I had both hands free and could manipulate the Zip-Lock bag with relative ease.

This is where the scent article game began. I made a habit of keeping the bag off to my left and out of sight and scent from Ronin. I always tried to have the wind blowing away from him so as not to prematurely scent him on the bag's contents when I opened it. I would slowly bring the bag out to my side and just to the periphery of Ronin's vision. He knew this game well by now, and he grumbled in mock anger over not getting a full picture of what was in my hand. I would invariably have to press my knees even harder into his sides just to control him. I'd slowly bring the bag across my body and at full arm's reach just to tease Ronin a little more. Once the bag was in front of him completely, I had an almost impossibly difficult time holding him back. I had to use every ounce of strength just to keep his forward momentum in check. It was at just this moment when I would release the pressure from his flanks and lift my foot off of the long lead while simultaneously grasping it with my free right hand. As Ronin's nose came in close proximity to the scent article, I gave him the command to search: "Skit it!" I gave this command with the same energy that was coursing through the blood of my hound. The command should never be given lightly but rather with a sense of urgency and vigor.

As soon as Ronin took scent from the article, I noticed an immediate behavioral change. He was always fired up for every trail, and I never had to worry about his prey drive, but this was different, and he literally surged with emotion and purpose. There was no denying that he had scent, and there was absolutely no way I was going to be able to stop him. There was something about that scent article that sparked a drive in him that I never saw again. Ronin immediately began to canvas the area for a trail leading away from the car, frantically turning this way and that. I gave him the entire length of my thirty-foot bull-hide lead and hung on for dear life.

Ronin immediately found a trail leading away from the car and to the south just on the east side of the cattail-forested embankment by the canal. He seemed to hesitate at the edge, though, as if he had a second thought about something he may have missed. I could sense his indecision as his head popped to the left where the dirt field lay and then to the right along the cattail thicket. I anticipated his decision, I think, before he committed to it, because I remember thinking, "Oh shit, he's going to drag me through that thick brush and into the canal."

The thought of running into the canal was not very appealing. The water was not moving all that well and it smelled a little swampy. I had on my good boots and pistol belt with a brand new Sig 239 nine-millimeter pistol on my hip, and I immediately thought that it would be a real drag to get it wet. Lo and behold, Ronin didn't give me much choice. He broke through the thick vegetation, and I could not see him well, but I sure heard the splash; so much for keeping him out of the water. I knew what was coming as the long lead stretched out into the canal and both of my feet slipped out from under me. So much for my good boots and pistol belt, because they were all completely soaked as I found myself almost chest-deep in water. Ronin was swimming in a lazy circle at first toward the pond to my right and then back upstream, lapping up the water as he paddled. Normally, I would be concerned with this behavior, because I might have thought that he was taking a leisurely swim, but the way he was mouthing the water without drinking was disturbing. I had

Bloodhounds can follow a trail through water more easily than they can on a city street.

seen this behavior when we had trained for cadaver finds in water, and Ronin had done the same thing sans actually swimming. I literally had a chill run up my spine when it dawned on me that we might actually have a body in the water through which I was wading.

Ronin gave me little time to think at this point, because he seemed to make up his mind that swimming upstream was the way to go. Frankly, he was confusing me. At first he was indicating that something was in the water, perhaps at our very feet, and now he was heading off into the marsh and still swimming. I had no choice but to follow right behind him. I was soaked to the ears, and I knew I was going to smell pretty gamey. Ronin paddled along, oblivious to my predicament. The footing was not exactly treacherous, but it wasn't good either. Some steps were firm, while others caused me to sink into some primordial ooze that I could literally feel saturating the leather of my boots.

As we progressed upstream in the canal, I could feel the cattails thickening beside me. It was if we were being funneled into some gigantic aquatic jungle. The dragonflies or some such winged bug were almost as thick as the plants around us and constantly buzzed around my head, forcing me to keep my mouth shut for fear of ingesting one or more of the little beasties. I was really getting distracted from my main job of focusing on Ronin. He was still swimming, however, now in and out through the stands of plant life. I had to try and stay close, because my lead was constantly getting tangled, and every time I tried to free it up, Ronin was line checked in the process. This was a problem, because now he was acting frantic and I was hard pressed to keep up. I often thought of simply cutting him loose, but I knew that I'd lose him if I did.

Ronin and I made our way into this forest of greenery until we got stuck. There was no more moving forward. The cattails were so thick that I couldn't even push them over anymore. It was almost like trying to move a semi-flexible wall of vegetation. We had no other choice but to go back the way we had come, and Ronin was furious. I tried to drag him back by his lead, but he fought me for every inch. He continued to try and break through the plants and actually began gnawing at them with his teeth. I was forced to physically grab him by the harness and body and drag him away. He was scaring me a little with his determination, coupled with our situation. I was in really deep water and my footing was less than sure, and here I had my dog fighting to get away from me. But I knew we could not continue. We had no other choice but to find our way out and try to start on a land route.

I was able to bring my reluctant dog back about a hundred yards or so, where I found a break in the vegetation large enough for us to get out of the canal. We made our way back to the car and I recast Ronin in the area. He seemed to pick up a scent trail again but this time went in the opposite direction to some barns and outbuildings. Tons of manure and other distractions were prolific, and I was really worried that Ronin was off the trail and screwing around on me. I started to curse him a little under my breath, because he was picking up his pace now that we were on dry land, and I was having a hard time keeping up in soggy clothes. Plus my pants wanted to fall down, forcing me to cinch up my belt uncomfortably tight.

I was just about to pull Ronin off whatever it was that he thought he was on when I noticed really small shoe tracks in the dirt of one of the barns. They differed dramatically from the boot prints I had seen everywhere else; in particular, they appeared to be made by a woman. The length and width very small, and the impression in the dirt was not as deep as any of the other tracks. They appeared to be made by a woman of small to average size. I had not seen a picture of our victim, so I wasn't positive that these prints were hers, but I was willing to give Ronin some more time just in case. I was feeling a little pressure to produce, but much of that had been alleviated when I had lost my backup officer.

I had started my trail with a uniformed police officer as backup right around the time we left the car. He was supposed to protect us if something went awry. It was also his jurisdiction, so any paperwork would be his. However, I seemed to have lost the guy as soon as we splashed into the canal. I don't recall seeing him fall behind anywhere in particular, and, come to think of it, I don't think I heard a second splash of another tentative soul testing the waters with me. He never called out saying that he was going to do something else . . . he simply vanished. As a matter of fact, I never saw him again—ever. This backup officer was going to be the first of many backup officers who Ronin and I lost for one reason or another. The predominant reason for losing backup people was their inability to keep up. I used to receive all kinds of comments to the effect that I must be in incredible physical condition to be able to run so fast and so far. I smiled often and said that I worked out a lot. The truth of the matter was that, yes, I was in decent condition, but Ronin did quite a bit of the work. Hell, I was being dragged behind him at the end of a thirty-foot lead. Ronin was a frickin' draft horse and could pull a tree if he had to. Of course, I never admitted as much and let people enjoy their fantasy of my athleticism.

The other reason why we lost backup officers was because they insisted on carrying every manner of excess baggage imaginable. I started out this way, too. When Ronin was a puppy, I bought all of these cool tactical vests, guns, bullets, GPSs, etc. It got to the point that I was hauling about thirty pounds of extra gear. When Ronin was a puppy and we ran only a couple of blocks, this was no big deal. I could carry a lot of stuff and get away with it. But as the trail lengthened and Ronin's speed and strength increased, I shed the extra poundage on my back and around my middle. I encouraged my backup to do the same thing when I was briefing agencies about what we might be doing. I don't know what the reason was—perhaps male machismo or plain stubbornness, but most people insisted on carrying it all; backpacks, gallons of water, big guns, just tons of crap. I almost always lost them within the first quarter mile.

Well, my backup on this particular case was long gone, never to be seen again, so I didn't have anyone behind me to add to my feeling that I had to find something fast. I let Ronin have the lead and told him that he was a good boy. Ronin surged into the harness a little as if acknowledging my compliment, which only made my pants want to fall down again.

Ronin was now definitely on the tracks of those I had found before. He didn't have his nose right down on them, but I could tell that he was following their general direction. This heartened me considerably, because it leant credence to his work. He trailed to a small bridge used for foot traffic and farm equipment that spanned the width of the canal and gazed across. The footing was a little funny due to large gaps between the creosote-covered planks. Ronin didn't like to see through the gaps and always lunged across these types of bridges. He did the same thing on this day. He looked left and right just before crossing with this little worried look he used to get and then took two uncoordinated bounds and was over the bridge.

Ronin picked up the trail with absolutely no hesitation on the other side. This time, he was on a foot trail running parallel to the cattail jungle on the west side of the canal. He was picking up speed with every few yards we traveled, and his nose was coming up off of the ground a little more than before. In these conditions, he was telling me that we were getting close. When his speed increased to a modest sprint, I knew that he was on something very hot. Dogs can normally run a scent trail fairly quickly in most conditions as long as the trail is fresh. Ronin's speed let me know that this trail was pretty fresh indeed. The irony of that did not strike me until later. Ronin ran up to another one of the farm bridges about a half mile down the little footpath. The bridge was the same type—creosote-covered railroad ties about twelve inches square with several inch gaps between each. This time, Ronin did not even hesitate. He simply got to the bridge and leapt. This time it was completely graceful, and grace is not a descriptive word for normal bloodhound maneuvers. His jump took him almost all the way across the ten-foot span, but not quite. However, both his hind and fore feet met together on the same railroad tie about three quarters of the way across, and he leaped again, clearing the short remaining length to the grass on the other side. His commitment and complete lack of fear or concern gave him a type of balance that I had never observed until this particular day. Every muscle rippled across his flanks, and he was moving as if we were running for our very lives. Maybe he was running for a life, just not his or mine.

I was at the tail end of my thirty-foot lead and holding on with every ounce of energy I could spare. My breath felt short and thick, and I tried desperately to make Ronin slow down, but he would have nothing to do with that. I was trying to yell, "Slow down!! Please!" in between ragged gasps, but I think that my voice was little more than a soft squeal. I was frightened that I was going to lose Ronin, because my legs were failing and it seemed as if he was just pulling away a little more with each lunge. Our little foot trail was turning softly to the left, or east, and my lead was raking across the cattails on the canal bank, causing them to bend with the tension and force we were creating. Strangely, of all the things that were flashing by me at that time, I seem to recall the slight sound that our lead made as it scraped across the stalks of those water plants—a continuous "swoooooossshhh" sound like a kite racing through a windy sky. I lost sight of Ronin because of the bend in the trail and the cattails in between.

All of a sudden, I ran up on a slack lead lying on the ground and leading into the forest of green next to the waterway. This was the thickest part of the stand of cattails anywhere along the canal. They were taller, and each stalk was the thickness of two of my fingers. The lead was not moving any longer, and I couldn't see Ronin. I noticed the tufts at the top of each coblike sprout at the peak of the stalks in the interior swaying back and forth and deduced that Ronin was just a few feet inside, but I could see nothing. I was worried that something might have happened to Ronin and had absolutely no idea what it was that he was doing, so I quickly parted the reeds and bulled my way through. I encountered Ronin's backside first and could see that he had his front feet up on the shoulders of a person who was desperately trying to avoid his sloppy licks and kisses. She was covered in several thick ropes of bloodhound drool, basically from ear to chest, and had her eyes shut while makes noises of complete disgust. She was trying to push Ronin off, but he would have nothing to do with that. I have never seen a dog so happy. Ronin kept looking back at me between licks, obviously waiting for his reward.

It was right then that it struck me. Ronin had found the missing girl. Here she was, right in front of me, and I didn't know what to say. I gave Ronin a handful of cookies and dragged him off of the poor woman. She was frightened by Ronin, and I had to calm her down a little. Once she understood that he had no intention of hurting her, she reluctantly began to pet his smiling head. Ronin was looking up at the woman adoringly with bright eyes and copious quantities of drool dripping from his loose jowls. I have never seen a dog so satisfied as Ronin was on that day. As a matter of fact, the emotion of the moment set in for me as well. I couldn't help myself and sobbed a little, knowing that all of our work had finally paid off. The woman looked at me a little questioningly, and I tried my best to explain what it was that we had done or were doing. She spoke very sparingly, and I don't believe that I ever got a single full sentence from her. Her communication was made up of acknowledgments such as yes and no, but little else.

I looked the woman over and tried to ascertain if she was injured or not. She was extremely dirty, but, for the most part, she seemed unscathed.

When I asked her if she had been abducted or attacked, she said no, and she didn't want any medical attention. Regardless, I immediately called for paramedics and backup officers to respond. It took a little explaining to the search commander where we were, as I no longer had a cover officer to do the communicating for me. I didn't want to move the woman for fear that she might actually be injured in ways that I could not see. I told the responding emergency personnel to follow the east bank of the canal for about a half mile and look for my long lead snaking out of the cattails along the trail.

We did not have to wait for long, because I heard the truck shortly before it arrived. I was relieved of my charge and stepped back while the paramedics did their thing. It was a little anticlimactic for me, and all of the energy that had been recently coursing through my body just seemed to evaporate. I was so incredibly tired and couldn't wait to get back to my truck. I felt like I could take a nap right then and there. The half mile back to the starting point was slow and leisurely—a far cry from everything we had just gone through and done. I had trouble feeling every step. My feet were numb from all of the pounding they had received in soaking wet boots. With that, I began to look myself over the best I could. I was pretty wet and filthy, with scratches up and down the length of my short-sleeved arms. I was a mess and probably looked like a vagrant to any passerby.

I got back to the command post area to the congratulations of the few remaining souls standing by. I was also surprised to see Kat walking up to me with a huge grin on her face. I choked up a little. All of the training, sweat, and effort we had put in flooded my memory in the short space that separated us. I grabbed her and hugged her close for a moment and told her how much I appreciated everything she had done for us. For without Kat, none of this would have been possible. Not only did we have our first find on this day, but I had my mentor there to share it with me. It was a fine day, indeed, and I know that Kat was reveling in the moment with us.

I don't think I really analyzed what we did on that trail until several hours later. I had to hurry off to work in Alameda, as I had a swing shift to cover that night. I didn't even have a chance to go home and wash up. Judy had to meet me at work to pick up Ronin. I discovered that the missing woman had been avoiding searchers intentionally. She was suffering from a mental illness and had a fear of people and society in general. The location where she was hiding amongst the reeds was south of where her car had been found. The canal flowed from that location to where her car had been parked. I think that the reason why Ronin jumped into the canal and swam upstream was because her fresh scent was flowing with the current toward the pond. Ronin chose the fresh scent on the water over the older foot trail. The thick forest of cattails in which we became entangled was only a few yards from the spot where we actually located the woman later. She must have heard our frantic splashing as we were trying to break our way through. When we backtracked to the car, Ronin picked up on aged trails that the woman had made when she was wandering around the farm during the days she was missing. I confirmed that the tracks I found were the woman's, because one of the first questions I asked was if I could look at the bottom of her shoes.

It is hard to articulate how important this case was to Ronin and me. It was a huge emotional high from which I really never came down. Almost a year of extremely long and hard work had finally paid off. There were times when I had felt like it was all for nothing and that the training we were doing was for naught. Well, all of this changed on this day in May 1997. We were now a proven team with a real find under our belts. There were far-reaching ramifications to this find that I learned about later. Ronin and I received a nice letter of commendation from the agency responsible for the search, and I managed to sneak a copy into my chief of police's mailbox at work. I believe that the case also received some media attention, which shone favorably on the police department as a whole. I had a couple of supportive supervisors who often offered words of encouragement while also singing my praises to their own superiors.

Not everyone in the department was so supportive. I was told by an immediate supervisor who later became quite a mentor to me that there were forces actively aligned against me and the bloodhound program.

This warning sounded like it was coming from a line in a science fiction movie! These people viewed my proposal with disdain, and I was considered an upstart with no real credibility. I was encouraged to put all of the favorable comments, news clippings, and general compliments on Ronin and me into the chief's mailbox, which was locked and only opened by the chief and his secretary. I was advised that this might be the only way for the boss to get the straight scoop about what we were doing. Now, taking such action was actually a break in the chain of command. Technically speaking, everything that goes to the chief must first go

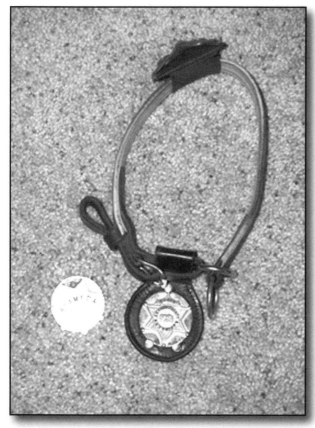

Ronin's collar and badges from the Alameda Police Department and the Amador Sheriff's Office.

through the hands of each supervisor in order of pay grade; in other words, sergeant, lieutenant, captain, and finally, the chief. By placing all of my cheese letters into the chief's box first, I was disrupting the chain. Obviously, this tactic paid off, because the order for my contract came directly from the boss himself, and none of my unnamed detractors seemed the wiser.

It wasn't long until I received an invitation to join the K-9 unit at my department. I had proposed this idea several months before, and although I received a lot of pats on the back for a fine proposal, there was no K-9 contract in the making. My proposal was obviously given a second glance after the successful find in Santa Clara County. I was offered a full-time position as the Alameda Police Department's first bloodhound handler. I would receive a little extra pay for my time taking care of and training Ronin, plus we had our own patrol car. In addition, his veterinarian bills would all be handled by the city of Alameda. To say I was ecstatic is an understatement.

The ink was not even dry on our contract when we had our first really big call out for our own city. This case, above all others, turned more heads in Alameda than any other.

ID card that Jeff gave out to the public while on the Alameda Police force.

Police Officer & K-9
Officer Jeff Schettler & Ronin

Jeff and Ronin became a team in 1996 when Ronin was just 11 weeks old. They are a specialized K-9 team in that they hunt for missing persons or criminals using Ronin's sensitive nose. They have worked a variety of cases throughout the country. "Ronin" translated from Japanese means masterless samurai.

In memory of: Sp-4 Robert Brede and "Bodia" KIA 1967
Combat Tracker Team #2
25th Infantry Division

Personal Message:
Kids! If you get lost, stop and hug a tree. We will be looking for you soon!

Sponsor: Raintree Studios
Alameda, 510.521.4900

Alameda Police Department
1555 Oak St., Alameda CA 94501 • 510.748.4508
©2000 House of Sierra, Inc. • 800-479-6062

ALAMEDA POLICE
DEPARTMENT

POLICE OFFICER & K-9
JEFF SCHETTLER & RONIN Year 2000 Edition

The Bank Robbery

I T WAS OCTOBER 1997, and I was at home on one of my days off. I had plans to train Ronin that day, but everything changed at ten that morning. I received a call from dispatch telling me that there had been a bank robbery on Park Street in downtown Alameda. Apparently, two armed suspects had robbed the bank at gunpoint shortly after it opened. The suspects had not thought out this robbery too well, because if they had, they probably would have picked another bank in another city. Alameda is an island connected to the East Bay city of Oakland by three bridges and a tunnel, all of which can be easily blocked off if something serious hits the fan. They might have also picked a better day, because everything seemed to work against them on this one.

The suspects were a male and female team who, after robbing the bank, fled on foot to a car that they had parked around the corner. Unbeknownst to them, there was an Alameda motorcycle cop right in the vicinity of the bank when the whole thing went down. The two were separated when they encountered the knee-booted officer riding his Harley. The male half decided that the better part of valor was to start throwing money behind him as he ran, hoping that the ensuing confusion created by the masses chasing floating Benjamins would get in the way of the pursuing officer. It didn't work, because there really weren't that many pedestrians in the area at the time.

The female half was chased around the corner onto Park Avenue one block to the east of the bank by a concerned citizen. The citizen was reportedly heedless of the gun-toting woman and her threat to shoot. He cornered her near a brick building, and, instead of shooting the man, the woman threw her gun onto the building rooftop and then tried to scale an eight-foot chain link fence in a parking lot just to the south of the office's brick walls. This was the start of our trail.

The crime scene investigators in my department were well versed in maintaining the scene for Ronin. We had only been on board for a short while, but they seemed to immediately understand how to protect scent evidence. This is the beauty of having evidence technicians whose only job is to investigate crime scenes for trace evidence. They are well trained and have many tools at their disposal. As far as they were concerned, Ronin was just another tool for them to utilize.

The CSI techs discovered the pistol by observing it through a window that overlooked the rooftop where the gun was lying. The area was then cordoned off for my arrival and dog work. The key to any trail, especially an urban one, was to protect the scene and scent evidence from contamination of any sort. Contamination in this case would be considered anyone walking in around the area where the suspect was last known to have been and handling the scent article on which I needed to start Ronin. The scene was the small parking lot with the chain-link fence, and the most logical scent article was the handgun. Everything was secured and left alone until we arrived at 11:15 A.M.

I can't tell you how relieved I was to have a relatively uncontaminated scene that was being protected the entire time. This was a huge case for me, because it was the first time that Ronin and I had been called out by my own department for anything really meaningful. A bank robbery was a high crime with state and federal implications. Everyone was involved in this case, including our local agency, regional task forces, and the FBI. It was a big deal, and again, all eyes were on me—especially the chief's. My chief took the ultimate responsibility for taking Ronin on. People were looking his direction, too. I was nervous about this case, because I knew that everything we had accomplished before was nothing if we didn't pull a rabbit out of the hat with this one. And pulling a rabbit out of the hat it truly could be.

The problems facing us were large. The incident had occurred a couple of hours prior to our arrival. We were going to be working in a naturally contaminated, inner-city area. The suspect could have easily run to a waiting vehicle or simply left the city, because she had ample time to do so. I was also nervous. It was time to "put up or shut up." I had done a lot of talking over the months, trying to gain the approval of not only staff members, but also of my fellow officers working their beats. I had done a fair amount of bragging, and I knew that this would nip me in the butt if we didn't come up with something here. I pulled up to the scene in my red Dodge Ram pickup truck in time to see the media arriving. Thankfully, the reporter and photographer were people with whom I had already worked, and I felt comfortable with them. I was still a little self-conscious, because I had no time to change into a uniform. I was wearing jeans, a gray T-shirt, tennis shoes, and a ball cap. I also had a big wad of chewing tobacco in my mouth. Looking back on it now, I can't imagine what people must have thought when they saw me show up: pickup, jeans, a hat, chew, and a blood-hound—priceless. I went immediately to work and canvassed the scene. My evidence technician showed me the undisturbed gun and the general location where the woman was suspected of trying to climb the fence. She apparently didn't make it over, and some witness accounts had her fleeing around the block instead. I collected the gun into a paper bag and tossed a sterile four-by-four-inch gauze pad in with it for a few minutes. I extracted the pad and placed it into a freezer-type Zip-Lock bag. I was going to keep a small scent article for use later just in case I needed it. I pulled Ronin out of the truck and let him canvass the area also, but with his nose. He'd peed a lot, too.

Ronin was a ham for attention. He loved to have people watch him, and it just added to his already huge prey drive. I knew I could count on him to give me a run for the money now. I harnessed him up in the general vicinity from which the woman had run and snapped his long lead into the D-ring, giving it a little tug in the process. I whispered a few sweet nothings into his ears that sounded something like this: "OK, it's all or nothing, because everyone is watching. Are you ready to go to work?" It was really the last words that fired up Ronin. You could immediately

Ronin in his patrol car, Alameda, California.

sense his body tensing as soon as I said ". . . you ready . . .," because he knew I was about to show him the bag with his prey scent. He was straining into the lead and I was holding him back with everything I had. Ronin almost leaped at the scent article as soon as I opened the bag with the gun, making me think that he may have not have gotten a good scent, because it all happened so fast. But he had it—his nose and body language told me so. He immediately began to sniff the area furiously up to the fence and back, up to the brick wall on the north end of the lot and back. He circled twice as if trying to confirm a sense of direction, then ran out onto Park Avenue on the east sidewalk, heading south. Ronin's nose was hovering about ten inches off of the pavement, and his head was swiveling slightly to the left and to the right. I could tell that he had a good scent trail because he was moving so well.

Paved trails are difficult, because the scent doesn't have much to stick to. It seems to blow with the wind and collect in little pockets here and there. In many ways, instead of having a continuous trail, it is more like connecting a bunch of imperceptible dots that only the dog can recognize. I expected this to be the case on this day, but not so. Ronin seemed to have a continuous trail almost as if it were on grass. I didn't understand this very well back then, but now that I have a little experience under my belt, I see what happened very clearly.

The female bank robber had just committed a crime that could put her away for much of her adult life. She had been chased down by a fearless citizen, had been separated from her male counterpart, was running for her life in a city that held few if any friends, and had the entire Alameda Police Department looking for her. She had picked the wrong bank to rob, and now she was scared to death. It was this fear that provided the glue for her scent to stick to the pavement. I know now that fear scent is the ultimate trigger for canids hunting prey. It tells them that the prey is weakening and that the pursuit could be over very soon. It is the scent of fear that gives the wolf the last bit of energy necessary to culminate a long chase with a deadly lunge for the throat. I believe that all domestic dogs feel this genetic memory at some point in their lives. Those that know it more often than others thrive on the feeling and grow powerful because of it

Ronin was on a powerful scent that only he could detect. He ran this concrete trail with almost a righteous purpose, negotiating obstacles without hardly a glance. I had to keep a tight lead out to about fifteen feet, though. It was a busy weekday morning and traffic was starting to heat up. Not only that, a lot of people were starting to simply stand and stare, and Ronin had to work through them. The beauty of a scent-discriminating dog that is on an actual scent trail is that he can work through all of these other human odors with little or no distraction. A well-trained dog just ignores these humans unless they physically get in the way or do something to disturb him.

Ronin ran to Central Avenue, the next intersecting main street. Central Avenue is almost smack dab in the middle of the very busy Park Street district of downtown Alameda. Many people were now walking around the area and traffic was heavy, getting ready for the lunch rush. Ronin wove his way through all of the pedestrians and obstacles like so many bowling pins. They did not matter, and he was sticking to his trail with little effort. He turned to the east and ran to Everett Street, where he hung a hard left directly toward the fence that the suspect had tried to climb. He alerted on the fence with a sniff of the chain link and a little wag of the tail but kept moving north toward Santa Clara Avenue.

Ronin alerted on the knob of a parking meter next to an empty parking space. This told me that the woman may have touched the meter or used it. The problem was that we were now almost around the block and back to our starting point on Park Avenue, which was the next adjoining street. There was another problem as well. Ronin was working a little slower and seemed a little less sure of himself. Of course, I couldn't know exactly what might have happened, but I had my suspicions. There was a very good possibility that Ronin was on the suspects' original trail to the bank. There was absolutely no way to confirm this, but we seemed to be heading back in that general direction. One other situation may have created a scent conflict for Ronin. The male suspect had been arrested in the general vicinity in which we now found ourselves. The two bank robbers had been working closely together, and their scents had definitely commingled. There was also a chance that the male partner had handled the handgun carried by the woman. I really had no idea, but I knew that if I didn't get Ronin back to a fresher trail, we would be ending this party pretty quickly.

I gave Ronin every opportunity to find his own way out—probably more than I should have. But I was still a new handler and didn't understand all of the nuances of good handler skills until much later in my career. If I had been smart, I would have taken Ronin off of the weak scent in which he had just foundered and brought him right back to the strong stuff that he liked so much. I was running with my own set of blinders on, though, and I couldn't see the forest for the trees. I didn't bring Ronin back to the hot trail until he ran out of trail completely—a little late, looking back on it now.

We went back to the northwest corner of Central Avenue and Everett Street and tried to pick up the scent again. Ronin hit the trail hard on the northeast corner of the intersection. I noticed an immediate change in his scent demeanor. He was focused again and pulling hard with an obvious direction in mind Ronin ran east on Central Avenue on the north sidewalk until he came to a very large, older apartment building with a white stucco front and thick vegetation all around. A nicely manicured lawn ran the length of the building front and was lined with palm and false pear trees. When Ronin got to the grass, his speed increased and so, too, did the sound of his snuffling. I let the lead out to the full extent because he was up against the building, on the grass, and in amongst the trees. I had little fear of traffic and knew that I could reel him in quickly if I had to. My backup officer was happy with our progress, and I could tell by the look on his face that he thought we had something.

We continued along the front of the building and Ronin hooked a hard left to the north side of the apartment complex and to the parking facility nearby. The vegetation got a little thicker when we cleared this area and turned west between a six-foot fence and the north side of the building. The wild grass was tall against the building and the fence, and a little cat path went right smack dab in the middle. Great! Ronin's arch nemesis might be nearby. We were in fairly tight quarters, sandwiched between the wooden fence and the stucco wall. Ronin was stretched out all the way to the front, I was directly behind him, and my backup was dogging my footsteps.

Ronin hit the northwest corner of the apartments and turned left. He didn't have a choice because another fence was directly in front of us. We got to just about the middle of this stretch of alleyway when Ronin's head popped to the left on the lower portion of the wall. He took a couple of more steps, doubled back, and promptly sat down at the same spot he had just looked at. He was still a few yards in front of me, so the only thing I could see was that he was sitting down and looking at the base of the wall and then back at me, wagging his tail. I had no idea what it was that he thought he had found, because to me, it looked like he had found, well . . . a wall.

I walked up to Ronin, reeling my lead into big loops in my left hand, and asked him what he had found. I was sweating a little but I wasn't too tired. However, my breath was a little short out of sheer anxiety. Here was my dog, sitting down in the middle of this narrow alley and no longer going anywhere. I could tell that no one was nearby, nor was there anything anyone could hide behind, so it looked like Ronin had found a wall. I asked him a training question that prompts him to give me a better indication of what it was that he thought he had found: "What is it?" Ronin didn't even hesitate. He lowered his body down almost to a prone position and pawed at a little screen vent framed in white-painted wood at the base of the wall. The vent was already a little askew, and Ronin just about knocked it off with his claws.

If I remember correctly, the vent was only about twenty-four-by-twelve inches, and I really didn't think anyone could fit inside of it. The only thing that I thought could fit was Ronin's nemesis, Mr. Kitty. My backup officer was one of our detectives. Pat was a veteran officer with many years of experience, and so far, he had been giving us the benefit of the doubt. He asked me what I thought we had, and I had to say that I honestly didn't know. Ronin also responded to the question and to our inactivity by starting to bark and howl while wagging his tail even more furiously. I was really worried that Ronin had found a cat. It was impossible for a human to fit into this little crawl space.

Because I was basically in civilian clothes and had very little equipment, I asked Pat if he had a flashlight. This was kind of a stupid question, because he was wearing his business suit minus the jacket and was carrying only a small sidearm. We had no light, and Ronin was getting

This is the area where the bank robbery suspect hid under a hotel.

impatient. He kept lunging at the wall and howling. We had to make an embarrassing call to dispatch on the radio asking for a patrol officer to swing by and give us a flashlight.

In the meantime, we just stood there, looking rather ridiculous with a howling dog that was getting extremely frustrated. Pat asked me what my opinion was of the situation, and I had to be honest with him. I said that I didn't think anyone could fit through the vent and that Ronin might be alerting on a cat or something else. He asked me if I was absolutely positive. I explained that Ronin was exhibiting behavior that was indicative of finding the person he was supposed to find. Pat suggested that we make an announcement as to our presence and see if we could get a response. What a great idea! Why didn't I think of that? I yelled into the vent for anyone who might be in there to come out slowly. I added that if they didn't respond, I'd be forced to send my dog in to get them. As soon as I yelled the announcement, I knew how stupid it sounded. My dog couldn't fit into the vent either!

By now, Ronin was frantic and getting pissed off. He didn't know what we were doing, and this did not fit into any of the training I had ever done with him. Normally, when he found something that was hidden, it was promptly taken from its hiding place and shown to him so that he could be rewarded with his Scooby snacks. Not so this time, and he didn't like it at all. Thankfully, the flashlight showed up right around the time Ronin was ready to eat the wall. Pat wasn't about to get down on his hands and knees in his nice suit, so the job was left to me. I removed the vent and put my arm with the flashlight in first. I followed it with my head turned to the right. The only things I saw were lots of cobwebs and cat poop . . . wonderful.

I had to remove my head and arm in order to look in the other direction. I stuck my arm in again, shining the flashlight to my left, and stuck my head in right behind. I immediately saw the whites of a woman's eyes staring me right in the face. I reacted violently the only way my body seemed to know how to respond—to sit bolt upright. The problem was that my head and arm were stuck in the vent hole, and the only thing I accomplished was to bounce the side of my head on the floor joist above it. Fantastic. Not only did I just get the fright of my life, but now I was seeing stars through watery eyes.

I hauled myself out of the hole and Pat asked me what the problem was. I told him that the suspect was in there and so close I could have touched her. Pat radioed in to dispatch and asked for more officers while I started to yell at the suspect to get the hell out of the crawl space. I threatened her with everything if she didn't come out on her own, which got Ronin even more fired up. He was howling to beat the band, and I think that's what ultimately got this woman's attention. She said that she was

The vent screen the robbery suspect removed to hide inside.

coming out and pleaded with us not to let the dog bite her. She didn't know any better, but the only thing Ronin was interested in was a puppy biscuit. The woman came out, empty hands first, and I grabbed them and hauled her out. I conducted a quick pat search of her person to ensure that she wasn't carrying any weapons and then handcuffed her. Pat advised the responding units and dispatch that we had one suspect in custody.

We walked the suspect out to the front of the apartment complex on Central Avenue just in time to see the press arrive. They had apparently been monitoring what we were doing by using a police scanner. The photographer took some good shots of the four of us on the sidewalk just before a transport patrol car arrived, and the photos ended up plastered all over the evening news. The woman bank robber never said a word. She kept her head down, for the most part, and didn't even acknowledge "yes" or "no" questions. But, I could care less. Ronin had found her and now she was going to jail. I was on cloud nine, and Ronin was enjoying copious quantities of Scooby snacks.

Regardless of the success of the trail, I would always try to analyze what we had done on the case in order to make the next one a little better. By the time our little suspect was packaged up and shipped on her merry way to jail, I had already concluded that we had made a couple of errors about which I've already written. However, I didn't quite understand everything that we had seen and done until later that night, after I wrote my report.

I believe that the suspect didn't make it over the fence when she was cornered by the good citizen who had chased her. She probably tried but failed, because even though the fence was chain link, the links had slats of wood slithered in between each one. It was really difficult to get a toehold in such a fence. Second, Ronin picked up a hot foot trail around the block on the other side. Yes, he alerted on it again, but it was probably because the scent passed easily through both sides of the fence. The problem began right here. There appeared to be a strong "pool scent" on both sides of the fence, because the woman had physically handled the fence. This always leaves more scent behind than when someone simply walks on the sidewalk. Because the fence was in such close proximity to the corner where the woman had obviously crossed the street while fleeing, Ronin couldn't help but check it out, because it must have been like a scent lighthouse on a stormy sea of contamination. Once he was in the scent pool, he didn't know that he had to go back to the corner to pick up the foot trail again; he simply moved in whatever direction instinct told him to go.

When Ronin ended up on Santa Clara Avenue, I believe that he encountered the original foot trail of the two suspects on their way to the bank. Their getaway car may have been parked nearby. He followed that trail until it ended up back on Park Street, which is where we stopped and went back to the fresher trail. Even though it may have been a mistake to let Ronin follow the weaker, original trail back to Park Street, he may have shown us right where the original trail had begun.

My biggest mistake was not having faith in my dog when he clearly gave me an alert on the vent at the base of the apartment building. Ronin knew, with no hesitation, that he had found the suspect, and every behavior that he exhibited was consistent with his training. I have written about how easy it is to rationalize a trailing dog's work to conform to just about any circumstance, but I haven't mentioned the other side of the coin.

It is simple for a handler to over-analyze what his or her dog is doing on a trail. Without years of experience following behind a dog, this is an easy rut in which to get stuck. This is especially true when a handler has the added pressure of peer scrutiny with a backup person. I was so worried about what the detective thought who was running behind me that I was ready to admit any transgression made by my dog just so I looked like I knew what I was doing. This problem most likely stemmed from the way I was trained as a police officer. During field training, a new officer is constantly advised not to rationalize a mistake that he or she may have made. If a rookie is caught rationalizing, he or she is immediately chastised verbally and often in writing. The reason for this training is to teach the officer that when a mistake is made, it must be admitted and dealt with appropriately. Ronin had not made a mistake, and deep in my heart I knew this to be true. Yet my fear of embarrassment kept me from trusting him. Imagine how bad it would have been if I had stuck with the cat-in-the-crawl-space theory and moved on.

An Officer Lost

MANY OF RONIN'S AND MY CASES HAVE BEEN QUITE PAINFUL, not only to those intimately involved in them, but to me as well. Ronin fed off of my emotions, and I know that he felt tragedy, too—perhaps not in the same human way, but in his own right, he, too, felt pain. As a police officer, I became desensitized to most emotionally compromising situations, yet there were times when no matter what face I tried to put on it, the raw energy of the moment broke through my best defenses. This was one of those times—a time I hope to never relive. I thought long and hard about writing this story. I thought that maybe it shouldn't be something for the general public to read. For the most part, I have only talked about it with some of my closest friends. However, as Ronin's and my story has evolved, I've almost become obsessive about writing. There has been a certain amount of closure for me in many aspects, and perhaps this is simply one more door to shut through revelation.

There is nothing worse than hunting for another cop, plain and simple. It is the worst of all possible scenarios. For good or ill, if an officer is missing, the circumstances are rarely positive. The date was November 13, 1997, and the sky was swollen with dark, billowing clouds that seemed as if they were consuming the very earth as they rolled to the east. It was raining, with ferocious, wailing wind gusts. There was a general feeling of malaise with this day, and I don't remember if it started with the call that morning or if it made itself known with the dawn. The only thing I do remember is that I felt horrible and wanted nothing to do with what we had been asked to prepare for.

The story had been in the paper for the last couple of days and the press was having a field day. A police officer's wife had been found dead in the trunk of her car and the officer was now missing. There were rumors of sordid relationships and other melodramatic details that so often find their way into daily rags. I had tuned most of this out until we became involved. We were called very early in the morning on that thirteenth day of November, and we didn't have any time to spare. The officer's car had been found at the base of a mountain in Santa Clara County, but the officer was nowhere to be found. The incident necessitated a full SWAT call-out by the host agency. The officer had worked for a nearby community for many years in the county and was known by most of the responding emergency personnel. He was a well liked and respected police officer with many years of experience. This was no easy task.

I arrived to a cluster of people, equipment, and vehicles, all except the missing officer's car. So much for a scent article. The area was a parking turnout at the base of the mountain with several hiking trails that led in different directions. It was a dead end, and car traffic was forced to stop here. The location had been thoroughly canvassed by other emergency personnel long before I arrived. The car had been impounded for future CSI work, or so I assumed. I remember not having anything to work with, a contaminated scene, and lots of people who were in the way. Probably the worst part of it was that I had to interview a partner and friend of the missing officer in hope of finding a scent article. The officer's partner and close friend was on the mountain with us, concerned for the welfare of his buddy, and here I was, trying to pry something out of him that might lead to his friend's arrest or death. I could not imagine how he felt and tried to tread as lightly as I possibly could. There was absolutely nothing I could say to assuage his concern; however, I needed a good scent article if we were going to have a snowball's chance in hell of finding the missing cop.

The friend was the consummate professional, and although he was wracked by the pain of having to help with the capture of a brother officer, he was willing and able to find whatever I needed to start our trail.

County of Santa Clara
Office of the Sheriff

55 W. Younger Avenue
San Jose, California 95110-1721
(408) 299-2101

Charles P. Gillingham
Sheriff

December 5, 1997

Alameda Police Department
1555 Oak Street
Alameda, CA 94501

Attention: Officer Jeff Schettler

Dear Officer Schettler,

On behalf of Sheriff Gillingham and the SERT Team, I would like to express our sincere gratitude and appreciation to you and your K-9 "Ronin's" efforts on November 13th, in the search and recovery of our missing person

Your professionalism and expertise, coupled with your partner "Ronin's" exceptional abilities were the key factors in the successful, yet unfortunately tragic resolution of our mission.

As we have been involved in numerous open terrain serarches and man-hunts in our jurisdiction, we are always envious of the agencies which possess such invaluabe assets such as you and your bloodhound. You and your partner literally "save the day" not to mention the wear and tear on the dozens of searchers.

Your Chief and your Department should be quite proud of and grateful to have such a team!

Once again, our sincere thanks for a job well done!

Sincerely,

Charles P. Gillingham, Sheriff
County of Santa Clara

By: _____

Sergeant Frank DeLuna - Badge 1137
Team Leader, Sheriff's Emergency Response Team

FD/nd

Board of Supervisors: Michael M. Honda, Zoe Lofgren, Ron Gonzales, Rod Diridon, Dianne McKenna
County Executive: Sally R. Reed

Letter of gratitude from the Santa Clara Sheriff's Office to Jeff Schettler and Ronin, December 1997.

I described to him that the article I needed should be an item with little or no contamination on it by another human being. If it was contaminated, it had to be by a person who had never been to this scene, or that person had to be present when we started the trail. I preferred a piece of dirty laundry that had been by itself. I had no other choice but to wait for a decent article, because the only other option was to start Ronin on one of the several trails and hope he picked up the right one. Needless to say, that wasn't going to happen, because I had no intention of following the trail of one of the many searchers who had already canvassed the area. We had to wait for more than an hour, because the scent article was ultimately obtained from the subject's home.

In the meantime, I received a briefing from the local SWAT commander. He was decked out in all that I expected someone to be wearing who had never run with a fast-trailing dog on a tactical mission. He had heavy fatigues and a load-bearing vest filled to the brim with essential accoutrements such as bullets, smoke grenades, radio, etc. He also had on a heavy helmet and an even heavier ballistic vest. The vest concerned me, because it was an extreme-duty vest complete with a ceramic center plate for the chest and back. This type of plate helps to absorb and deflect the initial impact of a high-velocity projectile. Over the vest rode a black canvas pack with a vinyl bag insert full of about two quarts of water and the accompanying tube and mouthpiece. The sergeant had a standard submachine gun strapped to his back and an issued semiautomatic pistol on a thigh holster. Overall, my guess was that this guy was wearing and carrying about forty to fifty pounds of gear.

The commander of the SWAT team was a mirror image of the rest of his team. They all were wearing very similar gear, including weaponry. Thankfully, they were relatively physically fit, and it was obvious by their demeanor that they were a competent, well-trained team. The problem was, no matter how good of shape they thought they might be in, there was no possible way they were going to keep up with us. My initial estimate was that I would lose all of them after the first 100 yards or so, on the trail . . . that is, if we ever got started. The briefing didn't take long at all, and it was pretty clear to me that the SWAT leader didn't understand exactly what we were about to do. He did know about tracking dogs, but he had never seen a dog like Ronin running on the trail. He explained to me that they would "move" in support of our operation and provide the necessary firepower and tactics should we encounter armed resistance. I could also see that the thought of this was distasteful to him as well.

Standard operating tactical police teams do not move anywhere near the speed necessary to work a high-prey-drive trailing dog. SWAT movements are oriented toward close-quarters missions inside or around an urban environment. SWAT teams are far more used to moving into buildings shoulder to shoulder, with weapons raised and ready. The idea of running behind a dog in a fluid, tactical formation was foreign—plain and simple. The whole idea that I was trying to impress on the man was that my dog was trained to move faster than the people we hunted. We didn't move slowly and methodically, because if we did, Ronin would lose interest. It was all about the hunt for Ronin, and speed was essential.

The normal reaction that I received when talking to tactical teams about how to move properly with a high-speed trailing dog was a mixture of raised eyebrows at a minimum and muffled "bullshits" behind gloved hands. In the eyes of a tactical operator, speed and distance between the team members was a mortal sin. Teams such as these were used to operating under very strict guidelines, where every operator's actions were known before they were made. The difficulty with a trailing-dog tactical operation was that there were simply far too many variables involved that most SWAT members had never encountered on a mission. Running for a long distance was the first obstacle for them to overcome, but I wasn't able to make that sink in. These guys also did not trust my dog all that much. While we were waiting, I overheard stories about other dogs that couldn't find anything. Their experience made it difficult to trust that this dog could not only find what they were looking for, but do it with a little bit of safety.

I had worked with tactical teams already by this time in my K-9 career, but I didn't have any formal education as to how it should be done. I didn't know that there was precedence for tactical dog-trailing operations with a group of men during the 1960s known as Combat Tracker Teams. I would meet some of these amazing people later in my career. In the interim, I was forced to improvise using tactics I had learned and been taught as a soldier in the U.S. Army. I had thought long and hard about how to properly integrate tactical operators into an effective, high-risk, fugitive trailing team, and I came to the conclusion that standard, close-quarter SWAT tactics just didn't apply. To begin with, we had the speed issue to deal with. Most important, operations like this one were conducted primarily in rural, uninhabited terrain that was impossible to completely memorize no matter how many maps and aerial photographs

Tactical training team practice session.

you viewed. In other words, everything was a variable with no clear definition. Tactical dog teams are also very much exposed to ambush and gunfire if the dog fails to provide a proximity alert as to the suspect's general location somewhere off in the distance. If the team ran up on a suspect who had ample warning of their impending arrival, the results could be horrible—probably for Ronin or me because we were out in front. Invariably, we would be on the receiving end of anything from a bad guy.

I decided that the best mode of operation was to incorporate basic infantry squad tactics at a faster pace. The team would move in a staggered column, or wedge-type formation, behind Ronin and me, and if we encountered an ambush, I would drop and reel Ronin in while the team dealt with the threat. I also thought that it would be best if the team had some semblance of an interval between them. I did not like the idea of shoulder-to-shoulder movement, which would be impossible on the run anyway, but the way I looked at it, it was a fatal flaw for the team if gunfire was really encountered. If we were shot at, the shots would probably be relatively indirect due to some distance between the team and the assailant. Unless the suspect was armed with a scoped weapon or the distance was within about twenty-five yards, the shots would not be too accurate. If the operators were close to each other, however, then accuracy wouldn't matter. Hell—even if the bad guy missed his intended target, the operators buddy at his shoulder would probably take the hit. No—shoulder-to-shoulder was just not going to be feasible.

I tried to explain this to the team commander, but he didn't buy it. He had tons of real-life experience, but just not with this. To make matters worse, I wasn't on a SWAT team myself and really had no street credentials to back myself up. I was told that we had to move as slowly as possible so that the SWAT team could keep up with us. I implored him to at least reconsider the gear that everyone was carrying, and I did succeed in getting the guys to shed a little bit. However, it would prove to be not enough. By the time we got the tactical operation order figured out, maybe not to my liking, but organized nonetheless, my scent article arrived—a Zip-Lock–bagged T-shirt collected as per my instructions. At least something was going right.

As we prepared to start, Mother Nature kicked it up a notch, just to make an already miserable situation a little less bearable. We were right in the middle of the line of a storm cloud on the west slope of a very large mountain in the middle of Santa Clara County. The wind was driving sheets of rain down on us in unpredictable intervals. Even though it was cold and wet, I knew that we were soon going to heat up. I stripped down to a long-sleeve shirt, a simple canvas pistol belt, my Alameda police ball cap, running boots, and my ever-present wad of chew in my mouth. I left my ballistic vest in my truck. I was confident enough in Ronin to believe that he would alert me to the presence of danger if the wind was right long before it could be a real threat. If the wind wasn't in his favor, well, at least I wouldn't be out of breath when trying to find a place to hide quickly. We were going to be running up a fairly steep slope for miles, perhaps. I, of all people, had to keep up with my own dog.

While the SWAT team lined up behind us, I saddled up Ronin, and he was anxious to be off. His whining was lost to the wind and clouds, but anyone watching could see that he was ready to go. I straddled him and opened the bag off to my side, slowly bringing it out to arm's length in front of his nose. I let the pressure off of the lead under my right foot as he craned his neck and head toward the T-shirt. Just as his nose got to within an inch of the mouth of the bag, I commanded Ronin to "Skit it!" and we were off.

Ronin circled the parking area and struck off to the southeast through a gated, dirt fire road. Shortly after hitting the fire road, Ronin encountered a small trail leading down to a rock promontory with a commanding view of the valley below. He alerted on the trail and started to go down but backed his way out after a few yards. It was if the trail went down and back. I had seen this behavior before and believed that our subject may have gone down toward the rocks shortly after leaving his vehicle, but then came back up after only a short distance.

Ronin was up on the dirt road again and the sprint began. I told the SWAT commander behind me that we had a hot trail and to get ready, not for action, but just to run fast. I could tell by his look that he didn't like what he was seeing, but I couldn't slow Ronin down even if I wanted to. Ronin was at his prime in 1997. He was the most powerful animal I had ever worked with, and even though he was a bulky 105 pounds, he was solid and had well-developed muscles. He was incredibly swift for a dog so large—perhaps not acrobatic, but fast. He reminded me of a big Peterbilt truck—not necessarily quick off the line but, once it got up to speed, was pretty difficult to stop. Ronin was upshifting to about fifth gear right about now, and our team was getting a little stretched out. I didn't know this for sure, but I felt it.

The rain had mired the fire road in sheets of mud that stuck to the bottoms of our boots and made each step a little more treacherous than the last. It got to the point where my boots were literally mud on mud, and I felt like I was slipping a couple of inches backward with every pace forward. I was far lighter than the rest of our crew, plus I had the luxury of Ronin's large frame hauling me along behind him. He was not having as much trouble as I was, because his large, splayed paws fell heavy on the soft earth while his claws found easy purchase. Each step threw up mud spray that splattered his flanks as he ran. My light shirt was quickly soaked, chilling me to the bone, but I knew that warmth would come from the exertion soon to follow.

I felt my team members become stretched out behind me and knew without glancing backward that they were having trouble keeping up. Their wet-sounding, slapping boot falls were quickly fading into the windy background. It wasn't much longer until the only thing I heard was the labored breathing of my SWAT commander, who, although he was struggling to keep pace, had absolutely no intention of letting me out run him. Chalk it up to personal fortitude, good conditioning, or just the fact that he was there to protect us—this man would not leave my side. I knew that he would be there no matter what happened and that he would die before letting me leave him in my wake. This was strangely comforting, because I was so used to losing everyone who ran behind us whenever the going got rough. I knew that I would not lose this guy.

We had a news helicopter flying overhead, and I made sure to tell the commander that the bird had to stay above us by at least 500 feet. I didn't want the prop wash from the copter blades or the related noise to disturb Ronin in any way. The news crew accommodated us quite nicely, but it was obvious that they were dogging our every muddy step.

We came to a small spur that the fire road went up and over when my loyal commander told me that we had to slow down because his team was too stretched out. I looked back down the slope just in time to see a couple of our team members make the bend in a turn that we had made about 100 yards before. The rest were missing. This was not good, and I knew it, but I was having a very difficult time with Ronin. His trail was getting hotter, if that could be possible, and he was literally pulling my planted but sliding feet through the ooze. He was at the end of his long lead, and I could see his thick leather harness biting deep into the sides of his chest and armpits. Ronin's breath was also labored, not so much from the run but from trying to drag me behind him. It was one thing when my 220-pound frame was being pulled along willingly but another when it was dead weight. We stopped momentarily and he howled, struggling to free himself from my restraint. I told the sergeant that we had to go, that we were close. He told me to go ahead as he noticed the rest of the struggling team making the bend in the turn behind us.

We began to run again now, faster and with far more determination. The wind was in our face now, and Ronin no longer had his nose near the ground. It was held high, nostrils flaring and ears streaming behind. Ronin had a fresh air scent now. It was difficult to determine how far away the source might be because the wind was so stiff, but I figured that he was somewhere within the next 300 yards. Right at that moment, the helicopter that had been filming our progress sped off ahead and to the south and began to hover. We could not see the pilot or anyone inside the aircraft, but it seemed that they may have spotted something. This was confirmed a short time later when the SWAT commander received a radio message from the command post that the news crew had located a body lying on that south slope, now only about 100 yards away.

I was not privy to the communication, as I could not hear the radio, but it seemed that the news was not necessarily good. The route to the new scene was made with tactical movements, but it was quicker than if we had expected any resistance. When we arrived, the reason for expediency was self-evident. The officer lay there dead of a self-inflicted gunshot wound. I'm not sure if Ronin realized that the subject of his search was dead, because he was acting out, trying to reach the body. He wanted to finish this search, and the only way that was possible, in his mind, was to smell or touch the find. I was loathing doing this. The enormity of the moment held us all in somewhat of a trance. It was hard to know what thoughts were going through the rest of the team's minds because we were all so quiet, but I knew that we still had to have respect for this officer regardless of the circumstances. I allowed Ronin to inch his way forward, wagging his tail a little faster with every foot until he was just able to nose the man a little. I immediately called him off and rewarded him with a quiet "good boy" and a couple of Scooby snacks.

Ronin wolfed down his cookies greedily but was obviously dissatisfied with something. He kept looking up at me, painfully raking his right paw down my thigh as if asking me, "Did I do right, Dad?" I normally react to his finds with unbridled enthusiasm equaling his own, and I know that my subdued behavior was having an effect on him. He was acting like he needed to make the find all over again and kept looking back at the officer's body, then at me. He was really confused, but I couldn't play the games I would normally play with him, for any exuberant praise that I might exhibit here would be captured by the film crew hovering above us and shown on that evening's news. I had absolutely no intention of embarrassing this officer's family or police department in such a fashion; Ronin may not have understood what my problem was, but he would have to wait.

I was trying to stay as composed and solemn looking as possible, as I think we all were. It was not a nice moment, and none of us felt any satisfaction, yet here we were, at the end of a very uncomfortable trail. While we stood there, talking in low tones even though no one could hear us, Ronin just would not leave it alone. He insisted on trying to get back to the body and was attempting to get around me by running from one side to the other. I kept him on a short lead, but with every little lunge he got a little more line. Ronin managed to generate enough space and lead length that he was able to move behind me from my right side to the left, trailing the lead behind him in the process. I wasn't thinking much of it, because I was listening to the other officer's conversation when Ronin took this opportunity to lunge again, thoroughly tangling his lead around my ankles and literally lifting me off of my feet. I managed to drag him back as I simultaneously fell on my ass, and I know that part made it on film, too. So much for trying to remain professional. My dog was acting like a lunatic and it was time to make an unceremonious exit stage left. I reeled Ronin in nice and tight, saying my goodbyes in the process. There was really nothing else to say. Damn, I felt bad.

Ronin, on the other hand, felt like it was time to get to the business of investigating animal odors, deer, rabbits, coyotes, and whatever other spoor or track he could find. I left him to his devices running off lead while I walked back down the mountain, lost in my own thoughts. I knew that the pilot of the news helicopter had spotted the officer, but his crew had followed us up the trail to him. I should have felt some satisfaction about Ronin's success, but I hated the situation. I dreaded going back to the command post to the officer's partners and friends. I did not want to look into any of those eyes or answer any questions. I felt like I had done something wrong, and knew I would have trouble talking to anyone.

As I meandered down the same fire road that we had just run up, I contemplated how I could leave the scene with as little contact with other searchers or bystanders as possible. I had little to worry about. As I made my way back to the command post, very little was left of the previous bustling, busy activity that had encompassed the command post before we left. A few folks were standing around, but it looked like almost everyone felt the same way I did; misery loves company until the company is ready to leave.

I spoke to the incident search commander for just a moment, telling him that I had to hurry off to work because I was late, and that I would FAX him a copy of my report. This was a lie, but I just couldn't face any questions and wanted to leave. My feelings were so convoluted that I didn't know quite how to deal with them. In the end, and true to form for that period in my life, I ignored my feelings, discounting them in the process, which ultimately messed me up just a little bit more. I can't do that anymore, and in order for anyone—myself included—to get a proper perspective of the moment at that time in our career, I find it strangely necessary to write about it here.

The way in which I dealt with loss or pain at that time was to ignore it or get angry. My family was the beneficiary of that syndrome. What I felt on that search once we began was the adrenalin rush of a potentially dangerous, high-profile case that had national attention, and I was right there in the middle of it. My pulse quickened with excitement every step we ran, and I felt strong and focused in a way you can achieve only during these life-and-death situations. Time seemed to move a little slower as I was able to categorize everything that was happening around us in a fraction of the time that it would normally take me. Ronin and I were completely in sync with each other, and I knew deep in my soul that he was going to find this officer. I was on a high that could not be duplicated by any form of drug.

Everything came to a thunderous, crashing halt when we came upon the officer's body. All of my original concerns for the case were flooding back in a tidal wave, coupled with guilt for the elation from which I had just come down. How could I be excited to do what I had just done? How could any police officer? I was disgusted with myself and couldn't share my thoughts with anyone. To this day, I feel guilty about what I did, even though I know that I did nothing wrong. I tell myself that I was only doing my job, but that doesn't make it feel any better.

APD bloodhound used to find police officer's body

The San Jose police officer's wife was found murdered in the trunk of her car last week

By Peter Hegarty
Staff Writer

In their search for the missing San Jose police officer whose wife was discovered murdered last week, investigators enlisted the help of Ronin, the Alameda police bloodhound.

The body of veteran San Jose police officer Tom Harris was eventually spotted Nov. 13 at around 8 a.m. by a KGO-TV news helicopter near Los Gatos. A fire-arm was found near his body, according to a Santa Clara County Sheriff's Department spokesman.

The sheriff's department had contacted Alameda police shortly after 5 a.m., asking to borrow Ronin—the only bloodhound with a California police agency that is available full-time.

"We sent him down there and he met with the investigators and members of their K-9 unit," said Alameda police Sgt. Jim Taranto. "Then they began the search."

Ronin was accompanied by his handler, Officer Jeff Shettler.

While the bloodhound was attempting to pick up the trail, Taranto said the news helicopter was monitoring the search from high above.

When Ronin made a sudden turn, apparently picking up the scent, the helicopter turned and followed. It was at this point that the helicopter crew saw Harris' body below, Taranto said.

Some 20 deputies and dogs took part in the search.

Investigators have so far denied that Harris is the prime suspect in the death of his wife, 48-year-old Judith Harris.

see BLOODHOUND, page 8

Clipping from Oakland Tribune, Oakland, California. Used with permission, Bay City News Service.

A Stolen Car

I WAS WORKING PATROL WITH RONIN at 1:55 on the morning of December 7, 1997. We had been a K-9 team on a daily basis for a little while now, with our own patrol car. Ronin was really enjoying coming to work with me everyday; he especially liked the attention he got from other officers and from the dispatchers. Unlike the protection patrol dogs, Ronin was pretty harmless and just loved to be given attention or snacks. He quickly learned how to ingratiate himself with everyone, but he liked the women up in dispatch the best.

We came to work for our midnight shift around 9 P.M. and got off at seven the next morning. We kept to the same routine most days, either parking on Lincoln Avenue as close as possible to the police station, or, if no parking spots were available, we had to park the truck about a block away in the county parking lot. I hated this spot, because all of the local dirt bags knew that this was where the cops had to park, and my truck had already been vandalized twice. Not even the "5-0" were safe! ("5-0" is a nickname the police have from the 1970s TV show *Hawaii 5-0*.) Ronin and I got lucky and found a space about a few car lengths from the entry gate to the back door of the station. Ronin liked this spot, too, because he was so close that I'd let him run off lead to the back door. He was itching to get out of the truck after our forty-five-minute ride from Livermore. More important, he was hoping to ditch me at the door and make a beeline for dispatch on the second floor. I had him figured out by now.

Ronin jumped down out of the right front passenger seat and didn't even look back as he headed for the door. I allowed him this little pleasure, and we made a fun game out of it, because he did the same thing every time—run for dispatch. Why dispatch, one might ask? It was simple: The dispatchers were the nicest people Ronin knew, and they had their own little kitchenette right next to their radio/phone consoles. They also started to bring dog treats to work just for Ronin. This evening was just like most others. Ronin had a sixth sense when someone was at the locked back door before we got there. He would have a couple of minute's head start if he could get inside with the Good Samaritan before I did. A couple of minutes translated to more Scooby snacks than I would normally allow him. The little shit had this process down to a science.

Of course, as I sauntered up to the door, it was shut and locked and Ronin was missing. No big deal, because I knew where the hell he was anyway and I smiled as I unlocked the door for myself. Rather than going to the basement to the dressing rooms, as I would have to do later, I walked up the stairs just to the left of the back door to dispatch. The door to the communications center was shut, but I could hear a couple of the dispatchers fawning over Ronin anyway, so I knew he was there. I looked through the glass partition and saw his adoring face beaming up at Patty with glowing eyes and loose jowls—a face only a mother or really nice dispatcher could love. The little ham got all the girls! Patty kept handing over little treats to my soon-to-be-fat bloodhound unless I intervened fairly soon. I opened the door, saying my salutations as Ronin grabbed the last of what once was an entire small bag of puppy snacks; great! Ronin knew that fun time was over and waltzed to the door and my side with great wags of his stegosaurus-like tail. This tail could be dangerous to fine china or any fragile item in any room.

We walked back down the stairs so that I could change into my uniform and make the midnight shift lineup briefing with our patrol sergeant. This process normally took less than half an hour. Ronin sat by my side while we listened to our briefing, learning of all the crime that had happened up to the point we started our shift; same thing, different day. Ronin was always impatient with briefing and, depending on the monotone voice of a particular sergeant, would assist with the briefing with

Jeff and Ronin on patrol in Alameda, California.

little "wooo, wooos" whenever he had a chance. Thankfully, everyone thought it was cute. Ronin got away with lots of little shenanigans that none of the other patrol dogs could even think of. He was the ultimate weasel.

Once briefing was over, Ronin and I drove to our beat on the west end of town, or the second beat. My call sign was 1L20. Because it was the midnight shift, I was the only beat unit on the west end. This was pretty normal for the dog watch, because we had only one patrol for each beat during this time of the night. The only difference was that I would probably catch the most "paper," because the west end of Alameda was the most economically depressed area of the town and accounted for most of the crime. "Paper" translates to police reports. Personally, I liked it, because it meant that I stayed pretty busy throughout my shift, and I could also knock out paper quickly.

This night was a little different, though. It was pretty slow, because it had been raining all night; the rain kept the criminals inside, I guess. Ronin and I had not been doing much of anything other than driving around. I tried to give him a few breaks here and there, but I didn't want to get out in the storm much myself. Ronin could care less and could have been a duck.

Another patrol had taken a recovered stolen car case on the far end of Main Street at the entrance to the Alameda Naval Air Station, which was now well on its way to decommissioning. We were quickly taking over the patrol responsibilities from the navy SPs; thus, Tom was taking this case near my beat. The car appeared to have been simply parked, and there was absolutely no sign that it had been damaged or tampered with. There were no keys in the ignition. This was kind of strange, because we expected the ignition to have been punched and it wasn't. Basically, this meant that someone had keys to the car.

Tom wasn't about to put too much investigation into this case, as it was our general policy to suspend stolen car cases with the recovery of the vehicle. Very rarely did any evidence arise to point in the direction of a particular suspect, and these cases just took up a lot of time. Since we had nothing better to do, Tom asked me if I wanted to run Ronin from the car and see what we came up with. It was still raining and I knew I was going to get soaked but—what the hell—I never passed up a potentially good trail with a good scent article to start off of. I made a quick inspection of the car, looking for the best possible source of the suspect's scent.

Stolen vehicles could be a little tricky, because the car was normally permeated with the owners' scent as well as that of the suspect. I had to try to isolate something that I knew the suspect had touched. It stood to reason that this suspect probably had touched the door handle, the steering wheel, the driver's door armrest and handle, and, of course, the seat. The seat would be the most contaminated article, but I didn't feel like getting picky. It was raining pretty hard and I honestly didn't think that we'd be going far. Most often, when a car was dumped this far from anywhere, the driver normally got into another car with a buddy who had followed him to the dump spot. I figured that this case would be similar. I expected to run a couple of hundred yards and get back into my warm, dry car. Well, Ronin, apparently, had other plans. Here I was thinking that I could score a quick stat showing that we did something— anything, it didn't matter—and he found a trail instead. It looked like I was going to get soaked and I had my dog to thank for that. As a matter of fact, this seemed to be becoming a pattern.

I scented Ronin on the driver's seat of the car with a little hand sweep to the seat cushion. He put his big, muddy paws on the opening for the door and took a good whiff of the seat. Ronin did not hesitate with the car at all and just turned around and started running back up Main Street, heading northeast. Ronin kept far from a straight course on Main Street and rather zigzagged back and forth from the north to the south, concentrating on the gutters where the rain was collecting. When it rains on hard surfaces, the scent is not necessarily washed away—it is just moved. In this case, I assumed that it had been moved to the gutters. We continued this way for about a half of a mile until we ran into the intersection at Singleton Street.

Once we made it to Singleton, Ronin checked the northwest and northeast corners before settling on a direction of travel, which turned out to be Mosely Street. He seemed to be banging the turns quite nicely on this trail, considering all of the rain. Everything was going just fine, aside from being pretty wet, that is, until I fell. Ronin was running in the road again and sheets of water were running to either side. It almost looked like we were running on top of a river in some places. Evidently, I placed a foot into a pothole and fell face forward, knocking the wind out of myself at the same time. The lead went flying out of my hand while Ronin continued to run, now with little resistance. His lead trailed through the water behind him like some water snake slithering to and fro.

It took me awhile to gather myself, because I fell really hard and fast, unable to break my forward momentum until the very last second. I remember feeling the road water filling through my uniform shirt and underneath my ballistic vest. I couldn't get up right away, but I did hear Tom yell at me asking if I was OK. I told him to hurry up and try to catch Ronin, because I was getting left behind. I watched Ronin turn east onto Cimarron Street right about the time I got to my knees. He wasn't even looking back!

During this stage of our career, Ronin didn't care much whether I was on the other end of the lead or not. I always tried to keep a tight grip on it, because he would never stop once he was on a hot trail. I could scream all I wanted to, and I'd be lucky if I got a backward glance. I even bought myself a weightlifters' lower-back-type belt with a big D-ring on the front of it onto which I'd snap Ronin's lead. I quickly got rid of the belt when I learned that, when I fell, Ronin just tried to drag me. This was really a pain in the ass if we were on a steep slope or stairs. It also sucked if there was a forest of trees anywhere on our trail, because he always tangled me up in trunks or branches. No, the belt didn't work, and neither did allowing Ronin to continue if I dropped the lead. We really started to work on recall commands after this particular trail.

Tom caught up to Ronin when Ronin got to Seahorse Street and a small navy condo near the corner. I don't think I caught up until they were both at the front door. I was hurt and soaking wet. I grabbed the lead just in time for the front door to open to reveal a young teenage boy and his elderly grandmother. Grandma inquired as to what it was we were doing while Ronin took the opportunity to enthusiastically greet the kid. Tom called in the location to dispatch and then advised me that we were at the house from which the car had been reportedly stolen.

Ronin was all over the teenager and kept trying to jump up on him but was having trouble because grandma was in the way. She really wanted to know what all the fuss was about and didn't seem to appreciate my slobbery-mouthed, dripping wet bloodhound very much. At this point, I figured out exactly what had happened. The kid had taken the family car on a joyride without permission, and something had happened to it at the north end of Main Street. Rather than 'fessing up to the truth, Johnny boy had told daddy that the car was stolen. Not an overly exciting case but a "walk-up find" nonetheless. I gave Ronin a few Scooby snacks along with tons of praise. As far as I was concerned, he was the greatest dog on earth, and I wanted him to know it. I was really not very comfortable, but Ronin had to have his "Ronin" time before we went back to our car.

Tom took over from here and cleared the case. Instead of a crime, it now became a civil matter. We were not going to pursue anything like falsely reporting a crime, even though it might teach the kid a lesson. The only thing I was interested in was changing my clothes!

Car Clout

MOST OF THE CASES THAT RONIN AND I WORKED TOGETHER were not all that exciting and romantic. Yes, we did have more than our share of crazy investigations, but for every interesting situation there were at least ten of the mundane variety. No problem here. The limelight had a habit of burning sometimes, so I was quite happy to do the simple stuff, too. This next case was similar to so many others, and rather than enumerate each one, I figured that one decent story could give you an idea of what we dealt with most every day.

It was April 1998, and Ronin and I were having a ball. What better job could an overgrown kid have than to bring his dog to work every day? I swear, if you believe in something strong enough, it's bound to happen. Working with Ronin was an extension of my lifelong dream that began with Belit eighteen years earlier. I never lost that dream. If anything, it grew into something else altogether. Ronin and I had been an official team now for a few months, and the city of Alameda was getting to know my dog pretty well. He had been on the local television news channels several times, and the papers picked up his cases as well.

Ronin was becoming very well known, indeed. A fellow officer and friend, Steve, told me that he had a pretty funny story to relate. He said he was on patrol in the Marina Village area of the island when he noticed a woman in a nice convertible sports car commit a minor traffic violation. Being the good officer that he was, he stopped the woman to explain the violation that she had just made. Before he had a chance to get a word in edgewise, the woman, thinking she was moments away from a traffic ticket, broke into a song and dance routine about how she knew another Alameda officer and the reasons why she did not deserve the impending citation. Steve let the lady say her piece, because it actually can be entertaining to listen to the stories people tell. She completed her dissertation, only leaving out the name of the officer whom she knew. Steve, being the cognizant investigator that he was, asked the young lady who her friend in patrol was. At this, the woman's face clouded with consternation as she stammered, trying to spit out a name. At last, and with a look of sheer happiness, she beamed and said that his name was Ronin. Again, the dog got all the girls.

I thought that the story was funny, but my laugh was just a bit forced because I was also slightly jealous of my dog! Steve recognized the look and told me not to fret too much because Ronin was obviously far more handsome. I went to work that night and could swear that Ronin must have heard Steve's story, because he was looking far too happy with himself. I decided that it was time for him to go to the navy base for some exercise.

Later that night we received a call to the 1400 block of Central Avenue for a report of a car break-in. These types of crimes were referred to as "car clouts" by the veterans. The victim in this case was a really nice guy who was a little pissed off that his brand new compact disc player had been ripped off from his Ford F150 pickup truck. Back in those days, CD players were still rather expensive and not everyone had one. This guy had just installed his system and was none to happy that some idiot had damaged the window of his car and made off with his sound system. He had just parked his car within the last couple of hours, so the crime was still rather fresh—easy enough for Ronin to pick up a trail from, at any rate.

The suspect had used a pry tool of some sort to access the small metal handle of the right-side wing window of the truck. He then had stuck his arm into the window and simply pulled the lock up and opened the door. Once inside, he had made quick work of the plastic frame of the stereo system by simply ripping it apart. He had unscrewed the retaining bolts and ripped the whole thing out, wires and all—very professional. His method told me that he was either a kid or a doper. I doubted that the suspect had been wearing gloves, but I didn't bother to take fingerprints anyway. My department had an unwritten policy that there was no CSI-type work done on misdemeanor cases. This case was classified as a misdemeanor petty theft because the value of the stereo was less than $400. The reason for this was sheer economics. We had plenty of thefts every day, and there was absolutely no way our technicians could work on every one of them. It just was not in the budget. I could still work Ronin, though.

I took a scent swab of parts of the stereo that I knew the suspect must have handled and placed it in a Zip-Lock bag. Ronin hopped out of the car, and I let him cruise the area, peeing on every bush in sight. When I thought he was done, I brought him over to the victim and told him to "check him." I do this to remove the victim's scent from the equation. This guy's scent was going to be all over the truck and he probably had installed the stereo himself. Ronin could just as easily run over to the victim and identify him as the suspect.

I harnessed up the movie star and asked him if I was good enough to run with him, and Ronin woofed "yes." This wasn't really the case, but I was still a little miffed that the cute blonde in the convertible could only think of Ronin's name. I scented Ronin on the gauze pad and we were off. He circled the truck briefly and headed east on Central, then north on Benton Street. He ran west on Santa Clara Avenue, then south on Morton, east on San Antonio, and north on Paru. He ran back to eastbound San Antonio and turned south onto Grand Street. I know that this sounds completely convoluted—and it really was—but there was a reason for it. The suspect was walking through the nicer neighborhoods, obviously looking for more loot, which meant that I was bound to get more car-clout calls that evening; wonderful.

Ronin was running south on Grand, heading toward the beach and the end of the city. Just about halfway down the block, he lifted his head and started to sprint. He had caught a fresh whiff of something. He ran into the driveway of an infamous house on Grand Street and started wagging his tail, looking around at everything. Ronin was particularly interested in a black, compact pickup in the driveway, circled it a couple of times, and then ran to the open front door of the house. Ronin tried to go in and I had a hard time restraining him. We couldn't walk right in, because I didn't have any backup and this was a house known for vice.

I called for a couple of more units to help me. Most everyone inside the house was an addict and on parole or searchable probation. My progress had been monitored on the radio by my beat partner, and he was there almost as soon as I called. As a matter of fact, by now everyone knew where we were going to end up anyway. Just about the time my beat partner walked up, Craig, one of the residents, walked out of the bedroom and said unceremoniously, " I knew that f—ing dog was coming here . . . I shouldn't have let that jerk in!" If that wasn't a spontaneous admission, I don't know what was. Ronin was happy to see Craig, but he didn't identify him with a paw strike to the thigh, so I had to give Craig a little credit.

Frankly, I trusted Craig as far as I could throw him. He was a big-time black-tar heroin addict and a major thief. He was on parole so he knew that we were going to toss the house anyway ("toss" is cop speak for "search"), but I still wasn't going to trust what he told me completely. I asked Craig who he shouldn't have let in the house and he told me that he was referring to John. John was also a heroin addict and thief who apparently wasn't in the house. This meant that he had probably jumped the fence as soon as we arrived. My best guess was that they were watching us as soon as we hit the driveway.

The problem with heroin addicts is that they have to support their habit in some way. Tar heroin can cost a doper a couple of hundred bucks a day depending on the grade of the dope and the connection from which it came. Addicts normally buy the tar in little balloons that the mule or transporter holds in his mouth until the deal is done. If the mule thinks that he is about to get stopped by the "5/0," he simply swallows the dope and poops it out later. Very rarely is a transaction made between the actual drug dealer and the doper. Dopers are just too unreliable and would sell their own mothers for a fix. If they are hard up enough for smack and they have no money, they either have to steal something or give somebody up. Cops pay for information, and even though heroin addicts are unsavory, they can provide some decent information from time to time. However, most of the time, guys like Craig and John simply steal, burglarizing homes, breaking into cars, shoplifting from the grocery store, etc. This thievery can be almost an everyday occurrence; therefore, it was not strange at all to be at Craig's house. Unfortunately for Craig, he bought some bad Mexican tar shortly after this encounter and overdosed while sitting on his toilet. What a way to go.

Craig told me a story about how it was that he knew my dog was on his way—something to the effect that he had driven past us in his pickup (the black one parked in front of the house), and he saw us on Grand. This was nonsense, because the hood of the truck was cool to the touch. Checking stuff like that was simply a habit when you walked up on a vehicle that might have been involved in a crime. I tried to narrow down Craig's story because the thief was Craig, John, or both of them. Just because Ronin didn't identify Craig with a claw paw didn't mean that Craig wasn't involved. Craig must have sensed this, because he did the next best thing a parolee can do when he knows he is had. If the bullshit doesn't work, he just shuts his mouth. Craig told me to go ahead and search the house. Of course, I accommodated him. We never did find the stereo, or John for that matter, but I was pretty well convinced that the stereo had been in the house just moments before we arrived. That was fine, because I found plenty of other stuff to take Craig to jail for that night.

Nothing was ever done with the circumstantial evidence we produced in this case. I'm sure that if some real effort or follow-up investigation occurred, the situation would have turned out differently. The bottom line, though, was that there were simply not enough resources for these misdemeanor cases. I had already done more than I probably should have; still, I did have a little satisfaction even if we did not get the stereo back.

A Life Destroyed

THERE WERE ALWAYS CERTAIN CASES THAT STOOD OUT FOR ME more so than others. The circumstances surrounding these incidents were such that I could never forget them. Ronin and I worked so many criminal and missing person reports over the years that they often bled into each other, or I have completely forgotten them. As I reviewed all of my notes on each and every case over our ten years of work together, I discovered quite a few successful trails that we had run, either identifying suspects or finding evidence that I have no memory of now. I found this extremely frustrating, because after reading my reports, I realized that the cases would have made great reading if I had some color to add to them. The problem was that I just had no independent recollection of the events that shaped our efforts, and it is the recollection that gives the story some flavor. You might think that the report in and of itself would provide all that I needed, but police reports are normally fairly bland, stating the facts and not much more. I also realized that most of my reports tended to be as short as I could make them in order to save time. This meant that my facts were only those that were necessary to prove the case, and they were actually quite boring to read.

On the other hand, there were still quite a few investigations that haunt me now that I have read them. The memories have probably been kept alive in the back of my little brain for many reasons, probably due to the pain endured by those whom we had been sent to help. I find it ironic that some of these cases affect me emotionally now when at the time I worked them, I felt so very little. This is one of those cases.

Officer Brian Kiel filling out trailing logs during a break.

I was working swing shift at this point in my career on June 8, 1998, and I finally had seniority enough to get off of the "dog" watch of midnight shift. Midnights kicked my ass in more ways than I could imagine. First, I had to get used to working from 9 P.M. to 7 A.M. The hard part was trying to sleep a full six to eight hours when I got home. The sun was up, lawn mowers were going, and the neighborhood kids were screaming, especially on weekends. Every little bit of light and noise was super annoying, and I had a tough time blocking it out. I went to extraordinary efforts to completely blacken my windows with super-dense fabric, but nothing got rid of the noise. The result was that I usually slept for three to four hours each "night" and felt terrible later. This went on for a couple of years. No wonder police work was stressful. It wasn't the job—it was the frickin' hours!

I was thankful when I left dog watch and moved over to swings. Not only did I get more sleep and live somewhat of a more normal life, I was able to work a lot more cases with Ronin. This case was one of our first on swings. I was working the east end of town, which encompassed Willow Street east to Eastshore Drive, when we got the call. This caper was actually in progress, and several units had been dispatched, code three (lights and siren), to respond. My beat partner, Jeff, arrived first, as well as an ambulance, which had hauled off the victim to the emergency room just before I got there.

The scene was at the intersection of Willow Street, which ran north to south, and San Antonio Avenue, which ran east to west. A compact car was stopped in the middle of the street just east of the east-side cross walk for the intersection. The driver had been heading west on San Antonio and appeared to have stopped just at the edge of the white lines of the crosswalk. The driver's side door was open and blood was all over the seat, steering wheel, and door. It appeared as if the driver had been beaten severely while he was inside his car and then dragged out. The rear hatchback window of the car had been smashed in, and I noticed more blood on the ground below this window.

The victim had been unconscious when he was discovered, so there was no story to go by. We just had to put the physical evidence together and take a stab at what we thought might have occurred. Based on the evidence at the scene, it appeared that the driver of the car may have gotten into a pissing match with a pedestrian or another driver. This other person had escalated matters and beaten the driver into a state of unconsciousness. Either our suspect or another person had vandalized the victim's car by punching or kicking the rear window and cutting himself in the process; thus the blood all over the ground below the back window.

I brought out Ronin and let him circle the area a little so that he could get a feel for everything around us. He was drawn immediately to the blood all over the driver's side of the car, so I let him check it out while keeping a tight lead just in case he wanted a taste. I dragged him back to the rear of the car, harnessed him up, and hooked the long lead onto his harness D-ring. I didn't have to say anything, because he was ready to go. I was pretty sure that the blood at the rear of the car did not belong to the driver, so I started Ronin there. He took scent and circled the car again, checking out the driver's side area. He just wouldn't leave it alone. I tried, repeatedly, to get him outside the scent pool of the car and onto an exit trail, but it seemed that there was just too much interesting scent from the suspect on and around the car. This was not the first time I had experienced problems like this. Often, when a large amount of pool scent is in a given area, coupled with a fear or other emotional scent, it is difficult for a dog to leave it. The scent simply is too strong.

I stopped Ronin for a moment to take stock of the situation. I knew that the suspect was also bleeding and hoped that he might have left a trail away from the car. I canvassed the street and sidewalk around the car in outward concentric circles until I found a couple of drops of fresh blood on the north sidewalk just east of the intersection where the car was located. This was perfect. I took a quick scent swab of the blood, placed it in a bag, and brought Ronin over. I restarted him on the blood, and he immediately found the trail running westbound.

We were running west on the north sidewalk of San Antonio Avenue when we came to a gated parking lot for a church that was situated right in the middle of what should have been the street. San Antonio actually continued on the other side of the parking lot. I found more blood in the lot as Ronin made it through the church's chain-link gate; good—we were on the right trail. Ronin ran out of the church to the intersection at Union Street and continued on a trail north to Encinal Avenue. He crossed the street diagonally and seemed to lose the trail at the southwest corner. I brought him over to the southeast corner and then to the northwest, where Ronin again indicated there was no trail simply by stopping where he was and whining.

While Ronin and I were checking corners, my beat partners, A.J. and Bob, were looking for more blood. I had radioed to dispatch the location of each and every blood splatter we found on the trail. Not only did we have a scent trail, we also had a physical one, so my buddies all got into the game. These new blood drops were getting smaller and the distance between them was increasing dramatically. This told me that the wound was beginning to clot and that we might be running out of this nice visual trail very soon. We were able to establish that the trail continued north on Union to Alameda Avenue. The suspect had been running on the east sidewalk but crossed over to the west side at the intersection.

I restarted Ronin on the last blood drop we could find on Alameda. Ronin trailed to Central Avenue and turned west to the major four-way intersection at Grand Street. As we were working the intersection, another officer, Pat, detained a white male in his twenties just a block north of us near the intersection of Santa Clara Avenue and Grand Street. Pat had detained this guy because he had obvious fresh injuries to his face and was bleeding from the nose. The suspect tried to tell us that he had injured his face a couple of weeks before and that he had also been at his twin brother's house all evening. The brother's house was directly behind us, and a couple of officers checked it out for additional suspects or evidence. Blood was found on the doorknob and all over the sink in the kitchen inside the apartment—lots of evidence but no other suspect.

My friend and fellow officer, Pat, had been listening to our progress while we were trailing with Ronin and calling out the locations of all of the blood splatters we had found along the way. He knew that we were on the trail of the suspect and maintained a distance ahead of us at all times. This was a perfect strategy to apprehend a fleeing suspect running from a dog team. Smart officers employ this tactic whenever possible, because it means that they often get the arrest.

Everyone was fairly certain that our guy at the bus stop was the suspect, but my sergeant wanted a little more to go on. There was no witness who could positively identify our guy as the suspect from the crime scene, but I had an ace up my sleeve that my sergeant was very well aware of. We had talked quite a bit about scent lineups and how they could be used to pick out a suspect involved in a crime based on scent collected at the crime scene. I was a little surprised that my sergeant remembered the conversations and was the one to suggest that we try a scent lineup. I was happy to accommodate him, but I was a little nervous, too. We didn't have any really good location to do something like a scent lineup other than an open, paved street. I had normally practiced these on grass or other soft surfaces to ensure that Ronin had a nice scent trail right to where the suspect would be standing. Pavement was another animal altogether.

I set up the lineup as well as I possibly could. I had four officers and the suspect start from a central point and walk out onto the street with the wind for a distance of about twenty-five yards. They started at the same point but fanned out to prescribed locations, on line with each other and about ten feet apart. If you were to view their paths from above, the scene would look like five spines of a fan radiating out at angles from a single point to the edge of the fan. Once each person was at the end of his path, I had each one turn around and put his hands behind his back.

I started Ronin on the scent swab that I had taken from the scene, and he seemed to immediately find a trail between the path the suspect had walked and an officer just to his right. As Ronin came abreast with both, he turned to the left without hesitation, sat down in front of the suspect, and pawed him on the thigh. My sergeant was more than satisfied, and the suspect was on his way to jail.

I still did not know who the victim was in this case, but I had heard that he was severely injured and in a coma. I didn't think much of it at the time and really wasn't too concerned. I had quite a bit on my plate that evening, not to mention all of the paperwork—not only from this case, but from all of the other non-dog stuff that I had needed to deal with that evening. It just didn't pay to get too wrapped up with victims.

This all changed when I saw the poor man in court a few months later for the preliminary hearing of our suspect. I had a chance to talk to the man for a few minutes before I had to testify. He had no memory of what had happened to him—not the time, the date, the suspects . . . nothing. He had lost much of his memory regarding his everyday life. His memory and physical condition had been so horribly destroyed that he had lost his job as a computer whiz at a local high-tech company and his fiancé had left him shortly thereafter. And here he was, after everything he had been through, facing up to the bad guys in court. I was ashamed that I had not concerned myself with his condition on the day he had been attacked, but I also was proud to see that he had the courage to come into court today to watch his ambushers fry. I say ambushers, because our first suspect was being officially being charged, but his twin brother showed up in court with his right hand in a cast.

My part in the hearing was none too brief. No one had identified our suspect at the scene, and the victim couldn't even remember the night it happened. Everything we had was based on the work that Ronin had done and on the blood we found along the trail and at the suspect's house. The defense attorney thought that he had a great argument to use against the scent lineup we used that night to identify his client. I don't remember all of the details—but enough of them to still laugh over the situation.

The attorney asked me about all of my experience and training with Ronin in the couple of years that we had been together, pouring over all of my trailing notes, prior cases, and, in particular, the mistakes we had made. He handled every mistake like it was some grand revelation, which I suppose was his job. As far as I was concerned, all of the mistakes Ronin had made that I had kept track of are what kept us honest. Nobody would believe that the dog was perfect—I sure as hell didn't.

We got to the scent-lineup portion of my testimony, and the attorney had a little smile on his face when he launched into what he probably thought was going to be his grand finale. He asked me if I knew that his client was employed as a cook at a local barbecue joint and had been working the night of the incident, and I said, "No, I did not." He asked me if I had noticed that barbecue sauce was all over his client's clothing from his night of work, and I did not remember that either. He asked me if Ronin liked human food, and I said that he did; our dispatchers could attest to that. He then asked, if that was the case, wasn't it reasonable to presume that Ronin, in identifying his client, was actually interested in sampling barbecue sauce on his clothing?

I couldn't answer in one word and asked the officer of the court if I could give him an explanation on how I would see it going down if the barbecue sauce was truly an issue. He said "of course," because I'm sure he thought that I was going to dig myself a big hole to crawl into. I said that if the barbecue sauce was really there, then why wouldn't Ronin instead pick out one of the patrol officers who were also in the lineup? He didn't really follow and asked me to explain. I therefore continued with the fact that it was common knowledge that police officers loved doughnuts, and that invariably there had to have been doughnut crumbs or dust from the powdery ones on their uniforms. Therefore, why would Ronin pick out the barbecue sauce over the doughnut crumbs? The defense attorney said that he had no more questions and the judge just chuckled. That was the end of my testimony for that case.

Ronin at a citizen's event in Alameda.

Manhunt

B Y THIS TIME IN MY CAREER, I HAD BEEN RECEIVING TRAINING under the tutelage of some of the nations' finest K-9 manhunters and had really been taken under their wings. Ronin was a very good dog, and I wasn't too bad of a handler. What we lacked in overall experience, we made up for with enthusiasm and dedication. Ronin's work had received the attention not only of my peers, but also of the Federal Bureau of Investigation. The FBI's hostage rescue team (HRT) had been attending some of our training seminars around the country and quickly took a liking to the whole idea of using trailing dogs for high-risk fugitive manhunts in rural locations.

The brass at HRT decided to test the idea of a tactical mission oriented around the use of bloodhounds and invited a number of handlers and their dogs from various parts of the country to attend a training scenario in the Blue Ridge Mountains. The idea was to stage a mock fugitive manhunt utilizing a couple of HRT members as "suspects" who would hit the woods with about a six-hour head start. Trailing dogs and their handlers would be supported by tactical elements of HRT in an attempt to run down the fugitives. The plan was not only to test the dogs and handlers, but also to develop a protocol for just these types of cases. The 1990s had a string of nasty cases around the country in which armed and dangerous fugitives had been lost in rural locations after law-enforcement agencies had tried in vain to track them down. I believe that this was a federal attempt at planning for such cases in the future.

I was invited along as an observer for this trial. Ronin had to stay home. However, a number of other handlers and their dogs came to

129

play, and it looked like we were going to have a grand time. One of my mentors, John Lutenberg, was there with his bloodhound, and I was standing in line for a chance to watch them work. John had trained me at several schools over the previous two years and I was a huge fan. He was extremely conservative, and his training methods were largely responsible for Ronin's and my success. Now I had an opportunity to see him in action.

We had our briefings in Quantico, Virginia, and headed off to the mountains. It was a long drive, and tons of logistical support—helicopters, command posts, sniper teams, etc.—had to be accounted for. It reminded me of some military maneuvers I had been on during my stint in the army. This was very serious business and was not going to be a cakewalk. This really struck home when we made it to the mountains in West Virginia. The terrain was steep and incredibly thick. I had no idea that this training scenario and terrain were going to play heavily into Ronin's and my future. The terrain was not for the faint of heart. It was going to be tough going for everyone involved in the ground-pounding part of this game, and I had a few reservations about some of the people participating in the program.

I have always tried to stay as fit as possible by running and working out with weights ever since I was a teenager in the army. I felt that I was in better-than-average condition, but after looking at the mountains, I knew that I was going to be taxed, especially if the trails became incredibly long. I was a little worried about some of my peers, too. Most of them were far older than I was and were not very well conditioned. The only person about whom I wasn't worried was John, because he was whipcord thin and had the stamina of a greyhound. I knew this because I had watched him run behind many other handlers over the years and was privy to some of the actual cases he had worked in his home state of Colorado. No—I had no worries for John. The rest of the K-9 crew was another matter altogether. The HRT operators were all highly fit and lived for this type of work.

We all arrived on the morning of the first day of operations and set up the command post and the logistical support for the entire operation, including large military tents to sleep in if the scenarios went into the next day. The "suspects" had arrived before us and had been allowed to decide where and how they wanted to disappear. They had a six-hour head start in an immense wilderness area. It was interesting at this point, because we were all asked who wanted to volunteer to run the first leg of the mission. The plan had been to run a series of dogs on the suspects' trail, keeping all of the dog teams relatively fresh in the process. The only person who volunteered was John, and I quickly asked if I could be his cover man. I had absolutely no intention of being left behind. Here I had a chance to run behind one of my K-9 heroes, and I didn't know if this opportunity would ever present itself again. I pleaded my case to John, telling him that I was the only one amongst the group who had a chance to keep up with him, and I'd really get to see how something like this was done. John was never one for many words and simply said yes, I could tag along.

I was ecstatic as the tactical team was put together to support John and his dog. We were running with a five-man HRT team complimented by helicopter support as well as another K-9 handler/observer. Not only was I going to get to run with John, but I now had the chance to observe a K-9 tactical support team designed just for a trailing mission. The HRT operators had obviously done their homework and were prepared for the grueling pace we might face and the tactical situation we might encounter. I was 100 percent confident in their abilities. It was going to be a fine day, indeed.

It was a little cold—a little more than forty degrees—on this winter morning. The mountains were steep, and I could see that they probably were also thick with foliage in the spring. Visibility was only a little better with all of the leaves off of the trees this time of year. I was thinking about the terrain and how it would affect the speed and efforts of our "suspects." These operators were in fantastic shape, so I didn't think that a few steep mountains would slow them down too much. The slopes were traversed by several well-worn hiking trails, but the surrounding ground was dense with vines, brush, and trees. Even with most of the greenery missing, it was still rough country to cut through if you were to leave the trail. I figured that these guys would probably stick to the trails until they decided that they had created enough space between themselves and the dog team, and then they might become a little creative with their evasion tactics. Everyone on the team was aware of the advantages and disadvantages of trailing K-9s, and I'm sure that the suspects were going to do their very best to test the dogs' tenacity and endurance. Operations were slated to run for twenty-four hours or more.

Each team was outfitted with Motorola multichannel radios that had encryption capabilities; therefore, surrounding ham radio operators couldn't eavesdrop on the operation. This program wasn't exactly supersecret stuff, but it wasn't common knowledge either. Various members of the team also carried GPS units with them so that overall team progress could be monitored by the command post (CP). The CP consisted of many high-tech electronic pieces of equipment to monitor the field problem and communicate with the teams in the field. It was staffed by several HRT officers in charge and the K-9 advisor-liaison to the overall operation. This advisor was another mentor of mine, Glenn Rimbey. Glenn was responsible for much of my early training after my time with Kat. He had many years of trailing experience in his home state of Kansas and had worked with the FBI on high-risk fugitive manhunts in the past. His name was well known and equally respected in the K-9 trailing world and law enforcement in general.

The general plan was to start the K-9 and tactical support team on the trail of our fugitives and plot their course via GPS. As a clear path was determined and, more important, the direction of travel of the suspects, the staff in the CP would attempt to figure out how far ahead they were from the K-9 team. Sniper/observer elements would then be placed at key points to watch for movement and make an interception if at all possible. Air assets—fixed-wing and helicopter—would constantly circle the area in front of the dog team to slow down the suspects' movements. The possibility that the plane or helicopter would spot the subjects was pretty slim, but that wasn't the point. Any wary fugitive would do his best to

Ronin and Jeff with their tactical support team on top of the Blue Ridge Trail. It had been miles of hiking.

stay under cover when surveillance craft were overhead. Keeping them locked down was the point. The less time they had to run, the sooner the dog team could make up lost ground and time on them.

I knew almost from the start that we were going to have some problems with a couple of observers on the trail. The going was treacherous, primarily down the side of a steep mountain, but there were a lot of switchbacks and obstacles that had to be traversed. John's dog was moving at a moderate trot, which meant a slow run for the rest of us. The HRT guys were strung out in a staggered column with a few yards between each team member. I was acting as John's cover man and had to stay right at his belt at all times. This wasn't exactly easy, but there was no way I would fall behind. Unfortunately, two of our other K-9 handlers/observers were having a rough time of it. We lost the first after about the first half mile and the second shortly thereafter. We had no choice but to continue, as the test was not only for John and his dog, but for all of the other invitees as well; two down already.

I was running light, as John had always taught me. I mirrored him to a certain extent—jeans, boots, a T-shirt, and a ball cap. The only extra item I carried was a canteen and a small first-aid kit. The temperature had not risen much—maybe five degrees or so—but I was already sweating as my muscles loosened for the miles surely ahead of us. John maintained a grueling pace, but we were all keeping up fairly well.

About two miles into the first leg of the hiking path, and still quite far from the valley floor, John's dog paused at what I thought might be a little deer trail into a draw running parallel to our original direction of travel. This little bypass was barely discernible from the other terrain features along the trail, but it had the dog's interest. John held her up for just a second and crouched down to look at the loamy soil. He waved me over to him and told me to look at a couple of leaves that he was prodding with a twig. He asked me to look at the color of the leaves that were facing us, and I could see that they were dark- and moist-looking in relationship to the dense bed of leaves all around them. The rest of the leaves were shades of yellow and brown, plastered about the forest floor, while these leaves, now that I looked at them, stood out like sore thumbs. Just behind the overturned leaves was the slight impression from the toe of a boot in the damp soil pointing in the direction of the little draw into which John's dog wanted to descend. John told me that that was all the confirmation he needed to know that his dog was correct, and we followed her down into the thick brush.

The going instantly got tougher. Now, instead of a hiking trail, we were moving over loose, thick leaf beds amongst incredibly dense stands of saplings that all seemed to be connected by thorny vines. There were also storm-felled trees haphazardly strewn about this steep forest floor. John paused at one of these larger trees, which his dog simply crawled under. The entire top of the log was covered in thick green moss that reminded me of a finely manicured golf green . . . except for the spot that

John was pointing at. There was one scuff mark that was the approximate width of a shoe. The abrasion to the moss was about three-eighths inch deep, and the rich-looking black soil below its surface was piled toward the downslope side of the tree. John took the time to tell me that this was an indication that one of the fugitives had gone over the tree/obstacle, trying to be careful to not leave much of a mark. He showed me how the piled-up portion of soil at the tip of the abrasion was indicative of the direction of travel in which the man was moving. He also said that, with enough practice observing "sign" such as this, I would begin to be able to determine the age of the trail. This, in turn, would give me an indication of how far ahead our subjects might be. We continued down the draw until it abruptly emptied into the river bottom at the base of the canyon. We had just dropped about 2,000 feet in elevation, and I was feeling it—as were the rest of our party. We were undaunted by our fatigue, though, because of the supreme confidence we all had in John and his dog. Not only had we been moving with purpose and absolutely no confusion, we had found sign and ground disturbance to prove that our quarry had come this way just before we had. Now the problem was going to be getting across the river. None of us wanted to get our feet wet on such a hard trail, because that would inevitably lead to blisters. Thankfully, the subjects of our search had obviously had similar sentiments, because the dog led us downstream to a large tree that had conveniently fallen across the river.

For the entire time we had been running this trail, our progress had been continually updated on a large map at the CP. Our GPS coordinates had been radioed at prescribed times, allowing for a nice picture of our total trail. Better yet, it showed exactly what the suspects had done in an attempt to avoid contact and established their general direction of travel. The CP commanders took this information and air dropped tactical assets far ahead of us in the hope that we would run the "bad guys" into the blocking/sniper force. This is exactly what happened and the manhunt was finished in just a few hours. What had been slated for a twenty-four-hour mission was over shortly after it started and with the use of only a single K-9 asset on a single mission. There was talk about conducting another scenario; however, it was determined that the operation was a phenomenal success and that there really was no need to test it again. It was only a couple of months after this field-training exercise that I was asked to join the K-9 assistance team to HRT.

The timing was perfect, because I was selected for one of the first actual FBI/HRT K-9 Assistance Program's missions on July 15, 1998. The Eric Rudolph manhunt gained worldwide media attention that summer of 1998. Rudolph was the center of a major multi-jurisdictional agency investigation into a string of abortion clinic bombings that resulted in the deaths or injury of innocent civilians and law-enforcement personnel. Rudolph was also suspected of planting the explosives at the Olympic Park bombing. Our involvement came when Rudolph decided to disappear into the Blue Ridge Mountains outside Andrews, North Carolina, once he felt the heat from the feds.

I received the call while I was at work, and my agency was completely supportive of the request for my services. This surprised me, because I would be off patrol for an unknown amount of time and this would cost the city of Alameda resources and money. However, I think that my chief was looking at the larger picture of our involvement in an absolutely huge investigation with national implications.

Once my department gave the final approval for my departure, things started to move very quickly. The FBI arranged for a plane ride to Atlanta from Oakland the very next day. Better yet, Ronin was allotted a seat right next to me on the airplane and I was able to carry my personal firearm onboard with no problem whatsoever. I found it amazing what one little letter from the director of the FBI could accomplish in such a short period of time.

Ronin had been on planes before and had no problem traveling. He was a good boy and didn't even slobber as much as most bloodhounds. This was a blessing for my fellow passengers on the plane, because a scared bloodhound is a massively drooling bloodhound. I could have easily had to incorporate a beach towel just to keep up with his mouth.

Ronin was the talk of the flight. He immediately had all of the attention of the flight attendants and received all of the water and treats he could possibly want. He posed for numerous photo shoots, basking in the limelight while I simply watched from the background. I was lucky to get a Coke, and no one remembered my name. We landed in Atlanta on time and with no problems. One of the flight attendants even offered to babysit Ronin if I needed the resource in Atlanta. The dog always got the girls!

My good friend, "Bob," from HRT picked me up at the airport and we had a great time catching up on life events during the long ride to Andrews. Bob told me that Rudolph had gone missing about a week before we arrived, and the plan was to use Ronin and another team bloodhound belonging to a friend, Brian Joyner, to see if we could pick up Rudolph's trail or obtain some evidence. The scent material that we had were scent swabs obtained at my direction from Rudolph's boots. I asked for numerous scent swabs to be made just in case this thing went on for awhile. I guess I must have had a premonition, because this search morphed into a gigantic cluster in very short order; more of that later.

The first people on the scene were a relatively few command post personnel, HRT operators, Brian, and me. This was perfect, because it allowed us to function relatively easily with little to no red tape. I learned long before this search that keeping things simple usually translated into a far more efficient operation. All was perfect when we first got going. We were set up in a hotel for the first night in Andrews, but I learned that we would be moving as soon as we unpacked. The situation was a little estranged due to the fact that the majority of the local populace seemed to side with Rudolph and resented the intrusion of the federal government. I discovered that we would be changing hotels on a nightly basis for our own safety; wonderful.

I remember my first experience with a resident of Andrews when Brian and I were gassing up our vehicle at a local convenience store/gas station. I went inside to pay for gas and the attendant looked me up and down with a little sneer on her face. She asked me if I was in town for the search for Rudolph and I smiled, asking in return if it was that obvious. She said that it was and asked if I missed home. I assured the woman that I did, thinking she was just engaging me in friendly small talk. She then told me that if I missed home so much, it might be best for me to go back there as quickly as possible. So much for small town hospitality.

It had been discovered that Rudolph has been camping next to a residence outside of Andrews on a little hilltop overlooking the house and the road adjacent to it. The camp was not very well camouflaged, nor was it set up with any expertise. Apparently, Rudolph camped out at night, and when the resident of the house left for work in the morning, Rudolph would hang out at the house until the resident retuned later that night. Rudolph did not appear to be roughing it in any way, shape, or form. When he felt the heat from the feds, he disappeared, and one of the last sightings of him was in a pickup truck near a public camping area. These two locations were the starting points for Brian and me. I chose the original campsite. The search was going to be tough no matter how we did it, because Rudolph had been missing now for more than a week.

The first couple of days of searching ended up being the most productive days for the entire manhunt. This, I believe, was because of two factors. First, we were a relatively small team at this stage with little to no bureaucracy to deal with. When we made a decision to do something, we just did it. More important, we were also using the dogs in accordance with their capabilities, which would change drastically just a couple of weeks down the line.

Working in North Carolina had some really good points and a few bad ones. Some of the bad situations I had already encountered—much of the population detested us. I was hesitant to eat at any restaurants for fear of finding foreign objects in my grits. Consequently, the military "meals ready to eat" (MRE) became the gourmet alternative. It was amazing what a little Tabasco could do for cold-packaged GI fare.

Perhaps I allowed a few bad apples to spoil the fruit salad. Not everyone treated us like the convenience store clerk did. As a matter of fact, I met quite a few really nice folks in Andrews and really fell in love with the countryside. The problems were with the hard line "right-to-lifers" who were so militaristic in their views that it reminded me of present-day Islamic terrorists. Their ideology and fanaticism were similar, although I did not draw the parallels then as I do now in our post "911" era. The good, on the other hand, was quite dog related. The conditions, although warm, were wonderful. The vegetation was thick everywhere we went, including in the towns, and the air was always humid. Scent loves plants and moisture; the more of both, the better the trails would be. I could already tell that Ronin was in scent heaven here by the simple way he reacted to everyday circumstances. It seemed to me that every sniff he took told him volumes more than a similar breath back home. The climate where we lived in California was very dry, and most of our work was in the urban cement jungles of the San Francisco Bay area. A trail in downtown Oakland might last only hours, while here in Andrews, it could be days. Maybe we had a chance of doing some good after all.

I started Ronin at the original campsite, and he immediately picked up a good trail right to the house Rudolph had been using. At the time, I didn't know what house it was and simply followed my dog. Ronin was interested in everything in and around the residence, and I had a hard time getting him to find a trail out of the area. The little butt also found a new fascination for chickens, which were running loose everywhere. I had never proofed Ronin on chickens before, because, frankly, we just didn't have them anywhere I was working . . . until now. I was forced to put him through a crash "anti-chicken" distraction course just to continue working. I eventually resorted to walking Ronin in ever-increasing concentric circles around the property until he picked out an exit trail. It was my opinion that most of the traffic had been to and from the campsite to the home, but there also may have been a significant amount of vehicle usage. Ronin seemed to find a scent trail onto the highway heading downhill. Interestingly, he stopped and alerted on almost every mailbox along the way. I had seen this behavior before in

Alameda when dealing with mail thieves and felt that there was a good possibility that Rudolph had been stealing from mailboxes. I don't know if this was ever confirmed, but I had my suspicions.

Shortly thereafter, Ronin made a beeline for a dirt driveway that led to a home in the woods along a ridgeline. He ran to an open, rear-sliding door at the ground level at the back of the house and wanted to go inside. I put the brakes on at this point. It was obvious that the home was not occupied. No vehicles were present, and there was absolutely no sign of recent activity. There were even cobwebs between the sliding glass door and the frame. I got the impression that the home, although very nice and well kept, had not been occupied for some time. Ronin really wanted inside the house in the worst way, and I was pretty confident that he had detected Rudolph's scent up to the door and also from inside. However, I had no intention of running right inside, knowing Rudolph's violent history. Who knows what we'd run into? Well, our job was over for the time being, and this is where our backup came into play.

My backup team consisted of HRT tactical operators armed with M4.223s, an Alcohol, Tobacco, and Firearms (ATF) agent, and an explosives-detection K-9 handler and his Labrador retriever. I ran extremely lightweight on these missions because they became grueling in short order. The first few days were not too difficult, consisting of following trails with the dogs in the hills. Later, however, when we encountered the vortex, our time in the mountains lasted for hours at a time; again, I will have to explain "the vortex" later. I had brought my level III ballistic vest along with load-bearing equipment (LBE), which consisted of a web belt, a canteen, a first-aid pouch, and my holstered Sig Sauer 239 semiautomatic pistol with three extra magazines of nine-millimeter Winchester Black Talon ammo. I wore olive drab (OD), green field pants, a tan or green T-shirt, and good running boots—which I kept two pairs of. The canteen of water was for Ronin, just in case he needed it, but I wore Camelbak pack strapped to my back. It held two quarts of water in a vinyl blister bag with a hose and a mouthpiece running up over my shoulder and clipped to my collar. This piece of equipment was by far the most important item I had on this trip. Running with a bloodhound for miles on end is hard, thirsty business, and I drained that Camelbak on each and every trip. Many people might criticize my lack of gear or preparedness for contingencies in the field; however, most of the critics probably never ran with a dog that was as fast and tireless as Ronin. It would be tough keeping up with him in a jogging outfit, let alone with all of the other crap I had to wear.

After the first day in the field, I shed the ballistic vest and it never did see the light of day for the rest of the mission. Wearing that son of a gun kicked my ass, because it retained so much heat and sweat that wearing it for even a couple of hours made me feel like I had a water bed strapped to my chest. I was not the only one who felt this way; everyone soon lost their vest even though we were all supposed to wear them. It was just too unbearable. Even though the Blue Ridge Mountains were gorgeous, they were also deceptive. It did not take much to get lost, exhausted, hurt, or a combination of all three. The way I saw it, the risk of dehydration and injury far outweighed the possibility of getting shot. It only took one mission with my vest to figure that out.

The tactical team was there just in case shit hit the fan and we encountered armed resistance or an ambush. I was extremely confident in these guys, because they are literally the best of the best. I had enjoyed the benefit of working with them in the past and I knew, without a doubt, that I would never be left out on a limb or left behind. More important, no matter how fast Ronin ran, these guys wouldn't be left behind either. Their fitness level was top-notch; I thought some of them could even outrun Ronin.

Because Ronin alerted on the rear door the way he did, I advised the team that there was a very good chance that Rudolph had been inside the house at one time. I did not believe that he was in there at the time simply because Ronin was not frantic enough to get in, but we had to look at this house as a potential hideout. Due to the exigent circumstances of the situation and the potential threat to all of us present, the tactical team conducted a quick sweep of the interior of the house for possible threats and then repeated the process with the bomb dog. Nobody was found inside, but the Lab alerted on a couple of locations, the most interesting of which was the drain of a sink in a small bathroom. We discovered that the owners of the house were away on vacation and had been for some time, and nobody was supposed to be living in the house. That was the crux of the problem. The house appeared to have been used recently by someone. The kitchen appeared to have been raided, and we found a compound hunting bow on a couch in the living room.

The exigency of our search was over, and we all left the house with the intention of gaining consent to conduct a more thorough search from the vacationing owners. This never came to be. I was informally advised after we left that the residents refused to allow any other activity in or around their property without a search warrant; interesting. I never discovered what became of the efforts to investigate that house or what connection, if any, it had with Rudolph.

I tried to start Ronin out of the driveway and had a little difficulty getting him focused. He really didn't want to leave this house either and was treating it like a massive scent pool. As a matter of fact, the entire area for about a one-half-mile radius was like a giant scent pool. Ronin seemed to have scent everywhere. It wasn't so much like we were running a trail but swimming in a scent pond.

When I finally got Ronin moving again, he headed out the driveway and back up the highway toward the house where Rudolph had apparently been shacking up—or so I thought. Right when I was about to pull Ronin off his course toward the chickens, I bit my tongue and started to think a little more. He turned up a driveway toward a neighboring home and started to pull hard into the harness. He seemed to detect something more akin to the house we had just gotten kicked out of. Maybe we had more surprises in store?

This new house was similar to many of the others in the area—small, one story, with white vinyl siding and a metal roof. The house was situated in a little valley with hills on either side and had a fenced, well-tended vegetable garden to the rear. The southern slope of the hill behind the garden seemed to back up to the house where Rudolph had been staying. I estimated that it couldn't be more than several hundred yards from where we now found ourselves. The hillsides were thick with greenery, and it was difficult to see past the first wall of trees at the edge of this property's clearing. It was still morning, because we tried to get an early start and take advantage of relatively mild weather. However, I was starting to feel the sun beating down on my back, and Ronin's tongue was hanging out.

Ronin had a serious interest in the garden area. He walked all around the fence line and desperately wanted inside. I had never seen this behavior before, but then, we had never trained around vegetable gardens either. For all I knew, he wanted some of the goodies inside; or maybe someone else had been interested in the veggies long before we ever got there. Right around the time I thought about trying to work Ronin on the fringe of this new scent pool in an attempt to get a trail off of the property, we were met by the resident of the home. He was an older gentleman, whip thin and wearing coveralls. I was instantly reminded of the old TV show *Green Acres*—this guy really fit the part of the country farmer. With a deep southern drawl and not a hint of anger or suspicion, he asked us what we wanted on his property. The team commander explained the circumstances and advised the man that Ronin had followed Rudolph's scent onto his property, and we were hoping to take a look around. Without skipping a beat, the man told us that he didn't know anything about all of that and that the only people who stayed on his property were his daughters, who liked to camp in the hills above his house. Talk about a spontaneous statement! Now we knew we had something and that the trail was probably a good one. The man told us to go ahead and search to our heart's content, but we would never find Rudolph on his property.

I had to drag Ronin off of the garden and into the woods a short distance away. He seemed to understand that we had to find something else and headed up a hill in the general direction of the first house and Rudolph's original campsite. We made it to the top of the hill to an area overlooking the highway. Ronin slowed down and started to meander through areas amongst the trees that were a little too devoid of leaves and other forest debris to look natural. After looking a little closer, we made out several potential campsites and fire pits all within an area about 100 yards across. We also found long branches propped up against the larger trees, which had obviously been used to create lean-tos or other types of shelters.

Bingo—we found another potential gold mine of information. A couple of the team members started to sift through the fire pits after we had secured the location and immediately discovered opened soup cans and other camp garbage in the ashes. Whomever had used these sites really didn't try hard to hide their tracks. Frankly, if this was one of Rudolph's satellite hideouts, I was a little disappointed in his ability to keep a low profile. The fires could have easily been seen from the road, and the trash, although partially hidden in the ashes, was a wonderful tool to determine identity. We had been led to believe that Rudolph was a mountain man with almost legendary field-craft ability, or so the papers had written.

The problem with "finds" such as the "burglarized" house and these new campsites was that every time they popped up, our progress was stopped completely. The tactical team and bomb dog would conduct a hasty search to ensure our safety, then we would have to back out and wait for an FBI forensics team to come in and do its thing—which was inevitably slow. Don't get me wrong—I love what the CSI guys do, but my type of work is usually a little faster. Well, a lot faster. I don't do well in a traffic jam on the freeway, and waiting for forensics work to begin and end was just as maddening.

The campsites on the hill ended up being the last of our work for that day, and we probably didn't run more than a half mile in any one direction. However, I believe that we produced a wealth of information. Not only did the house produce evidence related to Rudolph, but his prints were found on garbage at the campsites. Everything we found related to Rudolph was close to a major highway, homes, food, and mail. It seemed that he had all of the modern conveniences close at hand whenever he needed them. I got the impression that he was also getting a lot of local help.

Brian and I worked together off and on for the next few days, but we never found much of anything else. We seemed to pick up isolated scent trails here and there, but there just wasn't anything significant. There was no end in sight, and I did not have high hopes for much progress in the future. The problem in my mind was that we had started a week too late and Rudolph was obviously getting help from people who did not want to see him get caught. It is one thing to get on the hot trail of a criminal shortly after he runs, but it is another thing altogether when he has at least a week's head start on you. However, our world was beginning to spin a little, as the vortex had just begun.

The vortex was not of my creation. It was a situation aptly named by one of the HRT operators who was beginning to feel the friction of too much bureaucracy and red tape. As I mentioned before, when we first set up operations in the hills outside of Andrews, North Carolina, we had relatively free rein on how we conducted ourselves. Not many support people were present yet and the command staff was minimal. So far, we consisted of a few operators and K-9 assets, and that was about it. The news media hadn't arrived in force yet either. Things were relatively light and breezy. Well, that all changed when the "army" arrived. What I mean by army is not the military in the traditional sense, although we did eventually get a contingent of national guard troops running around with us, but rather a very large, diverse group of law-enforcement personnel and all of their logistical support. We had the cast and crew of the FBI, the ATF, the DOD, the U.S. Army, the Georgia Bureau of Investigations, the local police and sheriff's departments, the U.S. Forest Service, the North Carolina and Georgia Departments of Corrections with their prison hounds, and probably a lot of other people I've simply forgotten about. We ended up with a proverbial tent city whose population soon eclipsed that of most of the local towns or villages. We had tanks and planes and helicopters and every other mode of transportation you could imagine. We had all of the latest technology, including FLIR, GPS, and every other acronym for high-tech. There also seemed to be a commanding officer for every facet of the search, from food to uniforms, and each one of them had to be consulted before an operation could move forward.

Everything that was being done to facilitate the search for Eric Rudolph was now being scrutinized to the umpteenth degree. For example, and hypothetically speaking: We got a tip that Rudolph may be hiding in an old cabin in the mountains, and a local was willing to give us directions. Rather than debrief the local and get on with the search in short order, we were forced to sit around while all of the local commanders got together and strategized about whose and what assets we would utilize for the search and how exactly they might be used. Sometimes crap like this took hours. In the meantime, Rudolph was getting tipped off that we were about to conduct a lengthy search in his area of operation and had skedaddled. Every time we went anywhere at this stage in the game, and a game it surely was, we would have another army of news media and Rudolph

View from the FBI helicopter during transport for the Eric Rudolph manhunt.

supporters tracking our every move. Why did this happen? It was simple: We telegraphed our every move like an amateur boxer with poor footwork. The local population probably knew what we were going to do before the information was handed down to the tactical teams and K-9 handlers. It had to be this way because we had a caravan of camp followers who latched onto our every move even before we moved!

This situation was quickly spiraling out of control like the "vortex" after which it was named. We seemed to be putting in more hours with fewer results, and I was beginning to think about going home. Don't get me wrong—every asset with whom I worked was great, but we were all foot soldiers out there together and had very little to say about what we were going to do.

What upset me more than anything was getting tailed everywhere we went, especially when we were not accomplishing anything. One of the grand schemes thought out in the brain center was to cut up the forest into grid squares that would be hand searched by a tactical team and K-9 assets. The forest wasn't a little park—it was the entire damned Blue Ridge Mountain range in our area and everything in between. We were asked to simply walk the dog through these grids and watch for an alert from the dog indicating that Rudolph was near. Depending on conditions, a grid could take up to eight hours to clear, and conditions could be treacherous. I knew that I had a scent-specific dog and all, but I had no idea how I was supposed to keep him focused for hours at a time in thick brush, with absolutely no scent trail to go by. I couldn't trust him to remember Rudolph's scent after running through the brush for hours at a time. The best I could hope is that he would hit on fresh human scent and decide to follow it.

The news media apparently got wind of our new method of operation and was there for every outing and each time we returned. I couldn't believe it. We would come waltzing out of the woods—well, waltzing out doesn't quite describe it; dragging ass out of the woods is a better description—and there they were, with all of their vehicles, cameras, and other accoutrements. More often than not, they outnumbered our entire

Ronin with the tactical support team on top of the Blue Ridge Trail. It had been miles of hiking.

tactical team. Thank god they were friendly. We navigated all of the terrain by GPS or by the old-fashioned map-and-compass method. I was far more comfortable with the map and compass, having been brought up in the army that way, but the GPS was a pretty smart tool as long as the canopy wasn't too thick. Once we had a good azimuth and our egress point was known, we radioed in to the CP for transportation back to tent city. This was easier said than done, because we either had to have a road for a wheeled vehicle or an open hilltop for a chopper. And, because the media had radio equipment that was just as good as ours, they would be there when we arrived. If they could track our every move, what were the militias doing?

I remember one of these events very well because of a picture that was taken of us for the *New York Times*. The picture shows the tactical team,

Ronin taking a break in a river somewhere on the Blue Ridge during the Rudolph manhunt.

Brian Joyner's dog Tanner and Ronin at play in our hotel just prior to operations starting on the Rudolph manhunt.

with Ronin and me right as we were stepping out of the jungle, sweating, dirty, out of water, and pretty hungry. I was physically exhausted, and when that condition is coupled with hunger, I get pretty grumpy. The look on my face for the news photo really spelled it out quite well: "Don't mess with us, because I'm not in the mood." However, mess with us is exactly what they did. The questions started flying as the camera shutters opened and closed. Even though I was pissed off, I still tried to be as polite as possible. Ronin handled the situation for me quite well, however.

We were just getting ready to load into our trucks for a long ride home when a cameraman got in front of Ronin as we were walking forward. He was carrying a fairly large movie camera with one of those fuzzy microphones sticking out of the front. He asked me if I minded him filming

Ronin and I said I didn't but asked him not to stick the camera in Ronin's face. The guy didn't even skip a beat. He lowered the camera while bending over so that it was just inches off the ground while he walked backward directly in front of us. The camera was only a couple of feet from Ronin's face. I asked him again to back off a little and he simply ignored me, continuing to film as he duckwalked backward. All of a sudden he stopped right in front of us, obviously by design, forcing Ronin to walk around the lowered camera. Now I was really angry and was just about to sound off with an expletive when Ronin took matters into his own paws. Ronin seemed to be ignoring the camera and hadn't even given it a second glance when the cameraman had stopped in front of us, but as soon as Ronin was alongside the camera, my red dog partner lifted his leg and gave that fuzzy little microphone a yellow squirt. You should have seen the look on the cameraman's face! It was priceless, and I truly wished that the picture could have made the front page of the *Times*.

The media was a distraction to a certain extent and they did get in the way from time to time. But, for the most part, they were men and women with a job to do and I could understand that. I got along with most of them and they generally respected what we were doing and tried not to be too difficult. The militias, on the other hand, were another story. Militia groups were a sidebar to the whole Eric Rudolph escapade. Rudolph had an affiliation with one or more of these American militant groups that seemed to be springing up all over the country during the 1990s, and they were flocking to North Carolina just to be part of the action or to gather intelligence.

The militias seemed to have several things in common. They supported Rudolph, they were "right-to-lifers," and they trained extensively in paramilitary style. Rudolph was even rumored to be holing up in one of the local militia compounds in the area at the time we were searching for him. I never had much of an opinion about these folks until they started following us to and from missions. They didn't necessarily advertise who they were and had no uniforms or T-shirts with their names on them, but it was obvious when they were checking us out. They all looked similar—white guys with crew cuts, faded fatigue pants, boots, and ball caps. I'm sure that each and every one of them was packing a gun or two as well. They never said much but always had little cameras or binoculars in hand while they scowled at us. I remember the look of pure hatred in their eyes, which was the most disconcerting thing to me.

I never really understood the mentality of these people. At the time, we had not yet felt the full brunt of extreme religious fanaticism, and our homegrown terrorists were never really taken seriously; that is, until Timothy McVeigh and Eric Rudolph started playing with explosives. Rudolph's background and the backgrounds of those who affiliated with him were fairly similar. They loved their communities, practiced their faith with utter sincerity, and seemed to have relatively humble roots; however, something went awry somewhere and it became "OK" to kill

Elusive Bombing Fugitive Divides a Town

Associated Press

Members of an armed team looked for the bombing fugitive Eric Robert Rudolph in North Carolina.

An armed team searching for the bombing fugitive Eric Robert Rudolph in North Carolina. From the Associated Press; printed in the Oakland Tribune *about July 15, 1998.*

for their belief system. These zealots believed that abortion was tantamount to murder and that those who were involved with the practice were guilty of murder; therefore, their punishment was death. When I encountered some of these people in North Carolina, I had the distinct feeling that I could just as easily become a target; perhaps I was?

I remember one encounter with a group of militia people right after dropping out of the mountains from another mission. They were waiting for us and tried to strike up a conversation, asking about what we were doing with the dogs, if we had found anything, and what we had planned next. We did our best to sidestep all of the direct questions while trying to maintain some semblance of politeness. One of the men was taking pictures of us, with particular attention to whatever patches or insignia we had on our hats or uniforms, while a young girl in her late teens or early twenties tried to weasel her way over to Ronin, as if posing for a picture. At the last minute, she tried to turn his K-9 police badge on his collar around so that it could be photographed as well. This was eerily reminiscent of military training I had received regarding the use of guerilla bands for intelligence gathering; however, it was supposed to happen in some foreign country and not the good old U.S. of A. These people were becoming a bit too cozy for my taste, and it was really nice to see our transport vehicle arrive just as I was telling the young lady to get away from the dog.

I was getting tired of this place quickly. The work was not going very well, there were far too many chiefs and not enough Indians, and we were constantly hounded by zealots and the media. To make matters worse, Ronin and I were now simply wandering through the woods two to three times a day with no clear trail to follow—just walking around trying to see if he could get a scent. It was on one of these "walks" that our last story came into being.

I can't remember exactly where we were, as every mountain was beginning to look the same as the last one, but this walk was memorable nonetheless. Ronin and I had our usual contingent of tactical operators and our ever-trusty woods guide, George. George was a U.S. Forest

Service officer and had been working all over the South for much of his career. He knew all of the trails like the back of his hand and was a hell of a visual tracker in his own right. George took a liking to Ronin, and I believe that Ronin really liked George, too. George had worked bear dogs for some time and had an affinity for hounds in general. The joke between us was that George was going to steal Ronin before I left and turn him into a bear dog.

The way we lined up for our daily walks was like this: Ronin and I in the lead, followed by a squad of operators behind us, while George took up the rear. We stayed in this loose column until an obstacle or potential threat was encountered. On this particular morning, we were walking in line down a grassy fire road in the forest, one foot in front of the other. It was going to be a long day, and we were all simply hoping that our water would last throughout the hike and that there would be hot chow for us when we returned. Each of us was lost in our own thoughts as we followed along behind the dog.

The fire road was about fifty feet wide and overgrown with about two to three feet of grass. Ronin was up to his neck in it, and I couldn't really see in front of him. We had been walking down the middle of this fire road for about a mile when, all of a sudden, Ronin turned hard to the left at a forty-five degree angle. He walked a few steps, turned hard to the right, took a few steps, then turned hard to the left onto the middle of the fire road again. The grass in the middle of this little ten-foot square was the same as all of the grass before and after us. It looked the same with absolutely no obstacle I could see. However, I thought nothing of it and just kept walking; so did all of the tactical operators behind us. We all walked the same way, right in Ronin's footsteps, one behind the other. From high above we probably looked like a slithering snake.

Not so, George. We had made it about fifty yards past the little detour when George called out for us to stop and come back to him. He was crouching in the little ten-foot patch of still standing grass with the beaten path half-circled around it, prodding at something in the middle. George said that he was fascinated by the way we had all been walking down the middle of this fire road with little or no detours when, all of a sudden, Ronin had simply seemed to circle around what appeared to be nothing more than an invisible barrier, and we all had followed happily along behind him like he was some doggy pied piper. George was so intrigued that he had to stop and see what might cause such behavior. He said all of this as his hand was busily working with something invisible to us in the grass. Quickly and with a dash of showman's flair, George withdrew from its nest the largest rattlesnake I had ever seen in my life—easily five feet long or more. The morning was fairly cool and the snake was far from active. It just hung by the tail from George's meaty paw as if it was a thick length of diamond-scaled rope, slowly flicking its forked tongue in and out as its Jacobson's organ "tasted" what we were all about. This snake was as thick around as my wrist and its wedge-shaped head was almost as wide as my hand.

I have always had a fascination for snakes and was far more interested than I was concerned, but most of the team behind me stepped back very quickly. Ronin saw the snake, too, and was with the rest of the team at the end of his thirty-foot lead peeking behind someone's legs. Now I knew what had happened and was instantly thankful for the anti-snake training Ronin had received as a puppy. George was surprised that Ronin seemed to know that the snake was there without seeing it and simply took a wide berth around it without showing any outward concern. Frankly, I was, too, because I had never seen this behavior before. It was the first time we had encountered a real rattlesnake on a trail since his early de-snaking training.

Eric Rudolph was not captured during my stint in North Carolina. As a matter of fact, I'm not so sure that we were even very close. We found plenty of evidence of his past activities but nothing really fresh. I believe that this was due to the simple fact that we got there so late—one week after he disappeared. I also believe that, during this phase in Rudolph's run from the law, he was being helped by sympathetic people in the community and others of his ilk with extremist tendencies. The campsite that we found so close to homes with fresh food and running water was evidence of that to me.

Thankfully, Rudolph's fans seemed to wane, as did his notoriety in the press. Once he was just a footnote in history, he was found dumpster diving in the back of a supermarket on May 31, 2003, by a sheriff's deputy.

Abandoned Baby Girl

I N AUGUST 1998, THE ALAMEDA POLICE DEPARTMENT received a report of an abandoned newborn baby girl found inside a cardboard box left in an apartment carport area. Police and fire department personnel responded to the scene and found an infant, dubbed Baby Girl Doe, alive inside an approximately three-foot-square box along with some towels and a shirt. She was found by the building owner, who was about to recycle the box.

The paragraph above was the opening statement for our department's press release for this case. It was also pretty much the entire story I received from dispatch when I was home on a day off. I packed up Ronin in the truck and headed into work for some overtime. I wasn't too worried about missing my time off, because this case sounded pretty interesting. I had never worked an abandoned baby case yet, although I had been hearing more stories on the news about just such circumstances. I never could understand how anyone would abandon a newborn; tossing one into a trash dumpster was attempted murder in my book and went far beyond the boundary of abandonment.

Ronin and I pulled up onto a block of Central Avenue within forty minutes of leaving the house. The news media was everywhere, and an ambulance was just leaving the driveway of the apartment complex in the area where the baby had been found; I presumed, correctly, that the baby was on board. I met my lieutenant and one of our captains at the scene, and they gave me a quick briefing of the situation. Thankfully, my department was pretty well versed in protecting scent evidence by this stage of the game, and the box and all of its contents were right where the apartment complex owner had set it down. Everyone had been careful about the contents, including the paramedics, although I was sure their scent was going to be in there. Unfortunately, they were gone with the baby, so I wouldn't be able to use the missing-member method of individual scent elimination prior to starting Ronin.

This area of Central Avenue is made up of individual houses, houses turned into small businesses, and several apartment complexes that are two to three stories in height. The area is fairly nice and well maintained, and the crime rate is below average. The apartment complex where Baby Girl Doe was found was a two-story affair with parking on the ground level on both the east and west sides. The driveways to both led to the rear of the complex, which housed the garbage dumpsters in which the baby had been found. The garbage dumpsters were side by side, about six feet by eight feet, and had large openings at the top. They smelled pretty badly, as most garbage containers used for years might smell, and had large, double-door lids that had been thrown back to expose the contents within.

The box in which Baby Doe had been found was sitting on the ground in front of the dumpsters with the cardboard lids open. The shirt and towels were still inside and did not appear to have been handled much, if at all. I conducted a quick canvass of the stall for any other evidence or obstacles I might have to work through, then ran back and harnessed up Ronin.

My backup officers for this trail were my good friend Tony and one of our two captains for the department. The captains rarely saw the light of day and could normally be found in their offices on the top floor of the police building. Their job was administration of the agency, and it was not an easy task. They had moved up through the ranks over several decades to gain the positions they had, and I often felt that they would have much preferred to be back on the streets with the rest of us. I was really surprised to find the captain here, let alone have him along for the ride. It was also a little intimidating, as he was only second to the chief of police in our command structure. Much to his credit, the captain said very little and really tried to stay out of the way.

Tony and I had come up together as new officers and had spent many a midnight shift making drug busts. Tony now worked in our Special Duty Unit (SDU), which kind of filled the gap between our Vice Unit and regular patrol. They executed lots of search warrants and worked various special projects that would otherwise not get much attention. SDU officers wore civilian clothes and drove unmarked cars for the most part. This was a great job for Tony, because he was an aggressive beat cop and considered to be the scourge of many a doper in Alameda. Tony was quickly following in the footsteps of his father, who had been a famous narcotics detective from the Oakland Police Department just over the bridge. Tony and I got along really well, and he was one of my only supporters during the initial phases of my trying to get Ronin adopted by the Alameda Police Department. I was happy to have him along for support.

I brought Ronin into the garbage area and let him get a whiff of all of the scents in the general vicinity of the cardboard box. He was gravitating to the box anyway, because it was exuding some odor that he hadn't been exposed to in the past. I had never trained Ronin with a newborn and really didn't know anyone who had, so I believe that he was really attracted to the strange scent. As soon as I snapped his long lead onto the D-ring, Ronin was on the box and trying to smell all of the contents. I gave him the command to search, and he went right back to the dumpster. He did a little jump and performed an ungainly bloodhound pirouette toward the top of the garbage dumpster and then away back toward the driveway. He ran down the driveway to the area from which I had seen the firetruck leaving and just started to circle and whine. I knew right away that he had either followed the scent of one of the emergency medical technicians (EMTs) or the baby. I would never know for sure, but it was safe to assume that Mom didn't leave in the ambulance and that we were after her.

I brought Ronin back to the box and let him get another whiff while simultaneously telling him to "find the other guy." This is a command for which multiple scents are on one article and we have to find the source of one or all of them. Ronin seemed to get the message and ran to the opposite driveway on the west side of the complex and along the redwood fence line. He paused at a loose board about fifty yards from the box and pushed at it with his paw. The board easily pushed inward, and Ronin simply hopped over the bottom rail and into another driveway area very similar to the one we had just left.

We all piled through after Ronin and ran around the back of an identical apartment complex to the west stairwell. Ronin didn't even hesitate and started to run up the steps. He hated these types of steps, too. The staircase was the type where each cement step appears to be suspended in air because it is held in place by the railing, which runs along the entire length of the stairs, leaving an open space between each step through which Ronin could see the ground. This is actually a common problem with quite a few dogs, and I had taken extraordinary measures to get Ronin over the phobia of walking up this type of stairway. There was a time when I had to literally drag him over to the first step to begin our remedial training sessions and then slowly but surely coax him up, one step after another, with Scooby snacks as bait.

Not so this time. Ronin had no trouble with the gaps in the stairs and bounded right up them without a glance. We got up to the second story, and Tony told me that before we arrived, he had generated a list of potential suspect apartments based on our police data base, and he wondered aloud how Ronin might be able to confirm or rule out a particular apartment. I told him that the best thing to do was to allow Ronin time to smell each and every door and hopefully he would alert on the correct one. We had trained extensively for just this situation on a regular basis. We had the luxury of using the Alameda Navy Base housing areas, which had been vacated the year before as the naval station was slowly phased out of existence. The military housing was similar to the apartments where we now found ourselves other than the fact that this complex was occupied while our training grounds were relatively uncontaminated. The contamination issue was a concern.

The problem with apartment complexes is the sheer amount of familial and individual resident pool scent in and around the area. Each occupant leaves "tons" of scent simply by living there, and family members or roommates exacerbate this by spreading "associated scent" wherever they go. Rarely is there one trail from point "A" to point "B"; instead, the entire apartment complex is kind of like an ink well of scent that spills over and spreads everywhere, rather than there being a distinct line drawn from one end to the other. When individuals live in a place like this, they leave scent trails every time they leave or enter their apartment; when they go to the laundry, to the carport, and to the garbage area, they leave scent behind.

Based on the fact that Ronin started the trail so easily on the other side of the broken fence, I assumed that the suspect probably did not live in that particular complex; therefore, her scent in that location was easier to follow because it was a single trail that entered the dumpster site and left. Now that we had arrived at the neighboring complex, Ronin's pace had slowed and he was working more deliberately, obviously wading through far more scent pictures than he had previously encountered. This told me that our suspect probably lived here and on this particular floor. True to our training, Ronin went into muscle-memory mode and flawlessly executed apartment door checks. The entire process took only a few seconds for each door and consisted of Ronin sniffing the base of the door up to the doorknob or handle, then moving on to the next one. When he encountered the proper door or a door with matching scent, he was trained to sit and paw at it. The worry I had was, if the mother of Baby Doe had a few friends on this floor, and if she had visited other apartments recently, Ronin could easily identify the wrong one. Thankfully, this seemed not to be the case, as Ronin was working past every door so far, with little or no hesitation.

Ronin was slowly heading toward the end of this row of apartments on the second floor when he did a double take on one particular doorknob. He seemed to work this door like all of the others by all outward appearances, and I thought that he was about to leave it and move on to the next. But just as his fat nose hit the doorknob, Ronin's entire body went rigid and his tail began to wag. He nudged the doorknob with the tip of his nose as if trying to reassure himself of something, looked at me over the top of his harness, and sat down with his slobbery tongue hanging out and a huge doggy grin spreading from ear to ear. Ronin wagged his tail furiously as he raked his paw down the length of the door from handle to threshold, leaving three nice-size scratches side by side. I asked him what it was he found and he let loose with a howl to beat the band. Tony was smiling as well, as if it confirmed something he had been thinking all along, and the captain didn't say or do much of anything at all.

Tony immediately knocked on the door, because he knew that Ronin had found the right one, while our captain just stood back and let us do our job. We waited a couple of minutes without hearing anything inside. The curtains were drawn and there was absolutely no light or sign of activity from within. Ronin seemed to sense something, though, because he cocked his head a little to the left while his droopy ears perked up just enough to cause his forehead to furrow into several lines of bloodhound wrinkles. His canine hearing picked up something from inside the apartment, because his demeanor and intensity cranked it up a notch with each passing second. I got the distinct impression that I heard someone inside moving toward the door. Ronin had very clear body language that just about anyone could read, so we three were well prepared as the door opened up, revealing a young teenage girl. By the look of her, she was obviously not our suspect. She was very young and had none of the aftereffects of recent childbirth.

The girl asked us what we wanted and Tony began to explain our presence. Ronin took this as a cue to run inside. I had the lead coiled up in my left hand with only a short length to the D-ring on the harness. The lead was ripped from my hand as Ronin sprinted through the gap between the girl's legs and the doorjamb. The teenager tried to say something as her head and eyes whipped to the left and behind her in a vain attempt at tracking this wild dog's progress, but the only thing she could do was gasp and put her hand to her mouth as she backed away from the door. She was obviously terrified of Ronin and was ready to leave the apartment as he ran inside. She pulled the door open further, and all I could make out was the end of Ronin's lead snaking out behind him as he ran for a staircase at the back of the apartment. I yelled for him to stop, knowing that it was like trying to command the wind not to blow, and set out after him as quickly as I could, with the captain and Tony pulling up the rear. I think I heard Tony say something to the effect of, "You don't mind if we have a look around, do you?" as Ronin launched himself off of the carpeted stairs to the next floor.

In hindsight, this situation put us in a slightly difficult position. Ronin had trailed a scent source from the evidence in Baby Doe's box right to the front door of a potential suspect's apartment and had identified the door as a scent match consistent with his training and my experience. Yet, we did not necessarily have permission to step inside, as we were in America, where the Fourth Amendment to our Constitution still applied and where we were bound to the proper etiquette of search and seizure rules. Technically speaking, we needed permission to search or a warrant to come inside, neither of which we had at this point. Ronin's mad dash into the apartment changed things a bit, because now I had to be concerned with the safety of my dog and anyone inside. We did have some exigency in this case as well, and that circumstance can override the necessity of a warrant or consent. We were dealing with a female who had given birth within hours of our arrival, and if she was inside, it was doubtful that she had sought medical attention. So, not only did we have the welfare of my dog to consider, we had that of the mother's as well. It was very safe to assume that if Baby Doe's mom was inside and had given birth alone and without assistance, her life might very well be at risk.

Of course, none of us were articulating these thoughts let alone thinking about them as we ran after Ronin. The thrill of the chase and the potential proximity to a suspect was exciting, and the three of us were caught up in it. The thrill quickly faded to caution as the apartment dimmed more the further we went inside. It seemed that the power was out and all of the windows were heavily curtained. The upstairs floor onto which Ronin had disappeared appeared to be nothing more than a black hole, and the short hairs on the back of my neck started to rise as

I yelled a little more frantically at Ronin to stop. The last thing I saw from the foyer was the handle end of my long lead disappear around a corner at the top of the stairs like a snake's tail slithering into its lair. And, with any snake hole, it is not always a smart thing to put one's hand inside without taking a look first.

Things had just changed again. The floor at the top of the stairs was pitch black, and we had no idea what we might be facing up there. As Ronin ran with abandon, we were forced to slow to a walk with flashlights on and guns drawn. I was the first up the stairs and grabbed the loop of the end of the lead just before it completely disappeared into the first bedroom on the east side of the apartment. This trail was rapidly taking on the aura of a "B"-grade horror flick as I reeled in the slack of the long lead in an attempt to feel if my dog was still attached to it. I couldn't see him yet, but I sure wanted to know if he was still there. As I choked up on the lead, I slowly approached the left side of the door frame, illuminating the room's interior with my Stinger flashlight; as with the rest of the house, it was a combination of a Spartan existence coupled with a dumpster. There was little in the way of furniture, sheets for the window dressing, and crap lying about everywhere. A soiled, rumpled twin bed dominated the western corner of the room, which smelled of things discarded and rotted long ago. Much of the odor emanated from the semi-shag carpet left over from the mid-1970s; however, there was an overtone of "fresher" filth that seemed to be coming from the corner where I now found my hound.

The lead had gone slack due to Ronin's preoccupation with the fluid on the carpet in that corner. Preoccupation is probably a subtle way to say that he was lapping up with abandon what remnants I could still see. And, it was at that particular moment in time that I instinctively knew what congealed fluid it was that he was enjoying. To make matters worse, as soon as Ronin detected my presence in the room, he seemed to peer over his shoulder in that doggy indication of guilt that he so very often wore, as he greedily slurped the last morsel from the filthy carpet, knowing from experience that I was about to yell at him to drop whatever it was that he had in his mouth. In so doing, he ensured that all of what was to be had from the vanishing pile on the floor would make it into his stomach long before he was forced to respond to my verbal command. You see, Ronin and I have played this very game on many occasions, and it was a rare day, indeed, when I won it. Ronin could be a sneaky dog right on par with the best burglars whom we so often chased. Still, I had to utter the useless command even though I knew he had finished his grisly little feast, because I refused to also give him the satisfaction of winning without some form of chastisement.

What little guilt my dog wore at the moment faded almost as fast as it manifested itself, because Ronin was not done perusing this wonderfully smelly room. As quickly as I snapped a wrinkle in his butt with the buckle end of the long lead for his unplanned meal, he did a little uncoordinated bunny hop 180 degrees and took aim for the rumpled bed in the other corner. He wagged his tail and waddled over to the foot of the bed and promptly jumped up onto the covers, which, in turn, received the remnants of his meal as Ronin rubbed his drooling jowls to the left and to the right. Not done with his ministrations, Ronin decided that the scratchy wool blanket bundled up beneath his big paws could double as a body scratcher, and he began to roll and rub his entire body to the point where he fell off of the bed . . . and not on his feet, either.

You must understand when reading this that all of the previous two paragraphs evolved in little more than thirty seconds of real time. My captain and Tony arrived in the room behind me just as Ronin unceremoniously rolled off of the bed and onto his back. He picked himself up off of the carpet, shaking himself off while rattling his K-9 badge against the dog tags on his collar as if signaling to us all that his work was at an end, topped off by a feast fit for a buzzard. Tony smiled as my captain asked what we had found. He had only been present for the ending of the K-9 gymnast move that Ronin had attempted and was focused on my less-than-agile animal rather than the scene around us. I briefed him and Tony as they examined the wet corner to which Ronin had previously been so attuned, and it became abundantly evident that the room in which we now found ourselves was more than likely the birthplace of our little Baby Girl Doe.

The mother of Baby Girl Doe turned out to be the sister of the girl who had graciously opened the door for us; however, she herself was nowhere to be found . . . at the moment. Apparently, after disposing of her baby, she decided to visit friends in Oakland just across the bridged estuary that separated our two cities. She was later arrested and booked at the Santa Rita County Jail on charges of attempted murder.

Quadruple Homicide

THE WORST CASES I'VE EVER HAD TO WORK involved the abuse of children. I've always had a special place in my heart for kids who've had it rough, but those who have been abused have always touched me the most. The use of a child for one's personal or sexual pleasure disgusts me beyond fury, and I know that there is a special place in hell for those who prey upon the youth of our nation. This is another story that I considered not writing about, because it still hurts to dwell on it today. I cannot even begin to imagine the depth of pain that the victim's family has been forced to endure.

Sometime during the year of 1998, Ronin and I had become a search-and-rescue resource for the California Office of Emergency Services (OES). We had been called out for numerous missing persons cases throughout California and had experienced a fair amount of success. In July, I received a call out from Chief Roberts of OES for a report of a homicide suspect on the run in Auburn, California.

A migrant worker on a cattle ranch in Auburn had gone on a methamphetamine binge over the course of several days. He had invited some family members over to his little shack on the ranch under the ruse that he had killed a deer and needed some muscle to recover it with the intent of having a barbecue afterwards. Two men and two children subsequently had been murdered and buried in the cattle pasture in a large stand of blackberry brambles above the little shack. A young woman and mother of the children had been sexually assaulted and tied up in the shack while the suspect buried the bodies of her children. The woman had escaped and called for help. As sheriff's deputies arrived on scene, the suspect fled on foot into the nearby hill country. I was called out from home for this case and response time was paramount. The suspect had already been on the loose for almost twenty-four hours. OES arranged for Ronin and me to be transported by a California Highway Patrol airplane to a small airfield north of the town of Auburn. Sheriff's deputies picked us up at the airport and brought us to the scene. The under-sheriff of the Placer County Sheriff's Office was heading up the search and had members of his SWAT team on site for deployment with us if we picked up a trail.

The California foothills in July are blazing hot, and it is not uncommon to have temperatures in excess of 100 degrees for several days in a row. This summer day was oppressive, but we didn't arrive until evening and it was beginning to cool down. Not only did we have the heat to contend with but the terrain as well. Summertime meant lots of foxtails, oats, and burrs throughout the grassy hills of the ranch. All three can hurt the dog, but foxtails were the worst. Foxtails, as their name implies, appear similar to the bushy tail of a fox. They grow on the end of a golden brown grass stalk and can vary in size from a fraction of an inch to several inches. The problem with foxtails is that they imbed themselves easily into soft tissue and literally can burrow their way under the skin in less than a day. A foxtail in the nasal cavity can work its way into the brain with relative ease. California also has an abundance of other nasties during the summer months, such as rattlesnakes, poison oak, scorpions, various spiders, etc.

I was looking at all of this as I was taking in the scene around me. The migrant worker's trailer was situated in a bowl-like valley surrounded by low hills topped with oaks. There was little brush other than a hilltop with an incredible amount of blackberry brambles all over it. The terrain was similar to many of the other working cattle ranches in the area that relied on lots of acreage to produce grass for stock. The fields were cross-hatched by five-strand barbed-wire fences, some of which were relatively new on steel T-posts, yet others were remnants from a bygone era when this was still considered gold country. These odd-shaped posts were made of split rails from oak and bull pine trees dating back to the turn of the century and were pockmarked as if they had been gone over completely by machine-gun fire, creating small holes just big enough to hold an individual acorn in each one. These seed-studded fence posts were the courtesy of the many red-headed woodpeckers that live and nest amongst the trees in the area and that use the fence posts, telephone poles, and wooden-sided houses for food storage. It is strange the little things you remember during the course of events that are far larger.

The under-sheriff pointed out the blackberry brambles and advised me that they had discovered hidden makeshift graves that held the bodies of two men and the children. He then pointed to the trailer/shack just to the west of the grave site, which had been the site of the sexual assault and home to our missing suspect. The trailer was roofed with a screened-in, homemade veranda on the east side under the shade of several medium-size live oak trees. Crime-scene tape surrounded the trailer, and work was still going on to gather evidence. I was a little concerned about good scent evidence, because the scene had really been worked over with a fine-tooth comb. Not much was left that had not been handled or looked at by investigators. The only items left that might be a little trustworthy as scent articles were the sheets on the suspect's bed.

I started Ronin in front of the front door on the east side of the trailer at around 9:45 P.M. The sun had gone down, but there was still a slash of red and orange on the western horizon. There was no breeze, but the temperature had cooled off to about seventy-five degrees as the stars began to make their presence known above us. I was immediately struck by the beauty here and found it hard to understand the horror that had just befallen it, staining the ground and the life of this place forever.

I expected Ronin to have a heavy interest in the trailer and surrounding yard, considering all of the suspect scent that had impregnated it for years. That, coupled with the emotional and physical stress of the crime, should seriously enhance the scent picture of the trailer for Ronin's nose. I really thought that I would have to literally tear him from the scene in an attempt to find a trail. However, as with many of my assumptions, I was wrong. Ronin seemed to feel the urgency that we all felt, and he wasted little time with the trailer. He took scent from the bed sheet and immediately ran to a fence corner as if looking for a way out. He seemed to do a double take at the barbed-wire fence and headed back past the trailer to a stand of bamboo on the west side. Ronin found a small break in the fence there and ran fast downhill into the pasture and a small creek with lazily running water. A very large stand of blackberry bushes grew along the creek, and Ronin circled it several times. He paid an enormous amount of attention to the creek and the blackberry brambles, yet I could see nothing that might be evidence. There were numerous sets of footprints, new and old, but this was a working cattle ranch and the trailer was just up the short hill from us; they might mean nothing at all. I told the SWAT commander who was running backup for me that this was an area they should hand search during daylight hours.

By now, it was getting pretty dark, and I was nervous about having flashlights behind me. I had already encountered several incidents during past felony searches with Ronin at night where illumination put us at a distinct disadvantage. I told everyone that, on this particular evening, we should run in the dark so as not to give our presence away from a distance; a flashlight can be seen from miles away if you were on a hilltop with a clear view. Nobody knew if the suspect was armed or not. Based on his background and the area we were in, I considered it very likely that he had access to a rifle and probably knew how to use one. Put a scope on the gun and one or more of us could easily be shot from a distance of 300 yards or more. No—we were going to have no flashlights on, and I planned on trailing by braille if I had to. I also asked the tactical team behind me to split up a little and run in a modified column formation with a few yards between each member. I did this because if the suspect did have a long gun and was a bad shot, yet we were all packed in close on the trail, even an indiscriminate shot would have a good chance of hitting one of us.

I was amazed at how well the SWAT commander and the under-sheriff were taking my directions. I was a little hesitant to tell them what they needed to do at first, because some people in positions of supervision don't take kindly to a new dog on the block pissing on their territory. Both men listened to everything I asked them to do and performed better than I ever could have imagined. The under-sheriff was running as my cover man to boot! He was the second man in charge of law enforcement in Placer County, and to find him in the field, running at night with a slobbery dog and a tactical team, was amazing. I wish that more leaders were like this man; the world would be a far better place.

Ronin broke out of the creek bed and headed up a small hill and into very thick cover. He found a cave-like opening in the brush and immediately ran inside. I choked up on the lead because I lost sight of him, and I was concerned about what we might run into . . . which turned out to be a face full of blackberry brambles. My clothes were snagged, as was the flesh on my hands and face. As I threw up my free arm to protect my eyes, I realized immediately where we were . . . at the grave site. I had become disoriented in the dark and had no idea that we were anywhere near the place until we were almost on top of the first plywood-covered grave.

The SWAT commander lit up the site so that we could examine it. I was not concerned about the light at this point, because the cover was so thick that nobody would see it from the outside. There were two large mounds of loose red soil near the plywood-covered hole, and it was explained to me what had happened. The suspect had obviously planned long and hard for what it was that he had eventually done. He had found a thick, almost impregnable location and had literally tunneled into it with a chainsaw. Once inside, he had carefully prepared two grave sites where he could easily dispose of the bodies of his intended victims and family members. I was sickened by the thought of two children and men killed and buried in such a place and with such malice aforethought. Ronin was frantic, though. He wanted into the graves in the worst way, and even though the bodies had long since been removed, their scent—which spoke descriptive volumes of technical detail to Ronin—was everywhere, perhaps permeating the place with invisible messages of sheer human terror and madness. Ronin's prey scent was also here, and

I could tell that, even though he was bombarded by all of the other odors, he still had the hunt in mind and was trying to find a way out. If anything, he was driven to a higher level of intensity by this man-made horror. I would be interested to know how a dog might catalog such smells as fear, terror, and helplessness. I don't believe that dogs have the same ability to feel emotions like humans do, but are feelings of empathy or vengeance completely impossible? After seeing these graves, I had only one thought in mind, and that was to catch this man; I could only hope that it might affect Ronin the same way.

I had seen enough, and as the SWAT commander extinguished the electric flame of his Sure-Fire lithium battery-powered light, I was thankful that my night vision was long in returning. We had no words to speak at that moment, and I think that, even though we were ready to leave this place, its history would haunt us forever. Just as I was able to make out the monster-like shapes of looming shadows, translating them into the outlines of the brambles they truly were, Ronin seemed to find a way out on the far side of the hilltop just to the opposite of the vine-formed cave we had entered. The tension eased as we all left the thorny cover of that makeshift graveyard. Invisible chains and anchors of pent-up, never-to-be-loosed emotion that we all had carried until this time dropped away to a certain extent, leaving only their memory to empower our footsteps. There was nothing more to do now than try to complete this grim trail.

This trail to me now is somewhat of a blur, made fuzzy not only by the events that had created it, but also by the fact that we were running in the dark. Certain moments come to my mind, and they are refreshed by my log book from that period, but most of the run itself is lost to time. I remember crossing through several barbed-wire fences and weaving in and out of various pastures until we came across the country road that Ronin and I had originally been driven in on. He took us to a four-way intersection and took the first street to the right. He then took an immediate left into the driveway for a new housing project that was still under construction. As we entered into the construction area, I could make out the shapes of looming buildings in front of us. Ronin deftly negotiated his way through various pieces of large equipment, piping, and lumber. All of this was difficult to see until we actually got to within a few feet of any particular object; however, I was nervous about the buildings and the suspect who might be inside. I wanted no flashlights brightening our path and was willing to take the chance of incurring a few scrapes and bruises.

Trailing by braille is a unique experience, because it requires that you have complete faith in your ability as a handler to determine the path ahead by feeling the subtle tensions and angle changes of the long lead connected to the dog. The lead can tell you how fast the dog is going or warn you about an approaching incline or decline, any obstacles, and barriers. I had a great working relationship with Ronin, and, in most cases, I could work in almost complete darkness with little or no danger. I was confident in my ability to define lead language—until this night.

Ronin had been keeping a good pace of about three to five miles per hour, and the lead stayed straight, with its angle slightly up toward me off of the top of his back. This told me that we were on relatively level ground with few obstacles. All of a sudden, the constant feeling of the lead that I had experienced for the last several minutes changed dramatically to something that I'd never felt before. I felt sudden, intense pressure on the lead going down toward the ground, followed immediately by a powerful jerk that almost ripped the knotted end of the length of rolled bull hide from my grasp. The sudden downward pressure made me grab the lead hard with both hands right before I would have lost it. The jerk that I felt at the end was stronger and harder than anything I had ever felt Ronin do before, and I was a little lost by the sensation until I felt the lead stretch and swing hard from the left to the right. I knew then that what I was feeling was the weight of my dog as he swung, pendulum-like, to and fro above some unknown chasm. This lack of knowing scared the hell out of me, and I called for some help to hold the line as I ran forward to see what Ronin had gotten himself into. He was not making a sound, which scared me even more, until I got to the edge of what looked like an immense trench. I didn't hesitate with the flashlight this time and shone my beam down on top of my hanging bloodhound, whose back paws were barely sweeping the surface of the bottom of this six-foot deep pit. I struggled to keep myself from laughing as Ronin's harness backed itself up and over the top of his head and gravity slipped it the rest of the way off of him. His back paws hit the dirt first and his front followed. He looked around and just sat down. Ronin was obviously not moved like I was about his situation.

Part of the problem with the ditch in which Ronin now found himself was that it was deep—at least six feet or so. Ronin was never incredibly coordinated, and a leap back to the surface was not going to happen. I'm sure that is why he decided to follow the best course of action and simply sit down. I was forced to jump in there with him and try to hand him off to one of the guys from the tactical team. I picked Ronin up by the butt and his chest as if I was cradling him and then made a clean and jerk-type maneuver in a vain attempt at getting Ronin's front paws onto the bank above us. I guess I did not explain this to him well enough, because the only thing he did was throw his big butt and dirty feet up over my shoulders, away from the bank. I lowered him back to the ground and tried it again, this time asking one of the guys to grab his collar as I tried to jerk his body upward. The second shot worked like a charm. Ronin made it up out of the ditch by kicking off with his hind legs, effectively launching himself off of my chest and into the waiting arms of a couple of tactical operators. I decided to take a short break and let everyone catch their breath for a few minutes. This time allowed me to give Ronin a good once-over to see if he had been hurt in the long fall into the ditch.

Ronin had alerted on a gate near the four-way intersection prior to heading up into the construction area. There was a driveway to the gate that probably led to a home or ranch. I thought back on this area, because even though Ronin had brought us to the area where we now found ourselves, he had identified the gate as having a scent match to his intended target. I had allowed him to bring us to the construction site because he had chosen to do so, and his body language had told me that he was on the trail. Now I had to decide where to start him again.

The trail in and around the ditch area seemed to peter out, so I didn't have many options. Theoretically, the suspect might have gone up to one of the houses being built and then walked back down the same road. I decided that the best thing to do was to restart at the gate identified by Ronin rather than try to make something out of a dead end at the construction area.

Ronin eventually worked his way through the driveway and to a canal that ran parallel to Mount Vernon Road. He worked a small path along the canal for quite a distance. I don't remember how far we ran now, but I do recall that the water ditch ran through a number of small housing areas and eventually led to the outskirts of town. We worked our way to the backyard of one of the houses, and Ronin seemed to be very interested in a garden hose. He checked it twice for scent and then just seemed to stop. He stood there and whined without looking in any direction or moving. I took him back down to Mount Vernon Road, but he did the same thing. No matter what I did or where I took him, he just wouldn't budge.

I called off the search at 2 A.M. and apologized for suddenly abandoning a good trail. However, I knew better than to try and force Ronin to work. We went home that morning in the same fashion as we had come—by air. Ronin was less than thrilled about the ride, but he was also far less uptight than he would have been normally. He was actually a little depressed . . . or so it seemed. The next day, Ronin began to sneeze uncontrollably, forcing me to take him to the vet clinic. A short exam proved that both nasal cavities were full of seeds, foxtails, and other debris. He had already developed a major sinus infection on top of it. I felt horrible about the problem, because I should have been more aware of the possibility of this happening. He had worked until he physically could not work anymore. He had started whining when he stopped, because he knew that he was supposed to finish and just couldn't do it. I had no idea how much he had suffered to do the job that he had done that night.

I received a phone call from the under-sheriff shortly after Ronin was treated. He told me that they had continued to investigate Ronin's trail all the way to town and had discovered evidence that the suspect had been at a drugstore at the bottom of Mount Vernon Road. He was captured on video at the store and may have used a pay phone there to get a ride out of the area. The suspect was later captured in Los Angeles as he was attempting to leave the country. During his interrogation after arrest, he recounted his escape route for investigators, and it matched Ronin's trail identically.

PLACER COUNTY

SHERIFF
CORONER-MARSHAL

MAIN OFFICE
P.O. BOX 6990
AUBURN, CA 95604
PH: (530) 889-7800   FAX: (530) 889-7899

TAHOE SUBSTATION
DRAWER 1710
TAHOE CITY, CA 96145
PH: (530) 581-6300   FAX: (530) 581-6377

EST. 1851

EDWARD N. BONNER
SHERIFF-CORONER-MARSHAL

STEPHEN L. D'ARCY
UNDERSHERIFF

August 5, 1998

Chief Bernham E. Matthews
Alameda Police Department
1555 Oak Street
Alameda, California 94501

Dear Chief Matthews:

On behalf of the residents of Placer County, I want to commend Officer Jeffrey Scheitler and
his K-9 Ronin for their expert assistance.

We recently experienced a multiple murder incident and called upon the services of Officer
Scheitler and his bloodhound. They responded as soon as we requested them and were
flown to Auburn by CHP aircraft. Once they arrived at the crime scene, they went straight to
work, following a track of the homicide suspect until early the next morning.

The suspect was later apprehended in Southern California. During follow-up investigative
interviews, the suspect provided a chronology of his actions that matched identically with the
trail Officer Scheitler discovered with his partner. This trail was established 26 hours prior to
Ronin locating it – a truly outstanding accomplishment.

Officer Scheitler and Ronin provided invaluable assistance to this department, and we
appreciate their tireless efforts and dedication to service.

Sincerely,

EDWARD N. BONNER, SHERIFF-CORONER-MARSHAL

Stephen L. D'Arcy
Undersheriff

SLD/crb

Thank you letter from Placer County Sheriff for work on the quad homicide.

Tunnel Vision

B Y NOW, RONIN AND I WERE GETTING CALL OUTS FOR MUTUAL AID from police and sheriff's departments all over northern California. The Oakland Police Department (OPD) was one of our biggest callers and supporters. I had been working with the OPD for sometime now in the development of its own fledgling bloodhound program as well as responding to various calls for service. The OPD bloodhound was only a puppy and had not yet begun to work real cases. Ronin and I found ourselves in Oakland almost as often as we were in our own city of Alameda. Don't get me wrong—I wasn't complaining about the work; as a matter of fact, I reveled in it. I loved working my dog and would be happy doing only that. The reason why we worked so much for Oakland and elsewhere was because my chief had been an OPD street cop and had strong ties to the community and to the department. Everything that Ronin did was assistance not only to Alameda but to humanity in general. My chief knew this and was very generous with our deployments.

I was working swing shift in August 2000 when I was dispatched to a block of Courtland Avenue in Oakland for a double homicide. It was summertime and the nights were mild. This evening was no different; the temperature hovered at just above sixty-five degrees as the fog began to settle into the Bay Area. This block of Courtland is a bad stretch of city streets in Oakland known for gang activity and drug deals. Two Hispanic men had been found shot to death in the front seats of their car, which had rolled to a stop at the west curb of Courtland Avenue. They had strong gang ties in Oakland, and their murders came as no surprise to local law enforcement. The only question was if this case was an execution by a rival gang, or if it was drug related; it could have been both, for that matter. When we arrived on the scene in my K-9 patrol vehicle—a 1998 black-and-white Ford Crown Victoria outfitted with a special aluminum K-9 cage that took up the entire rear-seat area—the street was packed with OPD cars. Our K-9 cars were set up with fairly nice equipment; heat sensors alerted the handler if the interior got too hot while he or she was away from the car and the dog was inside, and automatic door pops opened the door remotely should the handler need the dog quickly for an emergency. The cars themselves were normally the older fleet members that had already seen lots of miles and officer usage.

I met with the sergeant in charge of the scene, and he showed me what we were dealing with. The car had rolled to a stop with the left, front tire resting against the west curb of Courtland and was facing north, toward the Oakland hills. There, the left, rear door was open, and I could see the silhouettes of two figure in the fronts seats with their heads all the way back, as if the occupants were gazing at the ceiling of the car. It appeared strangely serene until you noticed the blood and gore splattered all over the interior of the windshield and the exit holes that the smashing bullets had made. The suspect presumably was sitting in the back seat of the car behind the victims and had waited for just the right moment when he was in exactly the right spot to shoot both victims in the back of the head from point-blank range. The two men had died instantly and never knew what hit them; the only thoughts they might have had were now all over the dashboard of the car. This was an execution, and the shooter knew exactly what he was doing and where he was going to pull his trigger. My guess, even before starting Ronin, was that this guy had another car and driver waiting for him nearby. I did not have high hopes of finding anything, really.

This scene was swarming with officers and crime-scene techs, and I had received numerous warnings that my dog was not to get anywhere near the interior of the car. The CSI guys really didn't want me in there either, but I had to get some scent material if I were to start Ronin. I took a sterile four-by-four-inch gauze pad and placed it on the rear seat, which I figured the suspect must have come in contact with to fire the shots that he did. I didn't need to rub the gauze pad on the seat, rather, I let it sit there for a couple of minutes to adsorb whatever scent particles might be there. After my pad baked on the seat for a bit, I recovered it and placed it in a new Zip-Lock bag, then went back to my car to get Ronin.

As I was walking back to the car, I once again gathered in the surrounding area to get an idea of the kind of terrain we'd be running through. Although we were in one of the worst parts of inner-city Oakland, this location was somewhat park-like, with a grass-covered field just to the west of the car and a eucalyptus-lined creek bed on the border. I knew the area intimately, because I had worked so many other cases here. The scene was deceptive because even though it seemed clean and relatively nice, it was in one of the worst parts of Oakland. The sniper trail that we had run after the Oakland police officer had been shot and killed from a Highway 580 overpass was just around the corner, and I had no illusions about the danger that we faced here. This was a crazy neighborhood where the police were less than welcome.

I let Ronin waltz around the area with his bloodhound waddle. He walked up to many officers whom he had met in the past for a quick, tail-wag greeting and allowed his bladder to empty a little. He had been stuck in the car a lot this particular night, because I had been so busy taking un-K-9-related calls for service in Alameda. He had to pee badly, and I didn't want that to happen right when we started our trail. Once he was walking a little lighter, I brought him over to the car, harnessed him up, and snapped the long lead onto the D-ring. Ronin had air scented all of the blood inside the car, and I knew that he wanted to smell that more than anything else so I was prepared to line check him if he wanted to jump inside after I scented him on the gauze pad.

Ronin instantly responded to my command to "Skit it!" and only gave the back seat and the car's interior a quick backward glance as he picked up the suspect's scent trail westbound down a small cement path toward the eucalyptus trees about eighty yards away. Ronin slid down a dirt embankment in the grove down toward the garbage-strewn creek bed, where the brown-tinged water was lazily running to the south and ultimately spilling out into San Francisco Bay. My lip curled as I prepared myself to get wet in water that I knew was far from clean. Broken glass, fast-food containers, and human debris were everywhere I looked. It was obvious that the homeless in the area used the creek bed for a campsite, and the heroin addicts liked it as well, proven by the discarded insulin syringes and ripped-open, tiny, colored balloons scattered here and there. I was protected, somewhat, by my Magnum boots, but Ronin's bare paws were another story. I had second thoughts about this trail and was ready to call it for fear that Ronin was going to be exposed to the danger of an impromptu garbage dump. He had sliced up his paws on broken glass in places like this in the past, and I didn't want him to have to deal with that again.

Ronin changed my mind by the time he was chest deep in the middle of the creek, casting for the trail's direction and obviously in strong scent. He seemed to be vacillating about which direction he should go and kept hopping back and forth upstream and then downstream. He checked the bank on the far side of the creek and came back to the middle, ruling out an exit trail to the west, but he was intrigued by the south-flowing water and made several aborted attempts at running in that direction down the middle of the stream. I had seen this behavior before and decided that he was simply following a scent that was running downstream on the surface of the water. As soon as I figured this out, it seemed as if Ronin did as well, and he began to work his way upstream to a large pool of water at the base of a six-foot tunnel surrounded by steep slopes of ivy on either side.

Ronin was alerting strongly at the mouth of the tunnel, and I confirmed his interest with the sight of crushed vegetation from human tracks on the east bank leading to a little cement weir at the tunnel's entrance. The tunnel ran underground for at least a city block beneath a portion of Courtland to Brookdale Avenue. I didn't know about the tunnel before this night and had no idea what to expect. Light was already fading as the sun began to set, which made the tunnel mouth appear nothing more than an ominous black hole. Ronin wanted in, in the worst way, yet I was hesitant to follow. As surreal as it might be, the entire scene reminded me of a horror movie from my youth, but in this instance, the monster was all too real and could be waiting for us inside. It did not matter if we used flashlights or not; the suspect would hear us coming long before we got to him. If he was in this hole, we were going to run into him. Ronin was acting like he had fresh scent emitting from the tunnel mouth as it belched its murky water contents into the pool at my feet. I was struggling to maintain my grip on the wet lead as Ronin tried every angle available to him to get inside—first into the pool with a jump at the weir, then a side trip to the ivy slope just to my right—and if that didn't work, perhaps he could tie up my legs by running around them, which might trip me up and make me drop the lead. He tried every trick he could with his little doggy repertoire, yet there was no way I was going to let him in there . . . just yet. In a weird way, my concern was really only for him. I knew that if someone shot at us, Ronin was going to be the target, and that frightened me more than anything else.

I remembered a dream that I'd forgotten about until this night. As with many dreams, this one was left unremembered until something I had perceived on this murderer's trail spawned it into being yet again. I don't recall what the trigger was—perhaps it was the inky darkness in front of me—but I was remembering the dream now. Ronin and I were working across a grassy field in broad daylight when suddenly we were both engulfed in circle of total darkness. I could tell that he was in front of me, as the tension in the lead did not slacken. Just as suddenly, the world around us was shattered by a flash of light and noise that left me not only blind, but deaf and physically numb. I could no longer feel Ronin on the end of the lead, and in my dream, I knew that I was totally alone. I had woken up immediately and had felt a sense of panic. It was not so much the sense of aloneness that bit so deep; rather, it was the sense of loss. In my dream, I had lost Ronin, and there was a sickening feeling that I would never see him again.

I felt this panic return as one of my cover officers asked me what I thought we should do. I had two highly trained and competent OPD tactical operators armed with M4 versions of the AR-15. Each weapon held a thirty-round magazine of .223-caliber ammunition and sported small, lightweight, lithium-battery-powered halogen flashlights mounted on a Picatinny rail just forward of the hand guards. The little light was operated by a pressure pad under the fingers of the shooters off hand on the hand guard. The questioning officer knew that we were on it and was anxious to proceed. I could not articulate my fear to him, or to anyone else for that matter, without losing their confidence in our abilities. It was his presence and eagerness that made me take the next step into the stygian darkness of that tunnel. One step turned into many more as our booted footfalls slapped into the shallow stream, tattooing an odd cadence that reverberated through the walls of the tunnel. I was not worried about light now and asked my backup officers to try and shine their intense flashlight beams out in front of Ronin in an attempt to blind any potential suspect who might still be inside.

Once we were through what I perceived to be about halfway into the tunnel, it opened up into a rock- and garbage-strewn area about twenty yards across. Ronin pulled hard into his lead as soon as we set foot into this place, and I could see what was drawing his attention. Directly in front of us, and still relatively dry, was a black-and-white, knit serape or poncho. The serape was clean and free of debris that would have otherwise covered any other object entombed in this place for any length of time. Ronin was all over this piece of clothing, and it was obvious by his behavior that it matched the scent on which he had started, and it was fresh. The serape gave him even more energy to get moving, and he was straining at the lead.

We made it out of the tunnel in short order, and Ronin picked up a fresh foot trail to Brookdale Avenue. He identified a house not far from the tunnel; however, nobody answered the door and we had no search warrant. I wasn't going to wait all night for one, either. The trail seemed to end right around the area of the house, so it appeared to me that the suspect either lived at the home or had left in a vehicle. Regardless, Ronin just didn't have any more scent to work with and we called it quits. The serape belonged to the suspect, as corroborated by a witness statement obtained later in the investigation. I'm not sure what happened with the case, though, because there were so many cases that we were working at the time and I couldn't keep track of them all. Suffice it to say that Ronin found the escape trail of the suspect, physical evidence worn by him, and a home that was possibly connected as well. This case was one of many where we produced great evidence but fell short of finding the person for whom we were looking. The bloodhound or any police trailing dog is simply a tool and not a miracle worker, and we were working in an urban environment—the toughest of all places for a trailing dog to work.

Colt .45

I N 2001, I DECIDED THAT I HAD EXPERIENCED ENOUGH OF CITY LIFE and work and wanted a major change in my life. I was not enjoying my job in Alameda like I used to, though I craved the K-9 work all the more. I was not sleeping well and had few friends outside the police department. I didn't trust people very much and had a hard time communicating with anyone other than for work-related issues. I lived and breathed police work and especially my K-9 training and duties. All of my vacations revolved around dog activities, and I was constantly called out on my days off. The cases we were working seemed to be becoming all the more gruesome and evil with each passing day. I was not a very happy person and probably not all that great to be around, either. However, I was the last person to recognize the primary causes for my mood swings.

The only thing I could think of was that I needed to get out of Dodge in the worst way. I had this overwhelming feeling of unease that could only be assuaged by getting away from everything that I had known before. I didn't realize that I was running from demons that I voluntarily brought with me when I finally did move. That realization did not occur until Ronin and I were lying side by side while I was healing up from a couple of major-surgery sessions. I internalized everything that we did and took it very personally if I did not perform. The K-9 work that we were doing was tough, and although we had a good success rate comparative to other K-9 tracking programs in existence at the time, it really was not all that high. Couple this with the fact that the cases we worked on a fairly regular basis were some of the most brutal cases a police officer could work, and you have a recipe for emotional instability.

At this point in my life I didn't care where I worked, but I needed to get out of the city. The city seemed to be my arch nemesis, and I felt that if I could move to the country, I might regain some of my sanity. Judy and I found a nice home in rural Amador County for our bloodhounds on about six acres of land far from any streetlights and traffic, and I picked the closest law-enforcement agency to work at. I didn't really care what the department was like—I just wanted to move. I continued to work with Ronin but on a much more limited basis.

One of the first cases I worked for my new department was an evidence search in the Sutter Highlands area of Amador County. Ronin was not officially on the department roster yet, and most of the people at my new agency didn't know what he was all about— nor did they really care, for that matter. I was literally starting all over again.

I had responded to a domestic disturbance on Colt Drive and had separated the parties involved—a man and his live-in girlfriend. Not much had happened other than a big argument and the girlfriend running out the back door screaming at the top of her lungs. The problem was that the woman had decided to teach her boyfriend a lesson and take his collectable and valuable Colt Commander .45 pistol and throw it as far as she could down 'a golden brown, grass-covered slope below the house—a nice little area where the neighborhood kids liked to gather and play.

We looked for the pistol for a couple of hours and had, predictably, no luck in finding it. The girlfriend was useless when it came to telling us where she had thrown the gun. The situation was serious, because the pistol was a danger in of itself, but it was also "cocked and locked." "Cocked and locked" is a term relative to single-action pistols such as this Colt. Once a round is jacked into the battery by pulling the slide to the rear, the hammer is cocked and can be fired with relatively light pressure on the trigger. The manual safety is the only thing that keeps this from happening. Consequently, if a child did find the gun, it would take little more than a flick of a small lever to create fatal consequences.

The hillside below the house was very large—at least forty acres of open space before any more houses. We tried to calculate the distance a gun would travel in the air if thrown from various vantage points, but without knowing exactly where the woman had run, it would be almost impossible to determine trajectory or distance. We searched until the sun set and planned to return the next morning.

I spoke to my sergeant about the case and explained that it would be impossible to find the gun unless we grid out the entire hillside and recruited a platoon of searchers to ground pound the area. The Amador County Sheriff's Department (ACSD) had patrol K-9s, but they were not trained for article searches or any scent-specific work at all. I volunteered Ronin's services and told my sergeant that Ronin was trained for article searches and had a knack for finding guns anyway. I'm not sure exactly what it was that Ronin liked about gun odor, but he did. He found firearms far easier than just about any other item. I received approval to bring in Ronin for this search.

Ronin had to prove himself all over again. My new employer did not have a lot of interest in the program, and they were more interested in the warm body of a deputy than that of a hound dog. This work, as well as other cases, would be on a volunteer and "as needed" basis. It was a bitter pill to swallow, considering all that we had done and been through together, but ACSD did not understand our program or its application. We had to show them.

We arrived at the house on Colt Drive the very next morning. It was about fifty-seven degrees with little to no wind—perfect conditions for scent work. I started Ronin a few yards from the boarded-up entrance to an old mine shaft, thinking that the girlfriend probably had lied to me and had really tossed the pistol down this impossibly deep hole that I had found in a small oak grove on the side of the hill below the house. If it was in there, I was doubtful that Ronin would alert on it, but what the hell—I had to try something. I let Ronin take a scent inventory of the area and gave him my special and unique command to find guns: "find the gun."

Ronin put his nose to the air and seemed to pick up something; he started zigzagging to the west, away from the mine shaft. Of course, he was going in the opposite direction from which I thought he might—proving, again, that if I could do the job *he* could, I ought to put the harness on myself. Ronin did this to me regularly, so I rarely articulated my expectations to interested parties because invariably I would be embarrassed and be wrong. Therefore, I simply rolled my eyes and made another useless mental note not to think for my dog.

Ronin's zigzag pattern started off wide—about twenty- to thirty-yard intervals—and narrowed as he got closer to whatever it was that he smelled. As his intervals shortened, his speed and interest picked up. If you were to draw Ronin's pattern from above, it would appear like a cone lying down on its side, with Ronin working the large end toward the point. Ronin was working down the hill and had traveled less than fifty yards when he stopped, sat, and began pawing at the oak-leaf-strewn forest floor with his big, goofy paw, looking back over his shoulder at me with his tongue hanging as if saying, "It's over here, dummy!"

The area Ronin alerted on was a hillside of ancient oak trees that had decades of live and black oak leaves in varying levels of decomposition blanketing the ground about a foot thick. At the time, the morning air had a special scent to it that I have always loved. It was a smell that I have only detected in the foothills of California and can only describe as a combination of a newly made oaken wine barrel and freshly mowed hay. I ran over to Ronin quickly and raked away the area that he had already started to uncover. Ronin thought I was having too much fun and started to dig next to me with both front paws, creating a snowstorm of semi-rotted oak leaves behind us. Our work was quickly rewarded by the sight of the grips of the Colt Commander. I was grinning hugely as Ronin began to rake the side of my hip with his claws, demanding his cookies. I had brought a lot of cookies, thinking that Ronin and I might be searching most of the day and I'd have to keep his energy levels up. I was so happy that I gave the entire handful to him at one time. Ronin was chomping away with sheer canine culinary pleasure as I made the weapon safe and commenced brushing it off.

As soon as I had stowed the pistol away in the cargo pocket of my pants, I got on the radio and let dispatch know that I had found the pistol and would be heading back to the barn shortly. My sergeant radioed back to confirm that I had found the gun with an incredulous tone to his voice, and I answered him with a quick and neutral "affirm." I don't think my sergeant, or anyone else for the matter, really expected me to do anything more than take a walk in the park. This was made pretty obvious to me by the fact that I was the only one at the search. Ronin's first find in Amador received little to no fanfare. I was a little surprised by this, because I thought that we would get at least a pat on the back or a "good job," but nobody said a word. This was disappointing, because that gun would probably never have been found without Ronin's nose. A large group of people searching by hand and foot would have taken days to scour the hillside and probably still would have come up with nothing.

A Hunt for Mushrooms

R ONIN WAS EVENTUALLY ACCEPTED into the Amador County Sheriff's Department as a full-fledged K-9 but with some pretty strict conditions. I was given little flexibility with our training regimen and even less time to train. I was happy to be working with Ronin as my partner again, but I could see that he was getting rusty with each passing week. The key to any good trailing dog is continuous training in ever-changing environments. It is imperative that the dog be given an opportunity to train in the areas in which he might be working and to be exposed to all possible variables. If not, new conditions on real cases could surprise the dog and degrade his ability to work well, because it is spending too much time becoming accustomed to the new environment. My captain in charge of patrol decided that we could train only at the fairgrounds in the city of Plymouth or at home. This was further complicated by the edict that we could not train with any civilians and only with ACSD's personnel. The rationale for this order was based on what the captain stated was a liability issue. So, here I was with a trailing dog that was supposed to be able to find missing people or criminals (all civilians), yet the only assistants I could use were other deputies who were never available for me to train with anyway.

The real reason for this decision was the fact that Ronin had been featured in a newspaper article in the county after we did a nice job on a search. The article mentioned my name as well as Ronin's, and it apparently sent the sheriff and my captain off of the deep end. A verbal order was given to the department that no single deputy's or K-9's name would be mentioned in public print without the express permission of the sheriff. My orders to train only at home or at the fairgrounds came shortly thereafter. Unlike my chief in Alameda, who thought that all good press for the department was great for his image, this sheriff felt that the only good press was when *his* name was mentioned.

Ronin and I paid the price for this problem for the rest of our career. Regardless of the restrictions we were put under, Ronin continued to perform, although not quite to the standard to which I was accustomed. The saving grace was that we were working in a primarily rural environment, which was far easier to negotiate than the city from which we had come. For the record, I complied with my captain's orders, but what I did on my own time was up to me. I continued to train, when possible, with other people and in other places, just not to the extent that I should have.

Just before Christmas 2002, Ronin and I were dispatched to a report of a missing man in the mountainous area of Sutter Creek. The fifty-eight-year-old hiker had told his wife that he was going to pick mushrooms in the woods near his home at around 2:00 P.M. that afternoon. His family reported him missing at 7:08 P.M. when he didn't return home. We arrived around 8:00 P.M., and I collected scent material from the missing man's home. His family was distraught and had been searching the hillsides in vain prior to our arrival. I did my best to console them without promising miracles. I told them that we would do the best we could and that we'd search all night if necessary. The hardest part of my job was talking to the family. Expectant eyes followed my every move. They would often see Ronin, either in the car or as I was prepping him for work, instantly believing that their loved one would be found soon. How could I tell them that this was probably not going to be the case? That statistics actually spelled out just the opposite? I hated the media at times like this—painting the bloodhound as the dog always able to find his man. I could only say that we would work as hard and as long as possible.

The man's car had been discovered a short distance from his home. This was the most obvious place to start. I had considerable concern about starting at the car, but I didn't see much choice. The missing man's brother or cousin had been roaming the hills around the area where the car had been found for hours prior to my arrival. His scent was probably going to be laid on top of a portion of our target's trail, and this new trail would be fresher to boot. Ronin was trained to follow only the scent that I started him on, but it is tough for any dog to ignore another fresh human trail on top of the primary one. I did a quick visual search for tracks that would possibly give me an indication of a direction of travel, but I was not surprised to see that everything was pretty well obliterated by footprints of family members all over the place. I had expected as much but had to look anyway.

I could never blame family members of missing persons for doing everything possible to assist in the search, before and after the cops showed up. I understood the emotional hell they had to be going through and I knew that, if it was my spouse or child who was lost, I'd be pulling my hair out, too. Invariably, there was always a cousin, brother, uncle, etc. who had searched on top of the trail from which Ronin would have to scent. This made our work incredibly difficult because of two factors: new, fresh trail and family scent. Family scent is the worst, because unknowing searchers carries with them into the field not their own scent but a little of the missing person's as well. The closer the family member, the more target scent he or she might carry. Sometimes this is just enough to throw my dog off of the correct trail and make us run around in circles. Looking back on all of the missing people whom we did find over the years, the common denominator was lack of other searchers in the field before we arrived. There are many bloodhound handlers who claim that bloodhounds can always work through these other distracting human odors when they are working, but I beg to differ. I have too much experience working not only with my dogs, but with hundreds of others all over the country, that have experienced the exact same problem from time to time.

Well, on this trail, I was already looking at the distracting human-odor problem that was probably going to be an issue everywhere we'd be searching. The cousin or brother had been out searching the entire time prior to our arrival. Thankfully, he was with us at the car, so I could pre-scent Ronin on him using the missing-member method. It was pretty dark by the time we were ready to get rolling on this search and the temperature was dropping fast. There was no wind to speak of and that, coupled with the dropping temperature, provided great conditions for a trailing dog. It kept the scent low to the ground and relatively stationary.

I patted the brother or cousin on the leg and told Ronin to sniff him and then started Ronin on the pair of underwear that I had in a Zip-Lock bag as scent material. The guy started to follow after us and I had to tell him several times to stay back. He just didn't understand how confusing he was making it for us already. Ronin circled the car and started to head back to the house on the road for a short distance, seemed to think better about it, then came back to the car and followed a small footpath into the woods. This trail was obviously the one that the missing man had taken, along with all of the other searchers. Once Ronin was into the vegetation, he picked up his pace significantly and seemed to really be into it. He was so into it—like he was running a fifteen-minute-old trail versus a seven-hour-old one—that I immediately started to worry that we were following a family member's trail. We bottomed out into a draw, which eventually dumped into a creek bed in a deep canyon and then headed back up the hillside to the car. Ronin picked up his pace and became very animated as we broke out of the woods approximately 100 yards to the east of the car, which he spotted and toward which he started to run. He did exactly what I was worried he would do and obviously had jumped track onto one of the searcher's trails. Ronin did not run up to the brother or cousin whom we left at the car, so I was convinced that it wasn't that guy's scent we were following; however, we were headed back toward the house, and I'm sure we would have found a match there if I had allowed Ronin to continue, which I did not. Ronin was a little pissed off that I dragged him off the trail back to the house. The home had been searched completely, and I was positive that our man was not there.

Contrary to popular belief, the dogs are not always correct and will jump trails to other humans and especially to animals if they are allowed to. A good handler has to understand all of the subtle behavior and changes in body language that the dog manifests in order to determine if this has happened. It isn't easy, either. It takes years and thousands of practice trails around every possible situation—animals in particular— in order to learn how to read your dog properly. It also takes plenty of mistakes. The best way I have always learned is when I've made the big ones. I was usually so incredibly embarrassed that I made very large mental notes not to do the same thing again. I knew, based on my experience and training, that Ronin had jumped trails on me. He was acting far too much as if the trail he was running had just been put down . . . like it was fifteen to thirty minutes old. He was obviously following a human—his demeanor also told me this—but it was absolutely a fresher trail. If I allowed him to continue to run it, I ran the risk of not being able to get him back on the right one. The sooner this correction was made, the better off we would be. Unfortunately, I had allowed Ronin to run this one for far too long, but I had little choice without seeing an alternative route. I really hoped that I could get him back on track.

I restarted Ronin down the same trail, and he seemed to follow the same scent pattern down toward the draw. I was starting to worry—again— that we were going to repeat the exact same course we just finished. Just as I was about to give Ronin a little line check, he surprised me by hitting on a little deer trail just to the west of the little footpath that we had been on. Ronin was focused on the trail, but his animation changed slightly. He was a little more patient and moved a little slower . . . indicating that the trail was a little older than the one we had just left. This was a good sign as long as it wasn't the deer; however, I could see no crittering signs. Ronin's tail was up and rigid, his nose was to the ground, and he wasn't sounding like a Hoover vacuum cleaner sucking up a wad of wet gravel— the noise he makes when crittering on an animal. No, Ronin was moving a little slower but he was also looking a lot better and my confidence level was on the rise.

We were about forty minutes into our search and, instead of moving deeper into the woods as I had expected, we were running into an area behind some neighboring homes. This I had not expected. I figured that our man would be looking for ground less traveled to find the mushrooms he was looking for, but unlike the last trail we had just finished, I was not going to yank Ronin off of this one. He was working too "correctly," and everything felt right. It was best to just shut up and hang on at this point. We were in a relatively level old-growth oak forest with lots of varied ground cover—everything from poison oak to manzanita. It was tough to see much further than Ronin, because there always seemed to be some brushy barrier. A fair amount of ground fog was also beginning to linger just a few feet off of the ground. This trail was not exactly spooky, but it did remind me of a 1950s black-and-white werewolf movie. We were using flashlights and making quite a bit of noise. Unlike criminal cases, a missing person at risk needs to know that searchers are looking for him or her; noise and light are good things in most of these cases.

All of a sudden, Ronin's demeanor changed and he lowered his body and dug hard into the ground as he picked up speed. His nose was up, and it was obvious that he had air-scented something. I shined my Streamlight in the direction Ronin's nose was pointing and made out the silhouette of a body laid out on the ground about fifteen yards ahead of us. We were almost right on top of the man, and I could see that he wasn't moving. I had a sinking feeling in my gut as we moved in fast. Ronin got a quick sniff of the man, and I could tell by his behavior that our missing person had passed away. My backup officer and I knelt down next to the man and rolled him over onto his back. He was in full rigor mortis and had a pack of cigarettes clutched in his right hand, which was held tightly to his left breast. Lividity had set in, fully darkening all of the exposed flesh that had been lying against the leaf-strewn ground. There was absolutely nothing we could do.

My partner radioed our location and situation into dispatch while I praised Ronin and let him have his Scooby snacks. Regardless of the outcome on this case, Ronin had done his job very well. He deserved to be treated like the king he was, so I lavished all of the love and dog cookies on him that I had. We waited there until the paramedics arrived and then made our way back to the command post, which was far quieter than

W S   Ledger Dispatch, Amador County, Calif.

COUNTY CORONER

Missing Sutter Creek man found dead

By Sean Rabé

SRABE@LEDGER-DISPATCH.COM

A Sutter Creek man missing for over five hours was found dead by the Amador County Search and Rescue team only 250 yards from his house Tuesday evening.

An autopsy for Robert Settlage, 58, has shown he died of a heart attack.

Settlage had apparently gone looking for wild mushrooms near his home on Darling View Court.

When he had not returned after five hours, Amador County Sheriff' officials were called in to locate the missing man. Members of the rescue team, along with bloodhound "Ronin," searched the area for approximately 40 minutes before finding Settlage deceased in a heavily wooded area.

Undersheriff Karl Knobelauch said that there were no indications of trauma or foul play. Earlier in the investigation, he had said his office did not believe Settlage died from ingesting poisonous mushrooms.

"It is not likely he picked some mushrooms, ate them and died that quickly," Knobelauch said. "Wild mushrooms usually attack and kill organs, specifically the kidneys and liver. It is not like a poison where you'd die quickly once you've ingested it. You basically succumb as a result of non-functioning organs."

The cause of Settlage's death was determined after an autopsy was performed Thursday morning.

Clipping from Ledger-Dispatch, Amador County, California. Used with permission.

when we had left it. The search was a success but there was little to celebrate. I dreaded what was to follow.

I packed Ronin away into our patrol vehicle and slowly made my way back to the victim's home. I returned the scent article and met with the man's wife, who had already been given the sad news. I think that she had expected as much and was far more composed than I thought she would be. She was incredibly dignified at that moment—far more than I believe I would have been—although I could see the traces of dried tears around her eyes. She made a point of telling me how much she appreciated everything we had done and followed it up with a thank-you card to Ronin just a few days later.

Thank-you letter from the wife of the missing man to Ronin and me.

The Last Find

R ONIN'S LAST HIGHLY SUCCESSFUL CASE was just a couple of months shy of the time I was hurt on a SWAT obstacle course and our collective careers were simultaneously ended. I knew for a fact that Ronin was starting to slow down then . . . it was perfectly obvious even to me by that time. He had an old injury on his left rear leg that was starting to flare up more and more, and his back seemed to pain him many a night. He didn't like the idea of jumping into the back of the truck anymore and I lifted him each day, but he yearned for the harness all the same. When I put on that old draft-horse-style leather harness and his long lead, Ronin instantly regained his youth and could move mountains. He lived to work, and work was where he was happiest. I am sure now that it was this drive, tenacity, or simple will to do that hurt him so much over the years, but I failed to see all of the subtle signs that his body was hurting because his intensity hid it so well.

In August 2003, a teenage girl was driving her car on Ione–Michigan Bar Road and stopped at a stop sign at the three-way intersection with Highway 16 just west of the Amador County line. As the girl pulled out from the stop sign onto Highway 16, she failed to see another vehicle barreling toward her at an incredibly high speed. The driver of this other car was doing his utmost to evade pursuing police. The resulting collision and fire were horrifying, and a young Amador County woman's life had been lost to the callousness and thoughtlessness of a convicted felon.

The criminal's car was completely disabled, yet he and his passenger were able to jump out and flee the scene while leaving the young woman to her fate in the blazing inferno that they had created. The suspects hopped a barbwire fence and attempted to hide in a hilly, oak-studded cow pasture where they were later captured. Officers at the scene believed that the driver had thrown an object that he didn't want to be caught with; however, that object was never found.

In late August 2003, an Amador County district attorney's investigator asked me if I could use Ronin to find that object. It was now twenty-one days after the fact and in the middle of summer. I doubted seriously that we would find anything associated with the suspects, but due to the gravity of the case, I agreed to help. I didn't think we could find a scent trail of a suspect that late in the game given the environmental conditions. August is one of the hottest months in the Sierra foothills, with temperatures staying in the hundreds for weeks at a stretch. The heat, coupled with almost no humidity, makes running scent trails difficult at best, if not impossible. I told the investigator not to bother with a scent article and that the best thing to do was just use Ronin in an evidence-search mode. If an object had been discarded by the suspect out there, it might still hold human scent, but I doubted that the trail he had walked would.

We met at the scene at 9:00 A.M. and the sun was already starting to beat down. The temperature was up to seventy-five degrees, which meant that by midday, it would be pushing triple digits. We did not have long to work. Nothing was known about the suspect's path of flight into the cow pasture that night. There were no witnesses who saw them jump the fence. We had about eighty acres of ground to cover, and the only possibility of success was to find some evidence of the suspect's physical trail. The starting point was relatively easy due to the scorch marks still on the pavement of Highway 16. After the collision, the suspects had run north into the hills, which meant that they had to have hopped a four-and-a-half-foot field fence about twenty yards from the road. The fence was well stretched, unmarred, and taut to the point that you could bounce a ball off of it. I surmised that if the criminals had climbed the fence, they probably would have left some mark of passage. I started at the car, then moved to the fence and walked the length of it for fifty yards to the east and west. Just east of the collision site, I found bent wires on the fence, indicating that someone heavy had stepped on it in several places. It was the only place on the fence quite like it; therefore, I was fairly confident this was the spot where they had crossed.

I put Ronin over onto the north side of the fence and took the short lead off of his collar. When working in an evidence-search mode, Ronin ran unencumbered by me and was free to roam as he would. I allowed him to stay out up to around thirty yards in front of me when I would call him back and cast him in a new direction with hand and arm signals. My command to search was simple: "Find it." As soon as the district attorney's investigator was over the fence with me, I started Ronin on his search.

I sent Ronin into a patch of grease brush just north of the fence, figuring that the suspects had run straight for the hills and trees. I didn't have too much choice in the matter because the entire hillside was covered in the stuff. Grease brush is a nasty weed with yellow flowers and dark, viscous oil that permeates the stems and leaves. This oil is incredibly sticky, acting like flypaper when it gets on the skin. In less than 100 yards Ronin's legs, flanks, neck, and muzzle were so black that he looked like he was coated in tar. Twigs, leaves, and dirt were sticking to the oil so that his lower body became camouflaged and matched the grass and weeds through which he was running. Instead of laughing at his comical appearance, I groaned with the thought of giving him a bath when we got home; turpentine has a hard time cutting through that grease.

We were into the search for about fifteen minutes and the temperature was already up to eighty-five degrees. It was incredibly dry, and I could tell that Ronin was getting thirsty as his tongue hung down to his chest and he was panting heavily. The grease brush coating his hide didn't help the situation, and I'm sure that it was acting like another layer of insulation that he did not need. I called him back and let him drink out of my canteen, then poured the rest down his muzzle, neck, and ears. I hoped that this might cool him down and keep him working efficiently for a little longer. The cool water added some lightness to Ronin's step, and he waddled off to clear some more of the field.

I had mentally created a grid for the field that we were working and tried to work Ronin into the wind of each block on the grid. As he cleared one, we'd move onto another. When working an evidence search with a dog, it is important to keep the wind in the dog's favor as much as possible. The object of the search emits a small amount of odor as it is, but this odor is finite and diminishes with age. Unlike a human who constantly sheds thousands of cells per second, what is left on the hidden object is very small in comparison. If there is no wind or the dog is working with it, he may have to literally stumble over the object to find it. If the wind is blowing toward the dog, there is always the chance that a small amount of odor from the object might become airborne and therefore be detectable by the dog from a distance.

Initially, the wind was coming from the eastern hills to the west, but as the sun rose higher into the sky, the wind shifted to its normal easterly flow. I switched Ronin to a westerly search pattern as the wind shifted. As soon as I made the change, Ronin seemed to detect something in the breeze. His nose came up off of the ground for a moment, and I could see his whiskers twitching as he smelled something not too far ahead of us. The object was fairly close, because he did not zigzag as he normally would have for a distant object. Instead, he ran right to it just a few yards away. He nudged something in the two-foot-tall grass, sat, and looked back at me. Ronin looked at the ground in front of him again and hesitantly pawed it, then looked back at me once more. His normal behavior was to react with quite a bit more vigor, so I was confused about his timidity with whatever it was that he had found. I walked up to him and moved the grass aside, exposing a black fabric pouch on the ground. I smiled hugely and praised Ronin big time. I gave him a bunch of Scooby snacks and told him that he was the best dog in the world. Ronin obviously didn't think too much of the pouch, because as soon as he was done with his Scoobies, he decided that some piles of fresh cow poop were far more interesting.

I can only equate Ronin's lack of a strong alert to the age of the article he had found. It had been sitting in the hot, dry field for almost a month. Some human scent was obviously still on it, but it had to be slight. Ronin's feat was truly amazing. This was by far the oldest evidence item we had ever found on a search. The investigator recovered the pouch and looked at its contents with latex-gloved hands. The first item we discovered was a California identification card belonging to the suspect. Bingo—we had found what we were looking for. I never learned exactly what the importance of that pouch was, but it was apparently an important item for the suspect's ultimate manslaughter conviction.

The End of an Amazing Career

RONIN AND I HAD, OVER THE YEARS, WORKED IN EVERY CONDITION imaginable, and it was starting to show on Ronin. Always a very proud dog, I could see that he hated not being as strong and fast as he once had been. This was most evident when we were training with all of the young up-and-coming dogs. Ronin's back legs were starting to lose a lot of strength, probably from a spinal injury that he had received and that I had never caught when he was young. He would do his best on every search and would never quit, but you could tell that it cost him a little more each and every time. I should have started another dog a few years before this point, because I knew the day would come when I had to retire Ronin. However, I just couldn't bring myself to do it. We had been a team so long that I didn't think I could work with another dog—at least in the same way.

Apparently, Fate was listening to my inner thoughts and decided that the best way to handle things was to knock me off the street at the same time it did Ronin. I was trying out for our SWAT team in Amador County one fine November morning in 2004, running through an obstacle course that I knew I was going to ace. I had practiced for every facet of it for six months and was smoking it so far. The last section of the course was a place where I was supposed to run through a door, across a graveled area about ten feet across, and leap an eight-foot wall—easier said than done.

This wall had given me fits in the past. Normally, I would have had little problem negotiating it, but add the weight of a flack vest, helmet, firearms, and other accoutrements, and I was sporting about thirty pounds of gear after running a half mile that was spread out with all

From left to right: Morgan, Kalliroh, and Ronin at home in Plymouth, California.

kinds of other nasty physical tests. I had failed this portion of the test one time before, and I was damned if it was going to happen again. I had trained for this event. I had practiced the wall by running up to the right side and jumping in a basketball player's lay-up style, kind of catapulting myself up with power from my left leg, then throwing my right leg over the lip to help pull myself up and over.

Well, I made it through the door just fine and sprinted across the gravel separating me from the upcoming wall. I had all of this played out

Ronin and his puppy basenji, Aru, about eight months before Ronin passed away.

in my mind as I went for the lay-up. I compressed myself into a half crouch and fired off with all of the strength I could muster on my left leg. My quad contracted and exploded with energy and a "crack" that sounded like a lightning bolt. The next thing I discovered was that I was on my back, and my left leg was contorted in a weird fashion that I can't quite explain. Thinking only that I had to get up, I tried to gather my left leg underneath myself so that I could get up and start moving again. The problem was that the lower part of my left leg wouldn't move . . . and then the pain hit me. I have never felt anything to this day quite like what I felt that morning. It was excruciating.

Both Ronin and Kalli loved their basenjis and allowed them all kinds of transgressions.

The next thing I remember was being surrounded by my buddies, some encouraging me to get up, while a couple of others were making some wisecracks. I was yelling at this point, and one of the guys ripped open my pant leg. All of the joking and encouragement stopped. My kneecap was no longer where it was supposed to be. It was now centered nicely somewhere at the lower end of my quad. I don't remember much, because I couldn't look at it more than once.

The ambulance came, along with some morphine that I didn't think I needed but that somehow got injected anyway, and I was off into La La Land. The next year was kind of a blur because of several surgeries and lots of medication. Suffice it to say that I was not working dogs anymore.

Apparently, I had a 100 percent rupture of the patellar tendon that caused my kneecap to slingshot out of position. I had also busted the kneecap in half and broken off a piece of the top of my femur. There were other complications, but, to make a long story short, I had multiple surgeries and spent about three years rehabbing myself. I also lost my job.

The calls for Ronin kept coming in, though. I couldn't respond to any of them even if I had wanted to. There was one case where an Earth's Liberation Front member had firebombed a new apartment complex that was just being finished. The man started a fire for the sake of the planet, spray painted some graffiti, and didn't seem to think about the people in the apartments when he did it. I couldn't run with Ronin on this case, but I did farm him out to a local search-and-rescue friend to handle in my stead.

I told Mike to just hang on and not talk. Mike did well, and Ronin led them to a nice patch of poison oak and to a dirt parking spot nearby with a beautiful set of fresh car tracks exiting the area. Based on the degree of effort required to get through the patch of poison oak, I deduced that the suspect was going to have the worst rash imaginable. The trail had ended rather abruptly with the parking spot; however, I had a bit of intel to hand off to the FBI agent working the case. I told the agent that, if his team interviewed a suspect in the next couple of weeks, to be on the lookout for a very bad rash. The next day I received a call from the agent in charge, and he told me that I was never going to believe it. He said they had just booked a guy with the worst case of poison oak you would ever see!

I was struggling at this point with a lot of issues aside from rehab and surgeries. I had lost my identity and wasn't working Ronin. These two factors took their toll on me, and I wish I would have recognized it when it was happening. Ronin really began to slow down once we stopped working. He spent lots of time sleeping and very little time doing much else. In many ways, it was as if he just didn't care much anymore; I know

I didn't. I didn't understand it at the time, but dogs like Ronin simply need to have a job. Without one, they are shadows of their former selves. In many ways, I was suffering from the same malaise—the pot calling the kettle black. The final blow was the cancer diagnosis for Ronin and the fact that surgery was really not an option. He was tough as a trooper and fought with every bit of his being, but I could see that he was starting to slip away from me.

Epilogue

I T IS JULY 2007 NOW, and the coat hanger on the wall is still the special place for Ronin's leather slip collar and badge. It is displayed as proudly today as it was throughout our careers. I look at that collar most days, and although the pain of Ronin's death has subsided somewhat, I still feel a constriction in my throat while taking a deep breath to forestall the tears each and every time I remember various events, some of which I wrote in this book. The leather is ten years worn yet is still soft and pliable today. It maintains a variety of scars and stains, each of which holds a particular memory of their making. This invariably leads to a smile or a soft chuckle. I often take the collar from the wall, putting it to my nose just so that I can smell his scent upon it. Through the neat's-foot oil that I used to protect it, Ronin's essence lingers in the leather, as I hope it always will. The collar's place on the hanger is a permanent memorial to my Ronin. No words are inscribed there, and the average person might never know what that collar means to me, but perhaps that is how it should be. Ronin's life was vibrant yet humble. He was happiest when working or with me . . . he needed nothing more, and I miss him terribly.

Ronin's long lead still finds service even to this day. I bring it with me each and every time I teach a K-9 trailing school in various parts of the country. The lead is strong yet softer and more pliable than the day I bought it so many years ago. I remember how tough it was to learn how to wield that thirty-foot length of rolled bull hide. In the early days of our training, I would constantly struggle with it, tangling it in and around trees, bushes, fences, and Ronin's legs. A thirty-foot lead is difficult to master, but once you attain proficiency, it becomes the best tool

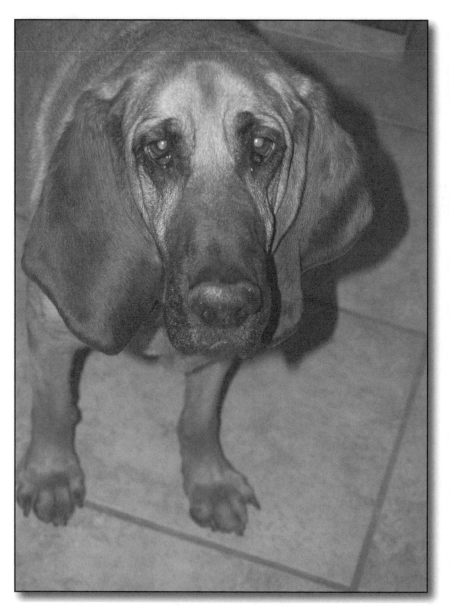

Ronin a couple of weeks before he passed away.

to allow a dog the freedom he needs to move and work while you still are able to maintain a modicum of control. I allow new handlers to try it on for size and laugh a little with their own first-time struggles, as I am reminded so strongly of how I, myself, once was. I doubt that I will ever wield this length of leather ever again in any manner other than demonstration.

Ronin's leather harness is now worn by another worthy bloodhound. I couldn't bear to see it hang idly, as such a simple yet memorable tool should stay in public service as long as possible. It always reminded me of Superman's cape or Captain America's red, white, and blue shield— not simply an old tool meant to be stowed away in a forgotten drawer

Ronin's harness, now worn by Matt Broad's Morgan.

Jeff's students, from left to right: Kevin Baughn and Zak; Matt Broad and Morgan; Jessie Grant and Athena.

in the garage when its bearer passed on, but more a symbol of an iconic dog who changed my life and the lives of many others forever. I passed Ronin's harness on to my very good friend and fellow bloodhound handler, Matt Broad. There is no better heir apparent than Matt's bloodhound, Morgan. I have worked with the pair for the last couple of years and am amazed at what an admirable team they make. Matt works as a deputy sheriff bloodhound handler for the county of San Mateo. Matt and Morgan are creating their own legacy now, and I couldn't have found a better home for Ronin's harness.

It took three long, hard years to regain some semblance of the strength and balance I once had, and my left leg will never be quite the same as it once was. The injury I sustained on that obstacle course was devastating and ended my law-enforcement career forever. It also made it difficult, if not impossible, to run at the end of a long lead with anything much bigger than a basset hound. I find that statement rather ironic, for one of my other early mentors was fond of remarking on his age and declining physical ability and had said much the same thing about his dog-working future. I also find it remarkable that my police career really began with Ronin and ended with him as well. There is little in my life today that compares to the excitement of my work with Ronin. I understand now that many of the brutal cases we investigated over the years had an impact on me emotionally, yet I yearn, still, for the excitement and adrenalin that such work carried with it.

Ernest Hemingway wrote:

Certainly, there is no hunting
Like the hunting of man,
And, those who have hunted armed men,
And like it.
Never really care for anything else thereafter.

I remember reading that quote at Kat Albrecht's home many years ago and was immediately struck by the truth of it. Those words were very powerful then and are absolutely haunting now. There is nothing in my life today that holds my desire and interest quite like the work I did with Ronin. I stay connected to the law-enforcement trailing world by training new handlers for the job. It is not the same as actually working my own dog, but I do enjoy watching their progress, and there is also a certain vicarious thrill when I hear stories of their own exploits on the job.

I worked quite a few child abduction and homicide cases over my years with Ronin, and my long-term goal was to provide a resource on a national scale for just these situations. I did not write about many of these cases in this book because they were haunting. The feeling I got from them was too brutal and, frankly, I just cannot relive those times right now. Perhaps one story haunts me more than all of the others, and maybe that's the real reason why I get writer's block. Ronin and I had been called out to search for a young girl in Pittsburgh, California, one evening. She had gone missing from a local church dance, and the only item discovered was her shoe on the side of the highway a couple of miles west of the church. Ronin trailed to a business that had lots of wooden pallets stacked against a fence with guard dogs on the other side. Ronin would not leave the place and shut down on me. I was absolutely convinced that he was stuck on the dogs, and I pulled him off. I tried to start him up again but he would have nothing to do with it. I even called Judy on to work the trail with her bloodhound Kalli with much the same result. We gave up and decided to try again the next day.

I received a call that they had found the little girl's body under the pallets to which Ronin had led us. I was dumbstruck and sick to my stomach all at the same time. I'm not sure if she could have been alive at the time we were there, and I could never bring myself to ask that question of anyone. I live with that on my conscience to this day.

I am a little melancholy and nostalgic about bloodhounds and what they have meant to me over the years. When I came up in this business, it was the beginning of the computer age and Google search-type engines. You still had to communicate by the normal means of verbal conversation, but information was just becoming available on a massive scale. Yet, bloodhound work was still personal and one-on-one. Not that many active handlers were out there. Or, if there were, it was impossible to find out anything about them, let alone call them. I was lucky enough to have been taken under the wings of some truly great ones, however. My handling education was more of an apprenticeship program than a formal education. Sure, there were plenty of seminars and classes on the subject and I went to all of them, but they were relatively disorganized. My real education came from the veteran handlers who snapped a wrinkle in my butt and made sure that I did things right.

Ronin's sister, Kalli, learning that she did not like water very much.

Kat Albrecht was my original mentor, and I owe her everything. Without her help, we never would have made it to where we did. There were others, though—all with tales of courage, hope, and loss of their own. I owe them all as well. Some of the original masters of our era with whom I had the opportunity to work were Glenn Rimbey, Bill Tolhurst, Jerry Yelk, Larry Harris, Al Nelson, Jerry Nichols, John Lutenberg, John Salem, Brian Joyner, and Morey Tripp. All of these people taught me everything I could soak up, and my handling style is nothing more than variations on their themes.

Sadly, some of the old-timers in the art of bloodhound handling are slowly leaving us. Their stories are more numerous than mine, and unfortunately, we probably will never have a chance to hear them. Most

Ronin and Aru shortly before Ronin passed away. Ru doted on Ronin constantly, all the way to the end.

were humble and quiet but infused with a burning desire to find people who were often thought to be lost forever. This is truly the link that bound us all.

I am trying to carry on their legacies by training in the fashion by which they trained me. I feel that the apprenticeship program is the best way to train a bloodhound handler. The trailing job is the most difficult K-9 business of all, and it takes an incredible amount of energy and patience to do a good job. Without the guiding hand of a mentor like Kat, we would have never made that first find in Gilroy, California, or any others, for that matter. I'm not sure if this type of training exists quite the way it used to, but I hope to pass it on in my own way.

The stories you have read are all real cases with as much factual detail as I could muster. They account for only a fraction of the incidents to which we responded over the years. Some stories are better left untold, buried in dusty boxes or file cabinets at various police or sheriff's departments, hopefully never to be experienced again.

Appendix:
Trailing Versus Tracking

THE FOLLOWING ARTICLE WAS RECENTLY USED in The State of California versus Deshawn Lee Campbell, docket # CC12649—a homicide trial where the victim was San Jose Police Officer Jeffrey Fontana. The Honorable Judge Northway at the Santa Clara County Superior Court heard this 402b motion on February 19, 2009; this was a motion to determine the foundation of proffered evidence.

A bloodhound, Zak, was used in this case to trail the suspect after he fled the scene. The K-9 evidence for this case was accepted after testimony by the K-9 handler, San Jose Officer Kevin Baughn, and myself as a witness for the discipline of trailing and scent evidence. This hearing was significant because, according to Judge Northway, the verbiage of "trailing" had not been used in the few California precedents where K-9s had been used to follow the scent of a suspect; the verbiage used historically had been "tracking." The judge determined that the definitions of the two disciplines were significantly different; therefore, the separation was necessary. Judge Northway has submitted this material to the California Association of Judges for rules concerning jury instruction.

The title is commensurate to its standing in various K-9 circles, debate, and conflict. There are purists on both sides with exceptional backgrounds and knowledge in both respected fields. Be that as it may, I believe that police K-9 manhunts of the future will be ultimately based on training philosophies regarding trailing. Why might I take such a position? Simple—trailing is ultimately and historically the much more effective method of locating humans with K-9.

K-9 TRAILING VERSUS TRACKING: A DEFINITION

By Jeffrey Hampton Schettler

To understand the conflict between the two methods, origins of the methods must be examined. The title of "tracking" comes from the visual art of locating sign or spoor of a subject through visual means and following it to a logical conclusion. Tracking was later used by early K-9 pioneers as a simple term to identify a complex canid behavior while working for man. Tracking is an easy way to describe what we see occurring when a dog chases a human or other prey animal via scent.

Early handlers took this belief system and adapted it to a series of training regimens that currently define the status of many modern police "tracking" programs, even though our current understanding of scent theory has evolved exponentially.

There are many variations on the same theme of "tracking," but ultimately they all have a similar definition: the dog's nose in the tracks made by a human on a soft surface. Once the paradigm shifts to that of a hard surface, such as any street in any modern urban jungle, the ability of the police K-9 to follow now-invisible footsteps is almost erased. This is not because of the breed or the dog's ability, but rather the nature of the training to which the K-9 has been subjected.

The theory behind tracking is generally twofold: (1) the footstep that caused the ground disturbance is the odor that the dogs follow, and/or (2) the footsteps are the location where human odor is most concentrated. It is easy to see why many early trainers felt this way. They trained on nothing but soft surfaces in relatively fresh conditions; thus, perception was reality—the dog's nose hovered close to the actual track of the human. Consequently, training regimens were created to subscribe to the training philosophy. If the dog's nose strayed from the prescribed height above the track, the dog's nose was promptly forced back into it without anyone ever examining the reasons for the behavioral change to begin with. It was automatically presumed that the dog was outside of odor. Many people believe that the dog must be within inches of the track to actually smell the odor. I believe that this perception came from our own scent-limited world and false rationalization. Nothing could be further from the truth, as simple tests have proven time and again that most dogs can detect odor from a fixed location and from a variety of distances—from inches to yards and more. You must simply ponder this one question: If it is proven that a dog can detect odor from either ground disturbance or from the human that created it, and from more than mere inches of the physical track, why must a dog's nose be forced into said track? I equate this with forcing a dog to smell his own feces when he soils the carpet of the house; it is bad practice.

Now let's look at what happens to human scent when the paradigm shifts. Step from the freshly plowed field of the corn farmer to his gravel road right next door. If you are lucky enough to see the track from the onset and, furthermore, can detect the faint changes of rock discoloration from the rocks' once sun-warmed face to its now darkened earthly bottom, then perhaps you might be able to determine the track and direction of travel of the human who tread there. Better yet, change the farmer's gravel road to the highway beside it. The track disappears, and it is now impossible to place the dog's nose into it. With that being said, the hard-surface trail rarely pans out for the average police K-9; that is a shame.

Trailing, although it is a relatively modern term, actually has its roots in English and early American history when bloodhounds were used to hunt criminals, and, in the case of our original colonies, Native Americans who were in conflict with early settlers. The hounds were "scented" on a particular human odor and allowed the freedom to follow that scent wherever it might lead. This information can actually be found in original colonial want ads in which colonists were looking for bloodhounds.

Trailing is a descriptive word for the art of allowing a dog to follow human scent wherever human scent might be—on the ground or in the air. It can also be taken one step further by adding scent discrimination to the equation. Each and every animal, human or otherwise, produces a distinctive odor based on species and other sub-determining factors such as infirmity, relative age, sex, and certain individual identifying traits. The amount of odor produced is dependent upon several primary factors: mental condition, such as fear or anger; exertion; and relative health issues. Frankly, some people simply smell more than others to our dogs. The more they smell, the better!

Unlike a tracking dog, a trailing dog is allowed more freedom of movement and, more important, a certain amount of independence. Independence in a police dog is normally considered an oxymoron; however, it is crucial to understand that scent is the dog's world, and there is a very good possibility that the dog might have a better grasp on locating it than humans do. Our job as handlers is to simply interpret their actions and hang on accordingly. This does not mean that the dog is allowed to go about his business in any fashion he sees fit; rather, it is a partnership based on mutual understanding of limitations and individual ability.

The Nature of Human Scent on the Trail

To understand trailing, a handler must become a student of scent theory in ways that are not normally considered. Each and every environmental or man-made condition has an impact on human odor and how the dog might detect it. Each element must be considered and evaluated not only before, but also as the dog works. Trailing might be a constant trail of human odor from one point to another, or it might be a complex game of connecting obscure scent "dots" in various locations to reach a conclusion. The ability of the dog to follow this "trail" is dependent upon his training and innate physical traits.

Trailing takes into consideration the fact that scent does not stay put in the "track" of the subject hunted, especially on hard surfaces. Depending on the conditions, human scent from a walking subject could easily travel hundreds of yards or more. It is illogical to force a dog to follow a scent path that simply might not exist anymore in the place where it originally fell.

Take, for example, an extremely hot, dry, windy day in the middle of any downtown city in America. There is little vegetation, if any, and the heat can be seen radiating off of the surface of the blacktop like a fast-order chef's grill. The heat of the blacktop itself is a reflector and destroyer of scent, and the scent will not stay where it falls, if it falls at all. Instead, the scent particles are dispersed by wind, heat waves, and physical manipulation to any barrier that might catch them. Barriers such as any moisture-bearing object—e.g., vegetation—attract scent particles more. It is my theory that scent particles, rafts, or whatever you might call them, have a tendency to be hydrophilic. They are attracted to moisture and cool places that are high in oxygen content. The reason for this is that any biological matter is subject to forces of biological breakdown. Carbon-based matter, or human particles that produce scent, are subject to the same aerobic type of bacterial action as any similar matter. As the matter degrades, so, too, does its odor. I believe that the odor also changes or "ages" as it degrades.

In locations with little to no vegetation, scent will still collect in areas that might keep it from moving or being destroyed. Cool, shady areas hold scent far better than flat, open tracks of hard surfaces that are subject to the sun's radiation or human manipulation. Certain gases, such as carbon monoxide, appear to have a negative effect on scent as well.

A scent trail is not something that can be determined by sight; rather, it is invisible and interpreted by reading a dog's physical reaction to its presence or lack thereof. Being able to read a dog when he is working is one thing; however, handlers often become tangled when they are reading a dog that is not on scent—or, more important, when he is not on the scent on which he was started. The ease with which a police K-9 can switch scent trails—animal or human—unbeknownst to the handler is absolutely uncanny unless the handler has a unique understanding of his or her dog's subtle behavioral changes when he jumps trail. Humans are visually oriented, and our natural habit is to rationalize things from a visual standpoint. Thus, when I discuss the nature of human odor, I like to find a way to make it visible, even if for only a moment and within our imagination. Picture, if you will, a person standing alone in the middle of a grassy park holding a red smoke grenade—red being the color that identifies this person above all others. If there is any wind at all, the red smoke will drift with the wind and collect against any object that might hold it, such as a small valley, a tree, or even blades of grass. As this person walks or moves about, so does the smoke trail. Changes in conditions, such as more or less wind, rain, high heat, or humidity, all have an effect on the scent trail to a greater or lesser extent.

Now let's add another human with a different color of smoke grenade who walks and mingles with the other person's scent trail. Both scents may still stay visibly separate, yet a clear division will be difficult to determine. Complicate this further with yet another person and then another. There might come a point when it is almost impossible to separate one color from another. Dogs, I believe, face the very same dilemma but in a different context. Rather than visualizing a scent trail, they smell it. Who has the easier job?

I like to keep the above scenarios in mind when I am training a new dog for trailing. One person, and perhaps, even two, can be easy for most dogs to negotiate through during early training sessions. However, adding a city street into the mix with thousands or millions of unknown scents can be a nightmare for any dog regardless of how good the scent might be. Trailing training is best done in small, easy steps with a clear goal in mind.

Trailing is often considered synonymous with scent discrimination, or the ability for a dog to detect an individual human odor amongst many. There are numerous schools of thought regarding this issue. Some people believe that dogs do not have this ability and instead work on a basis of the freshest "track" out of an area. In order to properly debate this subject I'd need to write an entire book. Suffice it to say, I believe that all canids have the ability to discriminate scent, and this is what sets them apart in our natural world as superb hunters. However, I do not believe that this ability is always 100 percent accurate. There are forces on the trail of prey that can confuse and distract a dog. This is especially true when a dog is required to wade through the melting pot of human aroma in the middle of suburbia or a downtown city street. The degree to which the dog works is commensurate with his training and native traits or prey drive.

The Scent Article

The key to scent discrimination, or ensuring that your canine locates and follows the desired trail, is dependent upon many factors, the primary one being (in my opinion) the scent article used to start the trail. A scent article is the object that holds a specific human's odor or scent. The scent article most often identified with this type of work is clothing of some sort. However, anything that a human has touched, held, or been in the vicinity of might be able to be used as a scent article. The average human may shed hundreds to thousands of scent particles per second, depending on his or her level of exertion, emotional state, and physical condition. The simple act of hovering over an object might impregnate it with human odor. It takes very little contact or exposure for an object to become a scent article. It also takes very little effort for the same object to be contaminated by other human odor, thus becoming a problem for any handler.

In the case of a crime scene, it might be rather difficult to determine what object, if any, is relatively uncontaminated yet still solid enough to be used to target your dog. The biggest problem normally encountered is when investigating officers contaminate the crime scene. There is generally a small window of opportunity to locate, protect, and utilize a suspect's scent to your advantage. Preferably, the handler should be the first one on the scene to discover and collect an appropriate article. In the absence of this luxury, knowledgeable first responders can also fill the niche. More often than not, everything at a scene might be contaminated. In this case, it is important to remember who was present at the scene and who had contact with the intended scent article. There is a method for using a contaminated article called "missing member." This is where the dog is allowed to pre-scent on the people who have been at the scene and differentiate between their scent and that of the missing person(s). My experience with missing member is extensive yet inconclusive. I have found it to be a necessary tool with a contaminated scene yet not wholly reliable. This might be due to other scent intangibles that were present on or around the article or to factors that investigators were just not sure of. Regardless, I have found success with this method, and I believe that it should be practiced when scent articles are seriously contaminated.

The scent article is not always necessary for a trail to be successful, but it is a useful tool that a handler should always be able to identify and employ. The "place last seen" is not always a good starting point, because the freshest trail could be that of an investigator or bystander. The use of a scent article is a highly sensitive subject, and solid scent-collection training is essential for proper utilization. At minimum, a handler should always keep in mind the sensitivity of a canine's nose and how little scent is really required for detection. If a handler maintains this mindset, he or she will be far more likely to collect uncontaminated articles and have successful trails.

Small- to medium-size scent articles need to be protected at all costs if they are to be used to start a trailing dog. I like to keep an inventory of various-size, heavy-duty Zip-Lock bags in my patrol car at all times. Paper bags just don't work because they are far too permeable, and any object inside quickly becomes contaminated. If an object is too sensitive due to evidentiary value to be moved and handled by a K-9 handler, the next best bet is to extract scent from the object. I also keep a supply of sterile four-by-four-inch gauze pads in my trunk at all times. Scent is easily transferred from most objects to the pad by simply placing the pad on the object and letting it sit for a few moments. A scent article does not have to be a movable or baggable object; it can be fixed in place, like a windowsill, a car seat, or the front-door knob to a residence. It might even be another human being. Take, for example, the scene of a strong-armed robbery in any city center where the victim was physically assaulted before being robbed. Nothing was left behind other than the odor of the suspect on the body or clothing of the victim. A person who has been touched by another person can be a scent article, too. This is not an easy method, but it can work.

Once a trailing dog is trained to discriminate scent and follow individual trails among many, it becomes increasingly important to stay cognizant of the viability of a particular scent article. It is absolutely crucial to understand that, if there is an article with several human odors on it and these particular people were all in the area where you are starting your dog, it is a crapshoot as to which one the dog might follow. Invariably, it seems that the dog will always take the freshest associated trail out or the one that is the most scent exciting. Fear or other scent that is emotionally charged comes immediately to mind. I think that this is often the reason why many traditional tracking-style K-9 handlers give up on scent-discrimination trailing practices. They find that their dogs work best on the freshest trail out or the one associated with strong emotion. Many handlers never take into consideration the sensitive nature of a scent article and how easily it can become contaminated. The scent article must have the overwhelming odor of the subject, and the subject's scent trail must be within the area in which the dog is started, if the dog is going to be successful. An extremely large part of our trailing training regimen is strictly on the nature of human scent, collection, preservation, and presentation.

Equipment

The quality and nature of the equipment used by a handler are critical. This is especially true if the K-9 team becomes proficient in trailing. Invariably, when this occurs, the call outs for service become more numerous and the types of trails more extreme—especially regarding distance. I can remember many trails that ran more than ten miles that were not only taxing on my body but also ruinous of my equipment. Within short order, I had changed to items that were stronger and more lasting. Also of importance was the ease with which everything was used. If I had trouble putting it on my dog in the dark with no light, I didn't use it.

The two most crucial pieces of K-9 equipment for a trailing dog are the long lead and the harness. A trailing dog must have a harness and never be run strictly on a collar. The intensity of the work, coupled with duration, would place far too much strain on the dog's neck and create health problems. I also think that, when the harness goes on a police K-9, it is a signal that the trailing job and no other is about to begin.

I prefer long leads of twenty to thirty feet that many consider far too long for control. I beg to differ and offer this instead. Any high-drive patrol dog has a tendency to work at a fast pace when he is allowed to trail rather than track. If the dog is not offered a modicum of freedom to operate, the weight of the handler becomes nothing more than a distraction and an anchor, increasing the probability of losing the trail, especially in an urban environment. A long, thirty-foot lead gives the handler the ability to allow the dog as much as thirty feet of freedom in large, open areas that can be narrowed down to just a few feet if safety becomes a concern. It is a simple matter of reeling in and reeling out. I equate it to catching a large trophy fish on a rod and a reel. There are times to let the fish have some backing, and there are other times when you need to strip line back in. The problem with most people is that they don't practice enough with the long lead to become comfortable with it. They ultimately switch back to a shorter line and bounce back and forth like a proverbial pinball. The keys to success are lead control and lots of practice.

Interestingly, my equipment came full circle to an old-school style reminiscent of the era of the turn-of-the-century manhunter. I started off with a harness that incorporated a narrow, wool-covered chest pad and a nylon, thirty-foot lead. I quickly learned that long, arduous trails through thick brush collected tons of burrs and nettles in the chest pad that rubbed my dog raw. Since my K-9 was a high-drive, fast-moving monster, the nylon lead burned many a groove into my soon-to-be-calloused hand. If the lead did that to my hand, I wondered what a nylon harness would do to my dog.

Ultimately, I changed the harness to a fairly large draft-horse-style, leather contraption that appeared bulky and difficult but turned out to be incredibly comfortable for my dogs and easy to put on. The breast pad was made of double-thick, twelve-ounce leather that was very wide yet smooth, spreading the force of resistance over a large surface area on my dog's chest and thereby reducing fatigue and skin abrasion. I switched to a leather thirty-food lead made out of rolled fourteen- to sixteen-ounce bull hide. This type of leather is rare and highly sought after. It is powerfully strong and resilient yet gives the handler a good connection to the dog. It does not knot easily, and, more important, it doesn't burn my hand when leather is rifled through a loose grip if my dog decides to open up full bore.

The cost of the lead fifteen years ago was $150, and the harness I made myself. It is difficult to find the lead leather that I am writing about now, but from what I understand, the Amish might still produce it. My understanding is that the original intent of this type of leather was for belt drives for very large, industrial-type sewing machines that are no longer in existence. I have three of these leads, varying in age from ten to fourteen years. They are as strong and pliant today as they were when I bought them. None of my other leads have ever come close to the quality of my bull hide leads. I make the harnesses myself now, but a fair price from any saddle maker would be about $200.

Many people might question the need for such strength and expense when it comes to trailing equipment for a dog, but I have discovered that you get what you pay for in this world. When it comes to the life-and-death work of a trailing police dog, no expense is too great. For my own equipment, I soon learned that lighter was better. If I anticipated that the trail I was about to run was going to be long and difficult, I carried very little. I always carried in my patrol car trunk a stripped-down pistol belt that contained my side arm, an extra magazine, and a canteen. I swapped this gear for my traditional Sam Browne leather that I always wore on patrol. Later, I switched to a Camelbak-type backpack for water. Boots were always important, and I had to be able to run in them for long distances and not get footsore. I quickly learned that appearance meant nothing and that only my own physical comfort should be considered. If I became tired or sore a short way into any trail, my ability to read my dog was compromised. Needless to say, traditional wool uniforms are horrible to wear for running. Polyester and cotton blends are far more comfortable. Of course, what an officer carries in the field is personal preference coupled with his or her agency's general orders.

First on the Scene

The best situation for a trailing team is to be first on the scene. If the K-9 handler has the luxury of arriving right off the bat, he or she will have the opportunity to quickly scan the scene and determine all of the factors that will affect the dog in a positive or negative way. It is nice to know how many people have been there and what they have done before you start your dog. If you know these factors, you will ultimately spend far less time following trails made by other people before you arrived. You will also have the opportunity to prep your scene for your job ahead.

Be aware of your surroundings and how they might have an impact on distracting your dog from working, be they scent, sight, or sound. If, for example, neighborhood dogs are creating a racket and might pose a distraction in case your trail runs right by them, see if there is some possibility of getting them put up for a little while.

If cops are working the scene, such as canvassing the neighborhood, see if you can slow things down a bit or even momentarily suspend them while you get your dog started and out onto the trail. If the K-9 has scent and happens to find a trail out, the investigation can get fired right back up again. There is nothing better than a good, scent-discriminating, trailing dog to help find evidence anyway, and the chance of disturbing evidence already present is minimal with a savvy handler. On the other hand, there is nothing more embarrassing than not knowing who has done what and where they might have walked. There are times when a well-meaning investigating officer will inadvertently touch or contaminate your intended scent article and leave his or her own scent trail out of the area. If the officer was the freshest scent on the article and has the freshest trail out of the scene, your dog will follow the officer. I know this for a fact, as I have done it—several times.

If you do not have the luxury of being on the scene immediately, ask someone in charge about those who have come and gone, where have they been, and, if possible, what they were doing. Better yet, if everyone is still present, give your dog a chance to smell each person before you start your trail. It is not difficult and can occur in a matter of a few seconds.

My technique when I arrive on the scene is to quickly obtain the overall story about how the crime evolved without getting into too many details. I do like to know directions of travel and certain witness statements as long as they are correct. Contrary to popular belief, witnesses do lie, often to suit their own ego or just to make an impression with police. Sometimes the information can be nefarious, and the "witness" is nothing more than an accomplice. I take all statements from witnesses with a grain of salt and read my dog's behavior for signs of the true exit trail. I have had cases where everyone, including other officers, insisted that the trail went one direction while my dog went another. If my dog is exhibiting body language that I can articulate, and it indicates that he has the scent of the person I started him on, I will follow my dog every time.

Once I know the general situation, I next look for my best possible scent article, collect it if possible, bag it, tag it, and keep it protected. If anyone touched my article, I try to make sure that they are present when I start my dog. In so doing, I stand a far better chance of finding my suspect's trail.

After I know what happened and have my scent article, I then canvass the scene to make sure that there are no hazards or distractions for my dog. If there are, I eliminate them or minimize them. The last thing I do is give my dog a break and let him canvass the area himself. This is a good time for him to void his bladder and allow him a chance to scent-inventory the scene. If time permits, I like to give my trailing dog several minutes to peruse the area with his nose before we start. The dog will do this anyway, so by allowing him to check things before I start to work, I actually end up saving time and distractions. I try to make one full circuit around the scene with my dog on a short lead and by the collar and then walk him by each and every person still there. This does not have to be over a prescribed length of time and can actually occur relatively quickly and at a trot.

It is important to watch the dog very carefully during this circuit, because, depending upon the nature of the crime and how emotionally charged it was, the suspect may have left a trail that stands out above all others. We may be walking along and suddenly my dog gives a quick little head pop in one particular direction. I catalogue this reaction but do not encourage it just yet. We are not working yet and the trail has not begun. The head pop could indeed, be an indication of a suspect's direction of travel, but it could also be my dog's best cop buddy; catalogue but do not encourage.

The starting point to scent your dog can be tricky. Many people believe that the best place is directly where the suspect was known to have been. This may not always be easy for the dog from a physical and/or scent perspective. The scent situation is often the worst situation. If the "place last seen" (PLS), is the suspect's home or a location that he or she frequents, large amounts of the suspect's scent may saturate the area. It is nothing more than a huge scent pool and could have many exit points with varying degrees of age. This can be confusing for even the best trailing dog. When the area is super-saturated with the target's odor, it is not as simple as finding the freshest trail out. The lines are blurred, and it might take a significant amount of time for a dog to work through all of it. There is also a chance that the dog just might not work through it. The common denominator for a dog not finding his way out of a large scent pool, or out of a distracting one, is simply due to the training regimen to which he was exposed. More often than not, handlers work their dogs in relatively "clean" areas or the same areas, over and over again. Very rarely are scent scenarios set up mimicking crime scenes that the dogs will be expected to work through later. Once my trailing dog is proficient with the basic skills of his craft, all of our future training is done with scent contamination and distractions in mind.

When I encounter a scene that my dog has trouble finding his way out of and the scent article is not to blame, I have to consider two major possibilities. First, the person I am looking for may not have been there to begin with; and second, the scent trail is too disguised or contaminated and it is time to work the perimeter.

I use an old visual tracking technique to help locate a new track when the old tracks simply peter out. I work my dog in prescribed concentric circles out from the starting point. The distance for each circle will vary with terrain and conditions; however, I like to keep it within twenty- to thirty-foot intervals. I will repeat the circles until my dog either picks up the trail that he couldn't find before or he finds nothing and it is time to stop. If you push a dog long enough, chances are he will pick any trail just to satisfy you. This type of work cannot be expected of a dog that has never been exposed to it. As with every task, he must be trained for it. I start with a trail being available for the dog on the first circuit, and once he is proficient, I increase the size of the circuit or add another.

Reading a Trailing Dog

The problem that most handlers have is their inability to read their dogs properly. This is especially true when the trail is a real one. It is essential to enlist the aid of a cover man on every real case you might have to work. The cover man is the eyes and ears of the handler, and this person watches out for obstacles, hazards, and distractions. This allows the handler to concentrate on watching his or her dog without distraction. Every trailing dog exhibits specific behavior when he is on a scent trail. However, every dog is different. It is a mistake to think that a particular tail position or head set is the same for each and every K-9. When a trailing dog is actively scenting his quarry, his body reacts based on instinct and on the physical traits of the breed and of the particular dog.

Depending on the animal's ability to detect scent, the head might be low or high to the ground. Environmental conditions play a part in this, too; however, a "cold-nosed" dog (weak scent dog) will often maintain a head level higher from the ground than his peers. When I'm looking at the head of a trailing dog, I find it prudent to also look at how the ears are placed. Are they pricked forward, laid back to the sides of the skull, or splayed wide? Even floppy-eared K9s such as bloodhounds, labs, or other hunting breeds will exhibit distinct differences in ear set, although ear set is not as self-evident in these breeds as it is in as their pointy-eared cousins.

When monitoring head position, handlers often fail to interpret the mouth of the dog. How open is it and what is the tongue doing? Normally, the dog's mouth will be partially open to fully closed in order to allow him to best utilize his nose and take up scent.

There is absolutely no set tail position for trailing that I have noticed. The most common is when the tail is held out and up, but there are many dogs with tails that droop, swing to the side, or wag incessantly. The most important thing to remember about the tail is the tail set when the dog is actively trailing his quarry. This will stay relatively constant unless there is an injury or some other issue.

The last body movement to consider is how the dog moves along the scent trail. Some K-9s tend to move in and out of the scent trail. I have noticed that Malinois have this tendency far more than any other breed. It appears to be relative to speed and a general impatience to find the quarry.

A savvy handler will take all of these subtle body language cues and catalogue them in his or her memory for future use. If the head, tail, and body language of the dog remain constant and there is little to no degree of change, it is safe to assume that the dog is actively trailing. It is important to be prepared for the time that one or all of the traits changes, which will indicate an interruption in the scent trail. Very few dogs will immediately stop when there is a scent change and will generally keep moving in the direction they had originally been heading. As the scent cone dissipates to nothing, the dogs will often stop or begin to quarter into the wind in an attempt to relocate odor. The problem with this is the length and breadth of the scent cone. In some cases, human odor might have spread over hundreds of yards past the original trail of the quarry or perhaps over a turn that was made. This is especially true on vast, hard surfaces such as parking lots and wide city streets. If the handler fails to register a subtle body language change as the trail is being overshot or the turn is passed in one of these situations, the dog could be so far off of the actual trail of the quarry that he might not find it again. On the other hand, if the handler registers the first of the body language cues as they become manifest, he or she will be far better prepared to remember or relocate the trail and cast the dog.

The biggest problem I have noticed with most trailing dog teams is the inability of the handler to read distraction behavior. Distraction behavior is any K-9 behavior that differs from trailing behavior or body language. This behavior is prompted by scent and sound. Scent, by far, is the most difficult to deal with. Sight and sound distractions—such as other dogs; heaven forbid, a cat; loud, surprising noises; or anything else that we know bothers our dogs—are easy distractions to catalogue and manage with good training. Scent distractions, on the other hand, are far less manageable, because most handlers confuse the distracting scent behavior with trailing behavior. In other words, most handlers can't tell when their dogs are following a human or another dog. The trail may start out following the person, but often even the best of trailing dogs jumps trail to something more interesting—like another dog or a hotter human trail.

Most handlers have difficulty reading K-9 distraction behavior based on scent, because scent is in a realm that is hard to understand. By far, most training that trailing dog handlers ever get is reading the dog when they are "on." Very little training happens when the dog is "off," because very few people recognize when a dog switches odor.

Just as every dog has a set of behaviors when he is trailing, so, too, does he have a different set of behaviors for almost every distraction that he comes across. The issue with these behaviors is that they are very subtle variations of the same trailing theme, and if the handler does not see or hear what made the distraction to begin with, he or she fails to recognize the trailing behavior shift to the distraction. The dog is encouraged by the handler's blind acceptance of the switch, and he happily runs with it.

I have devised a training program to deal with most distracting odors by providing a distraction trail that is an easily recognizable form for the handler to "see," thus allowing the handler time to correct the distraction. There are three phases to just about every distraction scent source.

The first phase is the initial detection of the distraction. This is normally a slight detection of the odor from a distance—air scent that is environmentally dependent. Most dogs will lift or shift their head slightly and their speed will adjust accordingly. The tail set might also change.

The second phase is when the dog crosses the offending scent trail or spoor. The behavior now becomes more aggressive. In the case of a second scent trail—human or animal—the dog's head will often pop to the distraction's direction of travel. The head and tail set will now have changed quite a bit. The third phase of the distraction is commiting to it. This is when the dog steps off onto the distraction trail or shoves his nose on the spoor.

The key to changing incorrect behavior is to recognize the dog's body language when he goes through the above phases and correct the wrong behavior before the last phase—or when the dog commits. If the handler allows the dog to commit to the distraction, it is often very difficult, if not impossible, to get the dog back onto the correct trail. This is exacerbated by the fact that many dogs simply forget what they were originally looking for when they are allowed to get off onto a distraction for too long a period of time. The determining factor for this time frame is the prey drive and memory of the dog. Some K-9s have a very poor retention time, and distractions kill their suspect trails.

I believe that it is best to correct the dog when you encounter the first phase of the distraction. This correction time is often fairly simple, because the distraction is not foremost in the dog's mind, and if he knows that the handler will not tolerate the distraction, the dog will readily leave it. On the other hand, if the handler waits until the dog has stepped off on the distraction and is following it, the distraction has now actually been reinforced by the handler.

So, how do you correct the distraction? It is easier said than done. If the distraction is recognized for what it truly is in a timely fashion, the handler should simply let fly with a quick and firm "leave it!" If the dog fails to respond, a second "leave it" command should be given in a more strident voice. The big handling faux paux occurs when the handler has to move onto the next level of correction, because now, sheer frustration has often set in.

By this time, the dog is usually far into the distraction trail or spoor for him to care about anything the handler has to say. The common methods of correction I have seen at this level are the following:

- Yank the dog off of his feet by a giving hard pull on the long lead.
- Run up and physically pull the dog off of the distraction.
- Yell from a distance in frustrated rage.

When a handler pulls a dog off of the distraction completely, he or she often fails to recognize that the original, correct trail may be very close to the distraction, and the dog may end up being pulled off of both trails.

When a handler runs up on the dog and physically manipulates him off of the distraction, the time it takes to get to the dog and then manipulate him actually reinforces the need of the dog to get to the distraction much faster in the future to avoid the handler's action that he knows is coming. This method actually reinforces the distraction.

Yelling at a distance speaks for itself . . . it is a waste of time and breath.

The best method to handle the last level of correction is to deal with it quickly and efficiently from the end of the lead. If the two levels of "leave it" fail to generate a response, follow them up with a loud "leave it" with a simultaneous "snapping a wrinkle in his ass." Snapping a wrinkle is easy but is not painful, and it gets the dog's attention immediately. You should already have a decent amount of tension on the long lead. Simply move forward just a bit to bow the lead some, then bring it up and down in a slight, whipping motion. The bow runs forward to the buckle on the harness and gently snaps the back of the dog. This quick physical correction with the loud command works in most situations. If it does not, the distraction is too big to correct in a trailing exercise, and you should take the distraction training elsewhere, without having the trailing equipment on the dog.

Most handlers are oblivious to subtle distracting odors that take their K-9s off of their subject trails, and even when they do recognize it, they are often afraid to really correct the problem because they are unsure about the distraction and the quality of the original trail. It is important that every service-trailing dog have distraction training where the distractions are diverse and known. I have established a distraction training regimen with all of my dogs that easily identifies the distraction for the handler so that distractions are easy to correct.

The second biggest problem with reading a trailing dog is the K-9's propensity to follow the freshest or closest trail regardless of a scent article. Most handlers, myself included, will follow a dog that is locked on odor when we read it. What happens when you have multiple trails leaving a single source point, and they all vary in age? If the dog has not been trained for the eventuality, he will invariably follow the freshest trail every time. This has given the false belief to many that dogs do not discriminate human scent and reinforces simple, soft-surface, fresh-scent tracking training methods.

A training regimen that works fairly well for this is called split trail training. This is where two trails are laid side by side and the subjects split at the end. The dog is forced to find the correct person at the end based on the original odor on which he was scented at the beginning of the trail. This training is usually pretty successful and easy to do. The problem is that it does not solve the age factor, and it is just that—easy.

The split trails should actually start from the source point and vary in age with training progression. They should also be practiced in small steps to ensure that the dog understands what is being asked of him. I normally start off on a soft surface and mark two trails that start close to the same point and gradually move away from each other at an angle. The dog is scented near the correct trail so that the choice is easy to make. If you remember the distraction sections above, you will also remember that dogs will detect source odors from a distance and do not have to have their noses right on them. If this is correct, then the dog will easily detect the presence of the second split trail when he is scented on the first trail. The first trail is positively reinforced by the scent article and encouragement by the handler. Repeat this process a few times and most dogs start to get the program.

Change the routine a bit by switching sides. Take the scent article and start near the bad trail. Most dogs will show hesitation on the first trail due to the earlier conditioning for the correct trail. It is important not to allow them to commit to the bad trail by allowing the hesitation to turn into commitment. It has now become a distraction. I recommend using phrases like "get to work" when I see that hesitation. You may also use "leave it" if necessary. Normally, this reinforces the second trail as being the correct one in the dog's mind, and he happily gets to work. Once the dog does this well, over and over again, it is necessary to add a third, fourth, and even more people to the mix. The last phase is to age the trails leaving from the source point until the correct trail is always the oldest. When a dog can successfully negotiate this scent nightmare, he is usually a pretty good trailing dog with a keen ability for scent discrimination.

The third biggest problem I have found for trailing dogs are intersections with traffic. The hard surfaces, coupled with wind, cause the scent to shift, pool, and eddy every place but the trail itself. I treat most intersections like barriers. A barrier is anything that stops the scent trail, and the team has to negotiate through it, around it, or over it. Intersections are no different. If the scent is not there in any meaningful way for the dog, it is pointless to mess around trying to find it there. The intersection will quickly become a distraction, and the dog will forget what he was looking for to begin with.

The key to working with the intersection is to move with speed and a sense of purpose. Let's use a four-way intersection for the sake of this model. The dog has run a good trail down the east sidewalk in a northerly direction until he comes to the curb of the intersection. Just prior to the curb, the dog's behavior begins to shift a little—perhaps his nose is starting to lift and his pace is slowing down due to the reduction of trail odor near the intersection. As the dog steps off of the curb (traffic allowing), his head comes all the way up, the ear set and the tail sets change, and the dog either tries to follow the direction in which the odor blew or throws his nose into the wind, trying to detect it. Either way, most dogs circle back to the place where the odor was starting to dissipate—the original trail and sidewalk.

In this situation, handlers will often err on the side of caution and allow the dog to circle the area for as long as he wants until he finds a way out. The problem with this is that, from a scent perspective, there may be no way out or the dog has not been trained for it yet. He may not understand that the scent is probably on another curb at another point in the intersection. The reason why the dog doesn't do this naturally is because he just doesn't think that way. We are placing human rationalization into the dog. On the other hand, if you expose a dog to the solution gradually, he will get it and solve the problem most of the time on his own. The key is getting there.

If the dog is allowed to circle at the corner for a long time, he will eventually pick up something—and not necessarily the correct something at that. It could be another person or animal. Then the team is off on a ghost trail. My method of training for this is, as soon as we get to the intersection and I detect the behavior change, I quickly run the dog across the street to the most logical direction of travel. I base this on the original subject's direction of travel. Once we are on the other side, I cast the dog out, telling him to get to work. If the dog finds the trail on the other side, great—we move on. If not, we saddle up and go quickly to the next corner in a clockwise fashion, so on and so forth. The keys are natural progression and speed. It is imperative that handlers not spend too much time at any location that lacks subject odor. To do so will ultimately lead to the dog giving up and switching trails.

These are just a few of the myriad of problems facing a trailing team. Trailing is by far the most difficult of all K-9 disciplines for everyone involved. The ease with which dogs lose the trail or choose a distracting one is indicative of this. A simple fact is that most tracks and trails in urban environments are failures unless they are very fresh. This is a shame, because a good trailing dog can usually overcome many obstacles such as age, hard surfaces, and distractions through smart, progressive training scenarios.

Trailing is almost as old as man's constructive use of the canine nose. Dogs do scent discriminate, they can follow scent trails that are many hours old, and they can negotiate most urban jungles as long as they have the correct training to do it. Occasionally, a dog comes along that defies all training and simply is a master at it out of the box. However, these dogs are few and far between. K-9s, like their handlers, work best through muscle memory. We work as we train, and if our training is lacking, so, too, will our work be lacking.

About the Author

JEFF SCHETTLER is a retired police K-9 handler who worked for the city of Alameda and county of Amador in California and was attached to the FBI's Hostage Rescue Teams' K-9 Assistance Program for two years. This program was designed to locate and apprehend high-risk fugitives on the run. Jeff has worked hundreds of trailing cases across the United States and is a specialist in tactical trailing applications. He and Ronin made numerous successful finds over their eleven-year career. Jeff has trained under many well-known manhunters, including Jerry Yelk, Glenn Rimbey, Jerry Nichols, John Lutherbert, John Salem, and Doug Lowry.

Jeff is considered a law-enforcement expert witness in the areas of scent evidence and trailing with bloodhounds. He has qualified as an expert in the counties of Santa Clara and Alameda in California.

After leaving the police force, Jeff founded TacticalTrackerTeams.com and later integrated it with the Georgia K-9 National Training Center, LLC, with his partner Kelli Collins. The Georgia K-9 National Training Center is a specialty K-9 training company with nationally recognized dog trainers and clients across the country. GAK9.com offers a variety of services, each tailored to fit the needs of civilian, law enforcement, and search-and-rescue dog owners and handlers.

Jeff rarely relaxes at his home and dog-training facility in Canton, Georgia; there are just too many dogs running around. He has branched out from his K-9 horizons somewhat and has begun to train basenjis to find narcotics and explosives. Jeff has written a series of nine articles for *Basenji Magazine* called the "Hunter Basenji Chronicles." These articles cover the use of the basenji for hunting and detector dog work.

Author Jeff Schettler with Ronin

For more information, please visit www.TacticalTrackerTeams.com and www.GAK9.com, and look for Jeff's forthcoming training book, *K-9 Trailing: The Straightest Path,* in which he will explain in detail the training methods mentioned in this book.